The School Library Manager

Recent Titles in
Library and Information Science Text Series

The School Library Manager

Surviving and Thriving

Blanche Woolls and Sharon Coatney

Library and Information Science Text Series

 LIBRARIES
UNLIMITED™

An Imprint of ABC-CLIO, LLC

Santa Barbara, California • Denver, Colorado

Library of Congress Cataloging-in-Publication Data

Names: Woolls, Blanche, author. | Coatney, Sharon, author.
Title: The school library manager : surviving and thriving / Blanche Woolls and Sharon Coatney.
Other titles: School library media manager
Description: Sixth edition. | Santa Barbara, California : Libraries Unlimited, an imprint of ABC-CLIO, LLC, [2018] | Series: Library and information science text series | Includes bibliographical references and index.
Identifiers: LCCN 2017024832 (print) | LCCN 2017047351 (ebook) | ISBN 9781440852572 (ebook) | ISBN 9781440852565 (paperback : acid-free paper)
Subjects: LCSH: School libraries—United States—Administration.
Classification: LCC Z675.S3 (ebook) | LCC Z675.S3 W8735 2018 (print) | DDC 025.1/978—dc23
LC record available at https://lccn.loc.gov/2017024832

ISBN: 978-1-4408-5256-5
EISBN: 978-1-4408-5257-2

22 21 20 19 18   1 2 3 4 5

This book is also available as an eBook.

Libraries Unlimited
An Imprint of ABC-CLIO, LLC

ABC-CLIO, LLC
130 Cremona Drive, P.O. Box 1911
Santa Barbara, California 93116-1911
www.abc-clio.com

This book is printed on acid-free paper ∞

Manufactured in the United States of America

Contents

Preface

This new edition emphasizes two threads throughout: leadership is a necessary attribute for all school librarians and school librarians must recognize the responsibility for ensuring equal access for all students. These two are the critical elements facing our profession today. The first chapter in Part I, "In the Beginning," explains the profession of school librarianship for anyone from the eager elementary student to the undergraduate who is ready to choose a school library education program. A typical day in a school library is described with three scenarios: an elementary, middle, and high school library, and gives options for choosing an education program. Chapter 2 provides a short history of both education and school libraries through the 20th century and moves into the present-day world with the explosion of information facing everyone connected to basic education. Chapter 3 details how to get that important license to practice and offers suggestions for finding, applying for, and accepting a position.

Part II, "Going to Work," suggests what the new librarian in a new school with a new faculty, facility, administration, and students should do that first week on the job in Chapter 4. Chapter 5 presents the role of the librarian in the school's education program, beginning with the traditional role in improving students' reading. It moves to analyzing teaching methods allowing the librarian to become a leader helping improve teacher assignments, understanding the learner, the curriculum, and inquiry learning. The school librarian in the role of teacher teaches all kinds of literacies, moves out of the library and into the classroom, and organizes and leads in the use of makerspaces and other new technologies and trends.

Evaluation and assessment is covered in Chapter 6 and includes qualitative and quantitative measures, the reasons one measures, what one measures including measuring to determine value. In Chapter 7 this volume brings attention to the business side of management, a model that many school districts are employing when they turn the management over to a businessperson rather than an educator. Information concerning creating the policy statements needed for a school library is followed by a discussion of budget and how to acquire materials and a section on cost accountability.

Chapter 8 discusses the management of library spaces and includes remodeling the library, planning new facilities, and moving into a new library. Several recent factors impact the facility, the declining need for shelf storage for hard-bound books, the new spaces needed for activities such as makerspaces, and the expanding need for different sizes of groups working together in the library. Chapter 9, on the management of information resources, covers creating a collection development policy if none exists, intellectual freedom and the right to privacy for all school library users. The need for expertise in copyright law is explained and policies for the ethical use of information. Building and maintaining the resource collection also covers de-selection or weeding.

Managing personnel, in Chapter 10, includes analyzing your leadership style to help you become a better leader. "Managing" also includes relationships with administrators and teachers as well as students and anyone who may be working in the library as a paid staff or volunteer. One aspect of management personnel that is often overlooked is the role in the community and other types of librarians and their libraries.

Part III describes keeping up. Chapter 11 combines leadership with technology and begins with infrastructure and access. The role of the librarian with technology includes the need to be willing to accept change, the need to engage students in helping with a Tech Squad, and building a technology plan. The challenges of social networking include helping teachers begin to make use of this communication method to meet their students on an even playing field. Suggestions are offered to help a librarian keep up with technology. Thinking about the level of impact of technology on education is briefly discussed.

Chapter 12 covers the leadership of the school librarian in professional development beginning with personal learning networks and helping the librarian and teachers move these into the school's professional learning communities. The librarian's role is described in helping coordinate the school's professional development. Ways for the school librarian to keep up include MOOCs, webinars, workshops, institutes, and professional associations.

The title of Chapter 13 is "Advocacy," but this chapter covers a business-like marketing approach to presenting the library to the school and community. Advocacy includes descriptions of activism with the school librarian becoming a participator in the political process, something that is essential if for no other reason than to provide a good model to other teachers and students. A short discussion features the potential of the school librarian as politician and closes with the role of the school librarian advocating in the global community.

Chapter 14 discusses the future of school libraries and librarians. It analyzes the future school library as a place, its content, its role in encouraging students to become lifelong learners as well as active, knowledgeable citizens in a democratic society.

Each chapter presents exercises for use in the classroom and in a workshop setting. Those designed especially for the library and information science classroom presume that students have ready access to at least one school librarian serving in an active school library with an integrated program. Beginning school librarians as well as veterans need to see good examples of teaching teams that are collaborating to develop and teach well-planned units of instruction that will prepare students for lifelong learning.

Acknowledgments

This volume, as were its predecessors, is dedicated to the many school librarians the first author taught in classrooms in Indiana, Maryland, New Mexico, Pennsylvania, Texas, California, and in the summers in Vilnius, Lithuania. You, and the school librarians I have met in other states and other countries, have provided both the suggestions for content and the impetus for writing. I would also like to acknowledge my niece, Marylynn Boatright, and my nephew, Robert Sutton, who, to varying degrees, followed in their aunt's footsteps. For the fifth edition, the timing was such that it kept creeping into family time, and I need to thank them for their patience: Don Fadden, Betty and Paul Woolls, and my granddaughters, Susan, Kelly, Shannon, and Laura, as well as the very grand great-grandchildren.

Throughout most of my professional career, David V. Loertscher has been there to support my dreams, to clear the better path through any woods, to tweak any faulty concept, point out errors, join in projects, institutes, teaching, and publishing. He is an incredible friend, not just to me, but to school librarians around the world. We all owe him a debt of gratitude.

Special thanks to a series of graduate assistants—Bonnie Black, Sandi Bianculli Miller, and Wendy Bethune—who worked with me on the first volume; Jo Falcon, who shared the second edition; and Dale David, for the third. For the fourth edition, Janice Gilmore; she provided not only research help but filled in some needed sentences when they were missing. These superb researchers found information, input data, checked headings, confirmed URL addresses, and brought sanity to chaos. For the fifth edition, two colleagues joined in the effort to provide the most useful text possible for new school librarians to begin their careers.

This sixth edition appears at a time when there is great uncertainty in the world. The school librarians everywhere who continue to work with teachers and students, the teachers who help students learn and grow, and students who learn so they can take over this world, and they will, very soon, are truly the best persons possible to make this world a better place.

Blanche Woolls

What a wonderful opportunity it has been to work on this important textbook with none other than Blanche Woolls, an icon to our profession. Thank you, Blanche.

I would like to acknowledge school librarians, LU authors, and friends throughout the country who contribute daily to my current understanding of school library management, particularly the librarians of the Blue Valley School District in Overland Park, Kansas, who let me visit and answered all my questions! A special thank-you to my son, Mark Coatney, journalist and social networker extraordinaire, for helping me always to understand the potential of the newest technologies, and to my daughter, Rachel Bailey, current LIS student, who helped me better understand what today's students need to know. And of course to my grandchildren, Natalie, Devon, Will, and Quinn—who always want to know why.

Sharon Coatney

Part I
In the Beginning

1
Becoming a School Librarian

People decide to become school librarians for a variety of reasons, examples of which are listed below. Some reasons might be perceived as more likely to produce a dedicated school librarian than others.

1. Students consider their school librarian one of the memorable teachers in their basic education experiences and wish to emulate this person.

2. Dedicated educators choose to serve all the children in a school rather than a single classroom; they not only love books but appreciate the opportunity to take a leadership role in the teaching and learning process of all students in one building.

3. Some librarians prefer the opportunity to work 9 or 10 months a year rather than 12.

4. Some teachers may elect to manage the library one or two hours a day rather than teach another section of a subject area.

5. Some teachers are "drafted" in times of school librarian shortages.

6. Furloughed teachers seek a permanent position when a school librarian's position becomes vacant.

7. Persons who have served in a paraprofessional position choose to continue their education and become a certified school librarian.

Choosing to become a school librarian is not an easy decision. Sometimes it is encouraged by a school librarian during those early years in classes where the information professional helped students not only find information for reference questions or research papers but information about which college or technical school offers scholarships and the specific career tracks to follow. Introducing students to public libraries opens the greater world of human resources to low-income families, the materials from the Library of Congress Library for the Blind and Physically Handicapped to family members with sight problems. A school librarian leading a field trip to an academic library introduces students to that information world.

Whatever the reason for choosing this role, the school librarian should not be building a program in isolation. School librarians are available to the entire school community: its students, teachers, administrators, and parents; and all of these users are a part of the design of the library program. This community expands with students and teachers in other schools who wish to organize experiences between students, even those in other countries. This means the managing of the school library program is centered on the users and their identified needs rather than creating a program and fitting the patrons into that box. It is designed around the experiences and skills the users bring to the library as well as their information needs. What do those users bring to the library?

Today's students come from all socioeconomic environments, but most will have a cell phone and will be avid texters. Some will feel uncomfortable if they do not have an earbud attached to their ear. Many live highly organized lives with sports teams and play dates while others need to have breakfast served after they get to school. Some may move from place to place because their caregivers have not paid the rent. They may be fluent in another language as well as English. Their families represent a variety of races, religions, and cultures, and while most will live in an urban environment, many still live in rural areas. It is definitely a world where no one size fits all.

Today's veteran teachers have lived through many different approaches to teaching their grade level or curriculum. Trends have been thrust upon them and almost before they feel they have mastered the new teaching method or curriculum or technology, another one is in front of them. They can feel unprepared after years of experience. New teachers may come from teacher preparation programs and hold degrees in education while others, because of their expertise or because of the need for additional teachers, were thrust into classrooms while they are finishing the requirements for their teaching license.

Your school library, its contents, and its program will be designed and implemented at all times to help students learn and teachers teach. Students will learn to read and add and subtract, but they also must have opportunities to practice skills they will use when they have completed basic education. They need to be able to distinguish between fact and fiction and how to research any doubts they might have. They need to learn how to work with others, acknowledging and respecting differences, collaborating and building new knowledge. They need to understand how to be successful adults who are useful, informed citizens in a democratic society.

School librarians help teachers model collaboration by co-teaching in the classroom, organizing units of instruction to make them interesting and appealing to students. If this leadership in teaching, collaborating, and helping students appeals to you, then this is the profession for you.

The other attribute you will need to develop is that of creativity. Many may feel they are not creative because they don't write novels or poetry and paint or play an instrument. One way to become creative is to try building a better mousetrap. To do that, you simply look at your mousetrap, what you are trying to do, and think about ways to make it better. When something isn't working, it needs to be changed. Sometimes being creative means giving up the old ways of doing something, which may seem to still work, but often it's just a comfortable way to act, and changing will open new horizons.

Sometimes creativity can be triggered by something read in an article, shown in a presentation, or observed, something that would be good to try, to make a change, to make things better. Observing good practice and then implementing it is creative. Observing good practice is perhaps the best way to help you decide whether to become a school librarian.

If you have no special example of what a school librarian can do, the following three scenarios may help you envision the role. They may also help you decide which level of school you would prefer.

A Day in the Life of an Elementary School Librarian

Arriving at school one hour before students will allow me to participate in planning with first-grade teachers during their monthly Professional Learning Community meeting, and we will be reviewing our month-long inquiry unit focusing on heroes. Teachers will evaluate students' work against the goals of their reading series, which features an inquiry focus (McGraw-Hill, Lead 21), and I will be looking for evidence of student acquisition of beginning inquiry skills. We will discuss our next project and look at the curriculum to make sure we are not overlapping with another grade level. As we have this new reading series, we need to do some adjusting this year; we are not yet familiar with the entire scope and sequence. Fortunately, I have been able to familiarize myself with the entire program, K–5, and can offer help and guidance.

School begins with the morning announcements. My team of fifth-grade "news gatherers" and I report on news of the day as well as lead the Pledge of Allegiance.

This morning, we have two hours of checkout with second- and fourth-grade classes. The teacher, my paraprofessional, and I assist students in choosing their books to check out. I do short book talks and "pass-arounds" with each class with the new books that just came in from central library processing yesterday. Because I had not seen these books since ordering them from my review sources several months ago, I stayed late last night to look at them. I am glad I did because I was able to "sell" them to students who were thrilled to take home the brand-new books.

During this time, one of the fifth-grade classes was in the library computer lab working on their Edmodo presentations for the annual Wax Museum of Famous Persons to be held later this month. Parents are thrilled with this part of the presentations, as they can access them from home and enjoy students' work again and again. Thanks to the help of the district technology facilitator, we were able to send passwords to individual parents. I check in from time to time, but the students have been working on these for some time and are just adding finishing touches. All teachers have been trained by me on this program at one of our monthly Wednesday early release afternoons when other specialists and I collaborate and furnish professional development training for the faculty.

It's now lunchtime, and the library paraprofessional and I make sure to leave the floor at different times, as small groups of kindergarten and first-grade students continue to come in to do daily book exchanges. While they are usually self-sufficient because we have trained them to do the self-checkout, it is good to have someone there to help if needed.

During lunch, I spend a little time with the PTO president, discussing and finalizing plans for the book fair coming up in a few days, confirming volunteers, training, and placement of the displays. All of this is part of our observation of School Library Month. The PTO is helping with an evening for families showcasing the library and its resources and services in addition to the book fair.

After lunch, the four sections of third grade will be coming in to begin working on their state research reports. Last week, I spent time placing the needed materials on our school portal with links to several useful websites. I placed World Book online and Culture Grams online, as well as several applicable e-books, in the portal for student use. We will begin our research with these online materials and expand to print sources next week. Students will produce a typical research report but will also give a persuasive speech about their state as a great tourist destination as a final higher level thinking and application project. It took a long time working with third-grade teachers to convince them to add the application piece to this project, but now they are pleased that students are being asked to do more than just report facts. This aligns with the new type of teaching and learning they have discussed in their district-mandated professional development meetings.

While waiting for each class to change, I go online and check my RSS feeds and LM_Net, always looking for new trends in education and school librarianship and important articles to bookmark and read later on my iPad.

At the end of this busy day, I must run off to a District Curriculum Committee meeting representing our building committee. I look at my schedule for tomorrow to check on the need for early arrival and things that must be done at home to prepare. I see that there is a webinar tomorrow on transforming your school library into the learning commons. I make a note to watch that in archive this weekend. Our school is one of the older ones in the district and is set for remodeling in a year. I want to be prepared to discuss my opinions with the architects. Checking the mail on the way out the door, I see a set of corrections from the district cataloging department that will need to be placed on materials tomorrow. I will need to tell my paraprofessional to check to make sure the corrections have been made in the library.

Driving home that night from the meeting, I reflect on how fortunate I am to have this job, the best job in the world!

***Special thanks to Ann Schuster (Valley Park Elementary, Overland Park, Kansas) and other elementary library friends for sharing insights into their day.

A Day in the Life of a Middle School Librarian

Arriving at school one hour before staff and students allows me a few quiet moments and an opportunity to get the doors unlocked, lights on, log into technology, and check email for emergencies and morning updates. I test the digital video feed to ensure the signal will work for the day's announcements. As I get materials set out for the library breakfast café and the day's lesson I will co-teach, the library clerk and I chat while she also prepares for her day.

Thirty minutes before school begins, we open the library early for the Library Café. Students come in early to read, utilize the technology, play our tabletop games, study, use the tools and resources in the makerspace, and socialize with friends. While the kids arrive for the café, the early risers on staff begin coming through for a morning greeting, an answer to a question, a resource need, or to schedule my time, resources, or a library space. Among the morning's needs: a class set of glue guns is checked out, a teacher is assisted in setting up her first online survey, a counselor schedules the multipurpose studio for a mentoring meeting, a classroom teacher and I schedule a time to co-teach next semester, and I share a calendar appointment with her for us to begin planning.

The students in buses and car riders are released into the building and the student news crew immediately begins arriving to prepare. The students have been trained, as we spent our first few weeks together developing skills, so they know exactly what to do as I supervise. I try not to intervene unless necessary in order for the students to develop their independence, teamwork, and leadership skills. This morning, the crew and I work through changes to the routine as we have guests, the speech team presenting a trophy to the principal, and a video to air, a music parody video to promote reading that the staff created and I edited.

At the beginning of the school year, I prepared a library schedule for one of our three instructional seating areas. Each class period has been split in half for 20-minute rotations, which ensures every language arts class has time each week to come to the library with the teacher for self-selection and reading time. Our student assistants run checkout while the clerk is at her circulation desk workstation helping individual students with issues, while finishing processing a collection of robot kits I cataloged after school yesterday. Whenever possible, I jump in and help students seeking or needing book recommendations.

In second period the eighth-grade exploration class comes in for day 4 of a seven-day unit on electricity and circuits. The students are maintaining notes and a list of new vocabulary in their personal learning journals. They are expected to use this technical terminology as we work through the unit. As is my practice when teaching, I have prepared a lesson with visuals, text, and verbal instruction in order to meet a variety of learning styles and reinforce key information. This is especially critical in this lesson as students will need to be mentally engaged and be able to clearly understand in order to be successful in their attempt to conduct electricity. When the bell rings for dismissal, the classroom teacher and I talk about the difficulty students have transferring their mental work into tactile form and how they struggled processing what they knew and wanted to do with their hands. We do a quick analysis and agree to changes I will make to tomorrow's lesson. I scribble some quick notes as the teacher leaves for her classroom.

A few minutes after the tardy bell for third period rings, the library is greeted by a very enthusiastic group. Today is one of our favorite days of the week as the CIP class comes in for story time and book exchange. The students loudly enter the library with their aides, place their return books in the book drop, and move excitedly to the couches asking for today's read aloud. The teacher brings the students' photo identification cards to the desk in preparation for checkout after story time. This class is an exception and we have a full period together every week so that we have enough time for the read aloud and checkout. Once story time is over, most of the students and aides head to the picture book collection to select new books for checkout.

Another reason this day is so much fun is that it is club day in the library. I offer a range of clubs that meet on Wednesdays in fourth and fifth periods during the students' lunchtime. I like hosting the clubs during lunch so that students who have difficulty coming to school early or staying after school can participate. Today it is Genre Lunch Club so I have the tables in the makerspace decorated for today's theme, sports stories (fiction or narrative nonfiction). The students come in with their lunches and books and sit down to eat. While they eat, students warm up to the subject by working in teams on a silly sports personality quiz I created. It doesn't take students long to eat, so we move to the project tables. While students are making a simple craft with a sports theme I found in one of our library books, each student takes a turn at "short attention span book talk." The rules are that the student has 30 seconds or less to try to talk others at the table into wanting to read the book they read without giving too much information about the story. Once lunchtime is over and the students are dismissed, I clean and reset the space for the next lunch group. After setting up, I help students entering the library on passes or go to my workstation at the circulation desk to check email and check in with the clerk. Once students begin arriving, I engage in the next genre lunch. I do this until all four lunch groups have come through.

Sixth period is prep for one of the seventh-grade social studies teachers. We are scheduled to meet, but he is not coming down immediately so that he can take care of a few things first. This gives me time to send an email out to the Family Read-In Committee with a link to the activities kit for proofreading, a list of tasks we need to complete next, and an online sign-up sheet. Once the social studies teacher arrives, we begin by talking about the social studies standards he wants to align, the intended student outcome for the project, and what lifelong and digital literacy skills we can effectively embed into the lesson along the way. As the bell rings, we agree that we have a good plan outlined.

I check email, take care of a few issues and needs that have come through, then outline the plan for the religions project. This includes the plan for which religions to include, the collecting/preparing of print and digital resources, the dates for the collaboration and the skill introduced or reinforced each day, what he will do to prepare himself and his students, and what I will do to prepare and plan. I email this to him to verify that we both had the same understanding before I will begin drafting the lessons.

In between helping students who've come to the library on passes, I make the agreed-upon changes to tomorrow's lesson for the exploration class and email it to the teacher so that she can review it in order to be ready and catch any errors to fix before tomorrow.

At the final bell, I step into the hallway to aid with dismissal while the clerk stays in the library to help students who make a quick stop to check out materials or return them on their way to the bus. Once the halls are clear, I go back into the library to set up for the Community Think and Make Committee. Nearly every month we host an evening family workshop. Each workshop has a specific theme, and we have a local expert come in as well as some school district mentors (usually high school students). The first semester's events have been very successful, but now we need to plan next semester's topics for each month. We quickly have our topics (computer coding, game design, and photography) and then move into brainstorming persons, organizations, or institutions that might be interested in donating time to one of our family workshops. Once the group breaks up, I follow up with an email to the committee about our plan. In the middle of writing this email, a teacher comes in slightly distraught about her day. We talk about it and ponder changes she could make for tomorrow's lesson to get back on track. Once the teacher heads out, I finish the email. I will also use this email tomorrow as my guide to begin contacting potential community experts for our family workshops.

I stay and post a picture to social media from the genre lunch. I finish my day by adding to my to-do list and going through email to deal with any questions, concerns, or needs from staff, students, and parents, and to see what is happening on my professional lists and e-newsletters from publishers and local organizations.

After my daughter's swim practice ends, she walks over from the high school. I pack it up for the evening, shut down my computer, and as we walk out to the car together we chat about the day.

***Special thanks to Leslie Preddy.

A Day in the Life of a High School Librarian

The director of the Information Center (iCenter) opens the door and glances at the countertop just beyond the circulation desk where the Tech Squad is meeting with a group of students who will serve at this "Genius Bar" all day, helping others with their technical challenges. Assignment to the Genius Bar is an honor given to students who have the skills necessary to be helpful to students and teachers.

The day's schedule is on the iPad at the circulation desk. Mid-morning, a group from a nearby high school has scheduled a visit to see the iCenter. The first thing on the schedule is a meeting of the iStaff to see who will be available to conduct the tour. A quick glance around the large room with bookshelves along the walls and open spaces elsewhere brings a chuckle because this won't look like a traditional library.

More early arrivals begin arranging their spaces for the day. Small and large groups have been scheduled into the iCenter, and each group understands where they will be meeting and the configuration of tables and chairs that will be needed. The drama club is making a circle of chairs where they will be holding their noon "listening lunch."

The normal stream of users is returning materials and equipment at the circulation desk while students are waiting to check out iPads for their presentations. Others are sitting at tables or in the informal seating area reading.

It is time for the librarian to check that units that will be used today are on the top of the virtual commons. Students began adding information into these units on the first day of the assignment and throughout the month. Today is the day for completion, demonstration, and publication of their findings.

When the warning bell rings five minutes before the first class, students finish checking out materials and equipment and leave for their classrooms. The agenda for the meeting of iStaff begins. Teachers who have requested space, materials, or equipment via email must be accommodated, and these requests are matched to the master schedule. Overlapping may be solved by the iStaff member going to the classroom or the activity being delayed for a short time before coming to the iCenter. For the visitors, the "guide" is selected and reminded to be sure they see the counselor's office just outside one corner with college catalogs, bound material about requirements for different professions, and computers dedicated to practice tests for the SAT. Another area they should visit is just outside the iCenter where the art classes meet and the small art gallery is located for exhibits of student work. After their morning tour, they will be escorted to the teacher lunch room for an "exit interview" with the librarian and the school principal. Other teachers who are there were asked if they would make comments about the iCenter and its programs.

The IT staff is asked to make any additional comments about particular databases before the vendor arrives to discuss the order for next year. At the close of this brief meeting, the librarian checks to see that all is scheduled properly for the visiting expert, who is coming to a social studies class.

A part of the afternoon will be used to talk with the district IT staff about the new software they are adding to the district. This will be held on-line rather than taking time for participants who are not in the IT building to drive to another location for the meeting.

As the school day comes to an end, the librarian makes sure the persons in charge of the after-school programs are there and prepared. They will need to use less space for these activities because the iCenter is going to be used for the school board meeting that night, and chairs will come out of their storage closets on their rolling carts to be quickly set up for the 60 people anticipated to attend.

School Librarian Competencies

An excellent school librarian should possess outstanding teaching skills and a contagious enthusiasm for learning and the continued accomplishment of students. A service orientation is necessary so information flows steadily from the library to the teachers and students, and a helpful positive attitude must be maintained at all times. Excellent communication skills, written and oral, are needed for the school librarian to work cooperatively with all. Foremost among these are listening skills. The steps of the reference interview to determine exactly what information the patron is seeking is exactly what must be understood to be able to help both students and teachers in the library.

As discussed above, creativity is essential for implementing the most effective methods and making the program exciting, ever changing, and ever challenging to students. Finally, good practice in leadership skills is essential if the library program is going to continue to grow and change in order to best serve the school. If teachers and the school librarian are to collaborate in providing instruction, the school librarian must be able to take the lead. If administrators, teachers, parents, and members of the community are going to consider the school library an essential part of the learning mission of the school, the librarian must gather and present statistics, provide training, and make presentations showing the mission of the library and the program's value in the accomplishment of students' learning goals as often as possible. Leadership in the area of advocacy is critical. This means an avid interest in taking a leadership role.

Before choosing the school library as their preferred "classroom" assignment, interested persons should decide whether they are willing to accept a leadership role in effecting positive achievement change for all students and practice flexibility and innovation in choosing methods to help students achieve success. They must also be willing to remain on the cutting edge of technology if they are to share these rapid changes with teachers who are quickly being left behind their students. The school library has grown far beyond the book collection to include information in a wide variety of formats and an ever-changing array of technologies. The school librarian's role must be constantly changing. An interest in trying new things is essential because the necessary skills to manage teaching and learning are constantly evolving.

As the methods of teaching students continue to change, content for classroom instruction continues to evolve. Teachers will be adapting and developing curriculum that is provided online to students or choosing the best from available programs to use with students. The librarian's role is critical in helping teachers prepare these new courses using the variety of resources available through the library. The school librarian assists in analyzing and choosing from what has been created or developed by others to determine what is best to use for teachers' classrooms. Here collaboration becomes critical. Once courses have been created, school librarians must help teachers remain aware of new resources available to be added to their courses and help them remove what is no longer useful.

In choosing to become a school librarian, one has many choices or pathways to follow. The bottom line is the personal decision to become a master teacher as well as skilled librarian. While this preparation may be started at the undergraduate level, it usually means more study in a master's degree program. The decision depends upon the choice of a library education program.

Choosing a School Library Education Program

Programs to prepare school librarians are offered in schools of education and schools of library and information science at universities and colleges at both the undergraduate and graduate levels. Courses are selected by or assigned to students to help them meet the certification requirements, sometimes referred to as credentials or a license, for the state where they plan to teach. The credential or license is discussed in Chapter 3.

Because persons attending institutions of higher education expect to be eligible for certification in a state upon graduation, university and college education programs respond to the certification requirements of their state and, whenever possible, meet requirements for adjoining states. State requirements, therefore, dictate the components of programs that certify school librarians. For many states, the certification program remains competency based; for others, specific courses are described. Many states require a practicum, which varies from a certain number of hours or days divided between elementary and secondary schools to a specified amount of time in a single location. Some states require both a classroom teaching credential and the school library credential; others require successful teaching experience before granting school library certification.

For those who are attending class in a school library education program, this section may be unnecessary to read. However, if you began your program in one location and had to leave or delay finishing, this section should be helpful. It should also be helpful to professionals who are asked by interested prospective students about possible institutions to attend.

In the past, deciding where to go to earn certification as a librarian usually was based on the student's ability to attend classes. As certification moved into a master's program, many who wished to pursue this profession already held full-time positions or had family responsibilities or both. Their choices were limited by the proximity of the institution. Older adults planning a career change with family responsibilities in one location found it difficult to move to a new location to take classes. Many colleges and universities offered full programs during the summer, when teachers who wished to become school librarians could move from home to campus to take classes for a shorter period of time.

Through technology and the possibilities opened by distance education, options for obtaining certification have changed. Many colleges and universities offer full degrees through a combination of possibilities such as face-to-face sessions on campus combined with online experiences. In these programs, students come to campus one or more times each semester and complete courses via the Internet. Many institutions offer complete programs online so students never need to leave their homes. As more institutions undertake this type of instruction, it will become increasingly easy to pursue both advanced degrees and continuing education experiences without leaving home.

When choosing a certification program, one must consider the curriculum proposed at any site. A major concern in the past was that school librarians be taught with other students pursuing another teaching credential or another type of library position in schools of education or in library schools. This has changed with the increase in online opportunities. However, school librarians are teachers and they are librarians. If they are in a school of education, they should be in some classes designed for teachers such as philosophy and psychology of youth, methods of teaching, selection of materials for youth and the curriculum, knowledge of the curriculum offered in schools, and current technology. If they are in library schools, they will complete the core curriculum with others who are going to work in all types of information agencies. In either case, to be isolated from others means that school librarians lose valuable opportunities to learn what they have in common with both teachers and other types of librarians.

Those who work with children and young adults must understand the learning processes and learning styles of their clientele. This is taught in educational philosophy and psychology courses and in classes on special-needs children, whether gifted or learning disabled. Understanding the growth of children from age six through the teen years helps the school librarian recognize different behaviors. These courses should provide ideas for maintaining discipline in the library. Schools with programs accredited by the American Library Association's Committee on Accreditation will have students in these classes who are not seeking school library credentials but will be planning to work in public libraries. Your introduction to their futures will help you understand their role, and you will be able to work with your counterparts in public libraries once you are in your school.

Because the school librarian is a teacher, it is essential to study teaching methods. Some colleges and universities may require a teaching certification before admitting a student to the school librarian program. Others offer teaching methods during the school library program. A program should include a practicum experience to allow the school librarian-in-training to teach in an actual school for no fewer than eight weeks.

Most library science programs offer courses in children's and young adult materials; these courses are mandatory for school librarians who will work in a school. The program should offer at least one such course at each level. In some schools, younger children are being admitted to prekindergarten classes. Because of the children's librarians in these classes, a pre-K materials class is taught; and if possible, school librarians should take this one also. The volume of materials published each year makes it difficult to combine two levels in one course, and certainly not all three levels. Further, the variety of types of materials currently being published for children and young adults must be reviewed, including new technologies for management of resources and database programs available. E-books are available, and their management has become a challenge because of the need for e-readers. Since some students have the ability to download books onto their cell phones or own e-readers, learning how to make these resources available to all students has become the only way to keep the have-nots from falling even farther behind.

Knowledge of the curriculum taught in schools with instruction in fitting the school library into the curriculum is another required course. Choosing materials is only one part of the process of integrating the library into the school's curriculum. In the past, school librarians learned how to work with curricula and teachers and how to blend materials in the library with materials in the classroom. This has expanded into the school librarian taking a leadership role in helping teachers use inquiry learning to expand their students' abilities.

One of the most important elements to consider in selecting a program is the kind of laboratory experiences and the types of technologies offered. It would be unthinkable for any school librarian program in the beginning decades of the 21st century to reject opportunities provided by constantly changing new technologies. To promote new technology applications as they arrive to school administrators and teachers, the school librarian not only must be familiar with the technology but also must have tested the technology and found it essential in the lives of students and teachers. It will come as no surprise that the students in K–12 schools are already familiar with and skilled at using these new technologies.

After researching schools, it may be helpful to ask other school librarians which school they would recommend. They may have had student school librarians from a specific school and can tell you how well prepared these students are to join the staff. They may also be well enough acquainted with their alma mater to know if their school is offering a cutting-edge curriculum for those beginning the program. Learning about outstanding, futuristic programs will help you begin to modify a more traditional program after you are hired rather than knowing only traditional programs that are lagging behind, which are those that administrators are more likely to downsize. It is your time to learn from the best which school you should choose.

School librarianship has a brief history, but one that is worthy of review. The history of school librarians and their role in the education of students is covered in the next chapter.

2
From Then to Now

School libraries are slow arrivals on the scene in comparison to academic and public libraries. They began to grow in the United States at the turn of the 20th century. This chapter discusses both education and school libraries then and now.

History of Education in the United States

American education has been, is, and always will be in a state of change. New theories are developed, refined, implemented—usually before they are tested adequately—and then discarded in a cycle that finds educators reinventing wheels. Administrators accept innovation; teachers follow administrative leadership; and students become recipients of each educational teaching theory, mode, and method currently in vogue. When an administrator becomes enamored of a new trend or idea and tries to implement it without exploring the innovation fully, changes are often forced into practice in schools with little buy-in by teachers. The successes and failures of such educational innovations continue. However, let's start at the beginning.

In the first schools in the United States, education was individualized, with the headmaster asking students to copy materials. Students did not necessarily learn how to read or write independently from what they were copying. Schooling was labor-intensive and open only to those who could pay; and the poor of our fledgling nation were basically illiterate.

For the masses, little formal education was necessary. Children would leave school to work in factories or on the family farm. The present-day "school year" was designed to allow students the summer free to work in agriculture.

To overcome illiteracy in some of the larger cities, societies were formed to provide free education. These 19th-century societies adopted a method called the Lancasterian system, in which many students were taught at the same time. The method was developed in India by Andrew Bell, who used it to teach Indian children whose fathers were in the British military. To maximize instruction, students were organized into groups based on ability.

15

Joseph Lancaster taught older children who, in turn, drilled the younger ones. Students sat in desks lined up in large rooms where they observed their monitor, who would state a fact and write an example on the blackboard. Students copied the fact, spoke it, and drilled it until they "knew" it.

This system of instruction through monitors meant the headmaster was freed from working with one student at a time and became responsible only for what was to be taught by being written on the blackboard, copied, and drilled and for training the first level of monitors. This type of instruction did require a trained teacher to plan the lessons, but ability grouping and rote learning became the norm, and free education for the masses began.

As the nation grew, theories of education were proclaimed, adopted, modified, or dismissed. These theories moved into the 20th century with the creation of kindergarten, adjustments to the legal age of leaving school, and changes in the length of the school day and term. In the early part of the century, the theories of Edward L. Thorndike and John Dewey led the way.

Thorndike believed that human nature, whether good or bad, depended on learning. He advocated a stimulus-response environment in which patterns of behavior could be established when a satisfying stimulus produced a satisfying response. Conversely, Dewey believed that education was life and learners react to their environment, solving problems posed from their environment. These ideas led to the concept of direct instruction, so common in many schools in the 21st century. Teachers lecture, students read the textbook, and then students take a test to see if they have mastered the material.

In Dewey's Laboratory School at the University of Chicago, Lancaster's drill and practice disappeared along with straight rows of desks in classrooms. The modern-day approach of project learning was based on a revision of Dewey's theories by William Heard Kirkpatrick. Here the teacher was responsible for beginning an activity, seeing that it was carried forward, and evaluating the results, but learning was in the hands of students who defined how to execute the assignment and solve the problem.

Theorist Maria Montessori's work offered a private alternative to public day care and kindergarten, and this concept remains in some private schools today. Montessori's focus was on the sensory perceptions of individual learners and allowing each child the freedom to investigate. The teacher provided relevant opportunities, encouraged independence, and allowed children to expand their inherent interest in learning.

Individualized instruction returned in 1919 with the Winnetka Plan in Illinois and the Dalton Plan in Massachusetts. Students were tested, allowed to proceed at different rates depending on ability, self-tested, and retested to check the progress made. Although group work was acceptable, the emphasis was on individual learning.

One of the greatest impacts on education in the 20th century was the ebb and flow in school enrollments. In the 1950s, schools were built to accommodate the baby boomers, children of GIs born after World War II. President Lyndon B. Johnson's Great Society programs instituted Head Start, free school lunches, and funding for new teaching methods.

The Soviet Union's launch of the Sputnik satellite in the 1950s produced an upheaval in U.S. education and caused Congress to provide funds for workshops, special programs, and institutes for training and retraining teachers. Funds also became available for materials and equipment to supplement classroom textbooks, especially in math, science, and foreign languages.

By the 1970s, it was apparent that enrollments were steadily decreasing. Schools in the late 1970s and early 1980s were closed and demolished or sold to the community. Neighborhoods changed as all the school-age children living there finished basic education. Funds for education were drastically cut as legislators responded to citizens' opposition to heavy taxes.

The Coalition of Essential Schools (CES), a project organized in 1984 and cosponsored by the National Association of Secondary School Principals and the National Association of Independent Schools, was chaired by Theodore D. Sizer, a faculty member at Brown University. The nine common principles of the coalition were an intellectual focus, simple goals, universal goals, personalization, student as worker, student exhibitions, attitude, staff, and budget.[1] Students were to learn to use their minds, to master "essential skills" in school, with goals applying to all students. Teaching and learning were personalized, with students participating in the learning process rather than absorbing what the teacher delivered as instruction. Final high school performance became an exhibition of what had been learned. After almost 30 years in existence, the CES Network website (www.essentialschools.org) shows the many schools remaining as members and the locations of its Affiliate Centers and continues to promote personalized teaching and learning.

At intervals, state and federal governments have become involved in education. In 1989, President George Bush convened the Education Summit with the nation's governors, and a set of national education goals were set. This framework, *America 2000*,[2] was designed to transform the United States into a "A Nation of Students" and make learning a lifelong endeavor.

> We will unleash America's creative genius to invent and establish
> a New Generation of American Schools, one by one, community
> by community. These will be the best schools in the world, schools
> that enable their students to reach the national education goals,
> to achieve a quantum leap in learning and to help make America
> all that it should be.[3]

Twenty years later, the National Governor's Association began another effort to transform the nation's schools. This new effort reflected the 1990s and a society concerned about both the cost and quality of education and a commitment to accountability, but it was affected by world events including the fall of the Berlin Wall, the breakup of the Soviet Union, the creation of the European Common Market, and the rapid expansion of technology with the opening of the Internet. The U.S. policy of free universal schooling, beginning in the 19th century to teach citizens to read, write, and do math, was followed by other nations, and some not only caught up but also surpassed the achievements of U.S. students.

The Education Environment Today

Challenges to schools today have increased; the economy continues to play a role in the numbers of staff per pupil, the ability to purchase new technologies and other resources for schools, and the maintenance of schools. The pressure given by testing and its results and its placement in the evaluation of teaching continues. The education environment today is more than ever a challenge to every educator, and solutions will require the best efforts of all.

The education environment is now two decades into the new century, and it is plagued by a severe, continued loss of funding with continuing changes in the government posing an even greater threat to public education. These economic concerns have led to budget cuts in basic education, placing larger numbers of students in classrooms; loss of many "special" teachers such as art, music, librarians, and counselors; and the cancellation of special high school classes drawing only small numbers of students, among others. The uncertainty of the situation makes it difficult for school district administrators to plan from one year to the next. Determining budget items requires as much information as it is possible to gather.

One method of researching these situations is the use of *environmental scanning*, a term used to describe the gathering of statistics about key factors influencing the school district. The external setting includes political climate; economic condition of the nation, state, and city; primary and secondary cultures in the community; numbers of children to be educated; family structure, income, and educational background of parents; and geographical location.

The political climate of a neighborhood changes rapidly when the decreasing numbers of children to be educated signal the loss of enrollment in an elementary school. Often, the effort begins to close that school. The tumult caused by parents whose children attend that school is formidable. The economic condition in a location may be one that lacks income, and the increase in single-parent families leading to increased class size brings little response from parents in the community. The opposite is found in other locations where parents and income lead them to establish school foundations and carry out fundraising activities to support positions in the school such as music, art, physical education, and a library. Bock[4] discusses how private schools have been joined by public schools in the effort to raise funds and offers the suggestion that if this fundraising can be done online, it will save much effort. He offers four websites to begin the process: Adopt a Classroom (www.adoptaclassroom.org), Digital Wish (www.digitalwish.com), DonorsChoose (www.donorschoose.org), and Schoola (www.schoola.com).

Among the external factors, the rising costs of consumer goods erode buying power. The transfer of services to other countries with expanded communication links means that personal questions about charges to credit cards may be answered from across an ocean. Costs of international conflict further erode the ability of the federal government to help fund many programs, not just education, and the expenses being transferred to state governments changes state funding in all areas. The loss of tax revenue from default closures on homes is a further drain when cities and counties must take care of these abandoned properties with the loss of income from the working adults who had lived in these homes.

Internal factors include the economic condition of the schools; the staff and their educational backgrounds; facilities, materials, and equipment; and the administration. The students themselves, including their performance on tests, the numbers leaving before graduation, and numbers going to college, affect strategic planning. A major consideration is the general mobility of the students. Schools in poorer communities must accommodate constant transfers of students for many reasons ranging from the need to move before the rent is due to parents' job changes.

As we move farther into the 21st century, in a noticeable change from the past, most students come from homes where both parents work or from single-parent households. In 2006, 30,717,000 children came from homes where both parents worked,[5] and as shown in the accompanying chart, there was an increase in both male and female single-parent households from 2000 to 2010. Few houses in any town or city have adults at home when the child is waiting to go to school or at home when the school day ends. In light of changing family dynamics, schools have restructured by providing extended services such as before- and after-school care, breakfasts and snacks, and flexible conferencing. School schedules now range from the traditional September to June to year-round and other modified schedules that suit the needs of families. Some school districts have adopted a movement called Small Learning Communities: schools within schools where teachers and students are grouped into more manageable-sized teams to facilitate connection, communication, and belonging.

Single-Parent Households[6]

	2000	%	2010	%	Change	%
Female	12,900,103	12.2	15,250,349	13.1	+2,350,246	18.2
Male	4,394,012	4.2	5,777,570	5.0	+1,383,558	27.3

School personnel have taken an interest in preschool connections and offer assistance in getting students ready for school. This interest can be traced to significant changes in kindergarten, which has moved from a primary focus on social skills and half-day schooling to teaching students to read and write. This means that students must enter kindergarten with significant skills that were not necessary in the past. Many school districts provide preschool programs with their elementary programs.

Preschool programs introduce foundation skills such as school readiness. Students become emotionally ready for school, able to leave their family and accept other authority figures. Children must be socially ready, able to tell adults their needs, get along with their peers, work in groups, and control their impulses. Teachers hope they will be behaviorally ready and able to sit in a circle, at a desk, and on the floor with a group and walk in a line. They should be able to answer simple questions; put together puzzles; and use pencils, crayons, scissors, and glue.

School librarians with preschool classes become a very important part of the teaching staff in these schools. They reinforce letter recognition, numbers, shapes, and colors, and also introduce nursery rhymes, songs and dances, and creative play. They work with public librarians who also offer programs to help preschool students become cognitively ready to recognize the alphabet, numbers, shapes, colors, and body parts.

Schools have undergone major restructuring, especially in leadership. In school-based management or site-based management, school programs have been decentralized and the decision-making process is placed with teachers, staff, and parents in individual buildings. No longer are central office administrators and staff making decisions across the district. Those persons who remain become generalists rather than subject-area specialists.

Perhaps one of the reasons for this restructuring is the change in tenure and tasks of superintendents. In 1993, the longest tenure of a school superintendent in a major city in the United States was six years. The American Association of School Administrators (AASA) publishes studies every six years. Its 2000 study dispelled the rumor that superintendents have a short tenure, maybe two and a half years. Rather, they usually have 14- to 17-year careers, but they work in two or three school districts, averaging five to six years in each. In 2006, AASA's State of Superintendency Study reported that "the mean tenure for superintendents is five to six years. The annual turnover is between 14 and 16 percent."[7]

The tasks facing many superintendents and assistant superintendents have become more business oriented, causing them to concentrate their efforts on relationships with teacher unions and the community at large. They now justify funding and seek outside sources of revenue, maintain buildings, negotiate with bargaining units, and oversee legal matters relating to students and teachers, among other tasks. They have little time to focus on curriculum and even less time to direct curricular reviews. In fact, one current idea is to replace the superintendent with a business person rather than an educator.

Another trend that is affecting schools and school staff is redesigning the evaluation of student performance, placing it back in the hands of developers of standardized tests. "Developers of scholastic tests have inadvertently become the overseers of a very powerful instrument of education policy making: achievement tests."[8] This means that "local control over schools is also being lost to private organizations, namely test developers. Despite the significant and growing role that their products play in educational decisions, these testing companies face little government regulation or supervision . . . governed by virtually no regulatory structures at either the federal or state levels."[9]

In the past, standardized achievement test developers created their tests on a generally similar curriculum scope and sequence not found in U.S. elementary and secondary educational programs because the nation did not have a national curriculum. In the past, the assumption of mass testing was that the education and thought processes of students were similar. Haney and Madaus suggest that "the term *educational testing* is something of a malapropism, since most standardized testing has far less to do with the teaching of individual teachers and the learning of individual students than it does with the bureaucratic organization of schools."[10] The focus on No Child Left Behind and the Common Core State Standards (CCSS) reinforced the era of testing student performance.

A new era of education in the nation is being created as this textbook goes to press, one in which school choice or charter schools are going to be proposed, which could greatly affect public education. Change is inevitable, but the degree or direction of that change is difficult to predict.

Challenges to Traditional Education

During the 1990s, an effort began to provide public funding for private education, long a greatly debated issue in the United States. One compromise was legislation for charter schools, a system in which private individuals are given the same funds per pupil for an approved school as would be given to the public school were the children attending there. According to the U.S. Department of Education, National Center for Education Statistics,

> A public charter school is a publicly funded school that is typically governed by a group or organization under a legislative contract or charter. . . . The charter exempts the school from selected state or local rules and regulations. . . .
> From 1999–2000 to 2009–10, the number of students enrolled in public charter schools more than quadrupled from 0.3 million to 1.6 million students. . . . In addition to the increase in the number of charter schools, the enrollment size of charter schools has grown over time. The percentage of charter schools with enrollments of 300–499 students increased from 12 to 21 percent during this period; the percentage with 500–999 students, from

9 to 14 percent; and the percentage with 1,000 students or more, from 2 to 4 percent.

In 2009–10, over half (54 percent) of charter schools were elementary schools. Secondary and combined schools accounted for 27 and 19 percent of charter schools respectively. In that year, about 55 percent of charter schools were located in cities, 21 percent were in suburban areas, 8 percent were in towns, and 16 percent were in rural areas.[11]

Charter schools, while publicly funded, are governed by a group or organization under a contract with the state. The charter exempts the school from some local or state rules and regulations. In return, charter schools must meet accountability standards, and their contracts are reviewed at intervals (usually every three to five years). If guidelines on curriculum and management or the established standards are not met, a charter school's contract may be revoked.

Although the first charter schools were privately funded, public school districts determined to initiate charter schools to keep education funds from the state within the district. Administrators and teachers were given the freedom to develop what would be an attractive curriculum for parents and their children to keep them in the local schools.

Another alternative to traditional education has been homeschooling. Many parents have adopted homeschooling as an alternative because they feel they can offer more individualized instruction at home. They do not believe a lock-step curriculum matches the learning styles of their children. Others homeschool so they can provide more religious training for their children.

Many students who are homeschooled take part in some school activities, such as band or chorus, and use materials from the school library. Meeting the needs of the homeschooled children is a new challenge for the librarian.

Proposals to offer parents vouchers to send their children to a specific school, either public or private, come and go. Parents can take a voucher for the funds allocated to their child for any school, public, private, or even church related. It is predicted that the voucher system will be increased in the immediate future.

Distance Education

Distance education is not a new concept. Correspondence courses were available to elementary students beginning at the end of the 19th century. As electronic transmission became available in the mid-20th century, students living on ranches in Australia were taught by radio. In Indiana, courses were available transmitted from an airplane flying overhead. In 1994–1995, a public school, the Utah Electronic High School, offered supplemental courses, with much print-based correspondence.[12]

In September 2003, the National American Council for Online Learning (NACOL) was created. Then, only two years later, in October 2005, the name was changed to the International Association for K–12 Online Learning (iNACOL), and the membership now includes school districts, charter schools, and state education agencies, among others. They have defined online learning as "education in which instruction and content are delivered primarily over the Internet."[13] Print-based correspondence was replaced by

Internet-based components such as videocassettes and educational software programs with significant instructional content. Christensen, Horn, and Johnson (2008), in their book *Disrupting Class,* predicted that the majority of K–12 students would receive their education by online learning within the next decade.[14] iNACOL states that "Online learning is becoming a common feature in public schools across the globe especially at the secondary level."[15] Their prediction was half of that of Christensen, Horn, and Johnson, that by 2012, 50 percent of all courses would be online. This was already being implemented in 2006, when Michigan required that all students have some form of online learning experience before graduating. Lincoln reports that "requirements have been implemented to give Michigan students the skills and knowledge to succeed in the 21st century and drive the state's economic success in the global economy. One of the requirements is that, beginning with the graduating class of 2011, all high school students will have had an online learning experience."[16] New Mexico, Alabama, and Florida have followed. This presents an opportunity for school librarians, who will be essential in helping teachers create these courses. While the teachers are developing their courses, school librarians will be preparing their information literacy, inquiry learning, and research modules that can be moved into the curriculum. These modules will be free of the need to bring classes into the library. The school librarian will be collaborating with the teacher, and while the librarian may or may not be at the side of the teacher, the librarian can also be present virtually during the online class session.

History of School Libraries in the United States

As stated at the beginning of this chapter, the history of school libraries in the United States is somewhat shorter than that of other types of libraries. School libraries are indeed an educational innovation of the 20th century. The first professionally trained school librarian, Mary Kingsbury, was appointed in 1900.[17]

Prior to 1900, schools had built collections of books into libraries to the point that, in 1876, *Public Libraries in the United States* reported 826 schools of secondary rank with libraries containing nearly 1 million volumes, or a little over 1,000 volumes per library.[18] Between 1876 and 1900, statistics reported the number of volumes but not the numbers of high school libraries, so further comparisons are not possible.

Growth in the number of libraries was slow, and growth of the collections was even slower. In 1913, Edward D. Greenman wrote, "Of the 10,000 public high schools in the country at the present time, not more than 250 possess collections containing 3,000 volumes or over."[19] He continued, "The libraries are well managed, and are frequently under the supervision of a trained librarian. The students are given practical training in the use of the library, in cataloging, classification and in the value of reference books."[20]

The condition of school libraries was further described in 1915 by Mary E. Hall, the second person to be appointed a school librarian in the United States, when she was named to the Girls High School in Brooklyn in 1903. She described her "modern" high school library:

> To have as your visitors each day, from 500 to 700 boys and girls of all nationalities and all stations in life, to see them come eagerly crowding in, 100 or more every 40 minutes, and to

realize that for four of the most important years of their lives it is the opportunity of the library to have a real and lasting influence upon each individual boy and girl, gives the librarian a feeling that her calling is one of high privilege and great responsibility.[21]

The activities were rapidly outgrowing a single reading room, and new facilities were being built that included a librarian's office or workroom and a library classroom. She offered all that was available in new technologies to her students:

The library classroom adjoins the library reading room and should be fitted up to have as little of the regular classroom atmosphere as possible. It should be made quite as attractive as the reading room and have its interesting pictures on the walls, its growing plants and its library furniture. Chairs with tablet arms on which pupils can take notes, one or more tables around which a small class can gather with their teacher and look over beautiful illustrated editions or pass mounted pictures and postcards from one to another, should surely form a feature of this classroom. . . .

There should be cases for large mounted lithographs . . . for maps and charts, lantern slides, mounted pictures, and clippings. A radiopticon or lantern with the projectoscope in which a teacher can use not only lantern slides but postcards, pictures in books and magazines, etc. . . . For the English work and, indeed for German and French, a Victrola with records which make it possible for students to hear the English and other songs by famous singers, will help them to realize what a lyric poem is. . . . This room will be used by the librarian for all her classes in the use of reference books and library tools, it will constantly service teachers of history, Latin, German, French, and be a boon to the departments of physical and commercial geography. After school it will be a center for club work. Reading clubs can be made more interesting. . . . Classes will be scheduled for a regular class recitation there when a teacher wishes the aid of the room in awakening interest.[22]

Hall goes on to say that this library had come a long way from "the dreary room with its glass cases and locked doors, its forbidding rows of unbroken sets of standard authors, its rules and regulations calculated to discourage any voluntary reading."[23]

Despite the enthusiasm of Mary Hall and others, school libraries developed slowly. The impetus to expand secondary school libraries accelerated in the mid-1920s, when regional accrediting agencies specified a high school library with a trained librarian as a requirement for all schools seeking to be accredited by their associations.

Although elementary school library standards were published in 1925, not many elementary schools had libraries or librarians. If monies were allocated for the purchase of library books, these books were kept in individual classroom collections and the size and quality of such collections varied greatly.

Mentioned earlier in the chapter, the Soviet Union's launch of the Sputnik satellite in the 1950s caused Congress to provide funds for materials and equipment to supplement classroom textbooks. Many school librarians were able to add to their collections to make these resources available to all teachers.

A Rutgers University professor, Mary Virginia Gaver, conducted two studies. The first, "Effectiveness of Centralized School Library Service (Phase 1) 1959–1960," reported the value of high school libraries. Her second, "Effectiveness of Centralized Library Service in Elementary Schools, 1963," researched that value in the elementary school. Her study was the basis of David Loertscher's doctoral dissertation in 1973 and the precursor of the Lance studies carried out at the beginning of the 21st century, which will be discussed in Chapter 6.

Several other events in the early 1960s had a great impact on the expansion of school libraries and the initiation of the concept of elementary school libraries in the United States. These are reported here because they show the successful methods needed to improve school libraries and confirm the efforts of the school librarians who led with these developments. The first was the completion in 1960 of *Standards for School Library Programs,* which updated *School Libraries for Today and Tomorrow,*[24] published in 1945.

Immediately following the 1960 publication of *Standards,* the American Association of School Librarians (AASL) received a grant from the Knapp Foundation to assist in the development of school libraries. Awarded in December 1962, the Knapp Foundation grant of $1.13 million was to be used for a five-year demonstration program to be conducted in three phases.

Another event that affected the development of school libraries was the publication in 1964 of a report by Mary Helen Mahar and Doris C. Holladay for the U.S. Office of Education showing that fewer than 50 percent of U.S. elementary schools had libraries.[25] The report attracted the interest of private industry, and additional materials were prepared to bring the plight of school libraries to the attention of the public.

These efforts in the early 1960s also caught the attention of Congress. Cora Paul Bomar, head supervisor in the Library and Instructional Materials Section of the North Carolina Department of Public Instruction (1951–1969), in her discussions with members of Congress, put on the "saddest face one could ever imagine" because she had "a vision of 10 million children going to 40,000 schools with no library."[26]

The lobbying efforts of the American Library Association's Washington office and the concentrated efforts of key school librarians across the country resulted in passage of the Elementary and Secondary Education Act (ESEA) in 1965. Funds were placed in Title II specifically to purchase library materials. These funds were then combined with local initiatives and volunteer efforts to build school libraries in elementary buildings and expand libraries in secondary schools.

Modifications in this law found federal funding guidelines rewritten and categorical restrictions lessened. Librarians now competed with other programs not only for declining federal dollars but also for declining state and local funding. The monies spent for microcomputers further decreased funding for other types of materials and equipment in school libraries; and in the early 1980s, the school library picture seemed bleak.

In the late 1980s and early 1990s, site-based management changes meant that many staffs did not include a school librarian as part of the essential programs for students. In other states, certification requirements came under review, and it was no longer considered necessary for the library staff person to hold a teacher certification.

Mid-decade, the DeWitt-Wallace/Reader's Digest Foundation funded a $40 million initiative to create model elementary and middle school libraries.[27] This Library Power project, administered by the AASL, involved 19 districts that received up to $1.2 million over three years to increase their collections, train staff, and improve facilities. While the foundation ended this phase of funding in 1998, the impact of these models helped librarians make a case for strong school libraries.

For the past 30 years, progress in school libraries has been affected by the development of new technologies. School librarians who were responsible for audiovisual resources in their schools were given the expanded assignment for microcomputers and related applications. Not only has the card catalog disappeared, but reference collections are mostly online. Access to electronic resources outside the walls of the library is readily available.

Within the past decade teachers came under pressure to demonstrate student achievement through testing and to implement the Common Core State Standards (CCSS) curriculum while meeting the guidelines of the standards movement through the content areas. These pressures were very frustrating to teachers who needed help in understanding the CCSS while keeping their students totally focused on the textbooks so they could pass the test. School librarians worked to help teachers understand and implement the new standards and to help change their approach to instruction as advocated by the CCSS. As with other "innovations" a change in government can predict a change in what has gone before. It is likely that CCSS will disappear.

The School Library Environment Today

Much of the library environment today follows the immediate past. The ease of use of Google, which offers free access to information, continues to build a perception that libraries are no longer necessary and that paying for resources, books, and databases is not needed. Because users are not aware of or even question the accuracy of information they find, an increased need for librarians to teach how to determine the accuracy and relevance of information located almost anywhere has become critical. Determining the fact from the falsehood seems of little interest, making it more important that librarians and teachers help students learn how to test what they hear, see, and read.

School librarians today need to continue to collaborate and co-teach with their teachers. In editing their landmark book, *Curriculum Connections through the Library,*[28] Barbara Stripling and Sandra Hughes-Hassell gathered articles from leaders in the field who discuss building independent learners, mapping the curriculum, teaching and assessing, and creating collaborative learning communities. They suggest that "in order to build independent learning skills, educators must offer a series of experiences in which students develop and use these skills to learn important content."[29]

The school librarian has a primary role in helping teachers teach independent learning skills and, through guided inquiry, helping students become independent learners. School libraries offer the laboratory for experimenting when opportunities arise. To meet this challenge, school librarians must continue to know the curriculum well and lead in the integration of all the literacy skills, information, technology/digital, and health, among others, in all areas of the school.

One opportunity is growing for school librarians to collaborate with teachers. With the movement of schools into an online environment to supplement their classes, basic education teachers are using course management systems to post information for their students. Some are even beginning to write e-books for their textbooks in their courses. School librarians are essential to help teachers find information, use it with respect to copyright issues, and continue to help teachers use new technologies as they evolve.

The school library physical environment is changing for some with new ways to collaborate. When a school renovates its library into a learning commons, the opportunity to gather other "special" teachers physically or virtually into the library expands the learning opportunities for students.

Another physical change is the development of a makerspace area within the library to allow students to build, experiment, work together in projects, and learn from volunteers in the community who are interested in helping students create. Other modifications are discussed in Chapter 8.

What is clear in the school library environment today is that this room is so much more than a place to come to get a book to read and return to the classroom. It must be a place for students to achieve, learn, and grow, developing a desire for lifelong learning.

After a chapter dedicated to preparing to take a position as a school librarian, the remainder of this text covers how school libraries should be managed. The leadership role of the school librarian is embedded throughout as is the need to provide access to information to all students.

Exercises

1. Study your local newspaper closely for one week, reading from cover to cover. Clip each article that would have an impact upon schools and school libraries. It may be as simple as a change in area code for telephones that would necessitate reprinting stationery for the school or as major as a report of a school board meeting that announces the closing of a school building or a change in grade level for that attendance center; an even more compelling announcement might be about a manufacturing company that was downsizing, which would predict loss of income for schools from both business profits and from salaries of employees. Also, if change is drastic, real estate values will decrease, further decreasing tax revenues for schools.

2. Respond to your principal who asks if you have any ideas for fundraising in your school. You may want to check the four suggestions for online fundraising mentioned in the chapter.

3. Prepare an entertaining presentation for a service club, such as Rotary or Kiwanis, that includes the history of school libraries and the history of your school library.

4. Prepare a five-minute presentation for the school board listing the reasons school libraries are important in student learning.

5. After reading the Bock article mentioned above and citation 4 in the Notes, check to see if the sites are still available, and if one is, how would you approach that site to discuss raising funds with your school staff?

Notes

1. Theodore R. Sizer, "Rebuilding: First Steps by the Coalition of Essential Schools," *Phi Delta Kappan* 68 (September 1986): 41.

2. U.S. Department of Education, *America 2000: An Education Strategy Sourcebook* (Washington, DC: U.S. Department of Education, 1991).

3. Ibid., 25.

4. Mike Bock, "Schools Tap into Online Fundraising to Expand Budgets," *Education Week* 32, no. 5 (September 26, 2012): 9.

5. U.S. Census Bureau, Housing and Household Economic Statistics Division, Fertility & Family Statistics Branch, *America's Families and Living Arrangements: 2006,* http://www.census.gov/population/www/socdemo/hh--fam/cps2006.html.

6. http://www.census.gov/prod/cen2010/briefs/c2010/briefs/c2010/br-14pdf 17.

7. http://www.aasa.org/content.aspx?id=74.

8. D. Monty Neill and Joe J. Medina, "Standardized Testing: Harmful to Educational Health," *Phi Delta Kappan* 71 (May 1989): 688.

9. Richard J. Shavelson, Neil B. Carey, and Noreen M. Webb, "Indicators of Science Achievement: Options for a Powerful Policy Instrument," *Phi Delta Kappan* 72 (May 1990): 692.

10. Walter Haney and George Madaus, "Searching for Alternatives to Standardized Tests: Whys, Whats, and Whithers," *Phi Delta Kappan* 71 (May 1989): 684.

11. U.S. Department of Education, National Center for Education Statistics (2012), *The Condition of Education 2012* (NCES 2012–045).

12. DeLaina Tonks, et al., "A New Kind of High School: The Story of the Open High School of Utah," *International Review of Research in Open & Distance Learning* 14 (2013): 255–271.

13. International Association for Online Learning (2011a, April), "Fast Facts about Online Learning." http://inacol.org/research/docs/iNADCOL$5ffastfacts--hrweb--April2011.pdf.

14. Clayton M. Christensen, Michael B. Horn, and Curtis W. Johnson, *Disrupting Class: How Disruptive Innovation Will Change the Way the World Learns* (New York: McGraw-Hill, 2008).

15. International Association for Online Learning, op. cit.

16. Margaret L. Lincoln, "Online Education in Schools," in Sue Alman, Christinger Tomer, and Margaret L. Lincoln, eds., *Designing Online Learning: A Primer for Librarians* (Santa Barbara, CA: Libraries Unlimited, 2012).

17. Blanche Woolls, *Ideas for School Library Media Programs* (Castle Rock, CO: Hi Willow Research and Publishing, 1996).

18. U.S. Office of Education, *Public Libraries in the United States: Their History, Condition, and Management,* Special Report, Department of the Interior, Bureau of Education, Part I (Washington, DC: U.S. Government Printing Office, 1876), 58. Reprinted in Melvin M. Bowie, *Historic Documents of School Libraries* (Englewood, CO: Hi Willow Research and Publishing, 1986).

19. Edward D. Greenman, "The Development of Secondary School Libraries," *Library Journal* 38 (April 1913): 184.

20. Ibid., 184, 186.

21. Mary E. Hall, "The Development of the Modern High School Library," *Library Journal* 40 (September 1915): 627.

22. Ibid., 629.

23. Ibid.

24. American Association of School Librarians, *Standards for School Library Programs* (Chicago: American Library Association, 1960); Committee on Post-War Planning of the American Library Association, *School Libraries for Today and Tomorrow: Functions and Standards* (Chicago: American Library Association, 1945).

25. Mary Helen Mahar and Doris C. Holladay, *Statistics of Public School Libraries, 1960–61, Part 1, Basic Tables* (Washington, DC: U.S. Office of Education, 1964).

26. Cora Paul Bomar, quoted in Bertha M. Cheatham, "AASL: Momentous in Minneapolis," *School Library Journal* 33 (November 1986): 38.

27. "Can Library Power Survive without Its Chief Funder?" *School Library Journal* 43 (April 1977): 10.

28. Barbara K. Stripling and Sandra Hughes-Hassell, *Curriculum Connections through the Library* (Westport, CT: Libraries Unlimited, 2003).

29. Ibid., xviii.

3
Going to Work

In almost all public schools, the librarian will need both a classroom teacher credential plus a credential as a librarian. The requirements vary from state to state so you will need to check them. Private schools may only require a teaching degree, and few charter schools even have a librarian. In this chapter, we help you think through your own professional preparation and getting a credential to practice in the public schools.

License/Credential to Practice

Once upon a time, a student called one of the authors to discuss obtaining certification. This student had graduated but had neglected to apply for certification immediately. The reason given was that no one had ever made it clear that an application process existed. This person assumed that the college granting the degree automatically sent an application for certification when a student graduated. This seems a little like assuming one would receive a driver's license after taking a driver's education course. Because most certification applications require a fee for processing, it is unlikely that such a process occurs automatically. Granting certification may be accomplished by one of the following means:

- The state department of education staff reviews the transcript of an applicant to determine whether the applicant's record meets state requirements.

- The school where you took your coursework may process the credential paperwork if they have been approved to do so by some accrediting body.

- A few states certify a candidate based on the passage of a test they have created.

Every state handles the credentialing process differently, and you can usually find the requirements online. The sooner you apply after the prescribed coursework, the better, since many of these requirements change over time.

State departments of education may grant certificates to persons with bachelor's degrees. The number of semester hours required at the undergraduate or graduate level varies greatly. While some states might require as little as 18 to 20 hours of library science at no specific level of instruction, others specify a master's degree. Such requirements are found through each state's department of education. Some states have added a requirement for a competency test. Some of these tests are administered at the state level, such as the California Basic Skills Test. Other states use the NTE Core Battery.

In some states, no specific college curriculum beyond teacher certification is needed because the state recognizes the scores on a PRAXIS test to be adequate to show that a teacher can work as a school librarian. The appropriate score on the PRAXIS test demonstrates competency.

Because each state's requirements are different, the person in charge of the school library program at the university can help with that state's requirements. The competencies acquired in the program may not make someone able to work as a school librarian in another state; those requirements should be on each state department of education's database.

You may discover that the name of the credential is different across states. Some may name it a school librarian credential, a school library media specialist, or a teacher librarian. Requirements as a technology specialist or instructional coordinator might be similar but may not be accepted for administering a school library. Often, the school or district to which you are applying will have the correct information.

Different types of credentials may be awarded depending upon the need for teachers within a state and the length of time before the credential expires. They have descriptive names such as emergency, temporary, or permanent or one of a variety of others. When the supply of candidates is much fewer than the positions available, persons may be able to begin working in a school library on an "emergency" credential. Graduates of undergraduate programs may receive a "temporary" certificate. Persons who begin their careers with a temporary certificate must replace it with "permanent" certification, usually within a specified time. The requirements for permanent certification also vary. Some states require teaching experience but no further education beyond a bachelor's degree with some library instruction or passing a test, and others demand a master's degree. Any certification may carry the requirement to update the certification through continuing education at intervals.

States seldom automatically recognize certification in another state. The most usual missing requirement is a course in state history, although it may also be completion of a higher degree. As stated earlier, some states require only a bachelor's degree and others require a master's.

Finally, many states require police checks for arrests. If a student has a conviction for driving under the influence of alcohol or a drug-related arrest, this student may not be granted a teaching credential. Such a check will also indicate whether an applicant for a credential has a record of child abuse or other crimes against children.

It is the responsibility of school librarians completing their programs of instruction to learn the requirements for certification and to apply for and receive their certificates as soon as those requirements have been met. Penalties may apply if this process is not completed in a timely fashion. In some states, one must complete the competency program in place when applying for the certificate. If certificate requirements change, it might be necessary to take more coursework or complete more requirements at a later date. Although these additional courses may be considered continuing professional education, it is preferable to choose continuing education experiences based on one's own needs rather than on making up some deficiency dictated by the state department of education.

One last factor may be critical in your own preparation. While the state may have minimal or extensive requirements for the credential, you might examine those requirements to see if they really prepare you for a 21st-century library learning commons job. For example, the state requirements may prepare you for a traditional library position, but lack coursework in technology and newer models of instructional designs that place you at the center of recent trends in teaching and learning. You need to ask yourself what kind of position description is being looked for in your area. Is the job that you have your eyes on a change from the traditional, and do you have the education and individual skills to make yourself attractive? You might want to supplement the required skills with others that demonstrate your ability to excel and lead an innovative program. And, even though the state may require additional professional development after initial certification, you will want to be a lifelong learner rather than a minimalist just to hold a job.

How to Find a Job

Sometimes, finding a job is a matter of luck, being in the right spot at the right time. Declining enrollments resulting in school closures and decreases in funding play havoc with hiring teachers and other school staff. Often, reduced funding for education means school librarians are furloughed or returned to classrooms and the library is turned over to clerical staff or volunteers or closed. Other times, an administrator will be looking for a dynamic new approach to the current school library and, noticing your excellence as a classroom teacher, will ask you if you are interested in making the switch.

Many universities providing the library credential offer some sort of practicum program in order to allow those without any experience to try out their skills under the direction of an exemplary mentor. Such an experience can be enormously helpful to you if the person who is your mentor is a true model of the latest practices in library learning commons. If you have a choice, investigate and try to find the type of school and mentor who will push your own skills and in turn write solid recommendations for your personal portfolio.

Next, the student should prepare a résumé and cover letter. These must be kept up to date because they contain the date the résumé was prepared, name, address, telephone number, educational background, schools attended after high school, and courses taken relevant to the job under consideration. Degrees received with specialization are followed by work experience, both full- and part-time, with emphasis on positions related to school library services. Examples may include library page or aide during high school, summer work at the public library, and experience in the college library. A brief description of related jobs and responsibilities should be included. Be sure to include your experience as a teacher that demonstrates how you can both support and partner with classroom teachers.

Finally, most administrators want to know a little about the applicant's interests and hobbies. One applicant might be chosen over another because of an ability to sponsor an extracurricular activity such as the tennis or debate team.

Résumés should be well formatted, attractive, and professional looking. The cover letter is addressed to the prospective employer, states the information understood about the position, and cites the reasons the applicant is interested in the job and is well suited for it. This letter must be carefully proofread to assure the reader that the applicant is articulate, accurate, and acceptable. A sample letter is found in Appendix A.

After the résumé is prepared and the placement file is complete, the student may begin the job search. Professors in the school library training program often have information about openings because school officials check with the training programs when they have jobs to fill. If the college or university provides a placement service, it will post job openings sent to the placement office.

Many state library associations provide job hotlines in their states. Although these may list more job openings for other types of libraries than school libraries, they are a good first place to seek information. The professional literature also provides information about openings in school districts.

Another job-search method used by some students is to request that their field experience or practicum experience be assigned in a school district where they might like to find a position. This is positive for both sides. The prospective school librarian can assess the school district at the same time school district personnel are reviewing the competencies of the student.

The network of school librarians is another source of information. These persons have immediate knowledge of resignations, transfers, and retirements in the school district and may have information about neighboring districts.

State department of education personnel usually are aware of openings in school districts in their state and can be called for help. Job seekers also can talk with persons in federal agencies responsible for library programs. These persons talk regularly with state department of education personnel, library school educators, and supervisors in large school districts and are aware of openings.

Professional association conferences are a source of information about job openings. Many students attend a state or national conference before they graduate to talk with school library and other technology professionals about situations in various school districts. These experiences may aid the decision process by helping match skills to preferences. Many professional associations also have an electronic list where their members post openings in their districts with information about the actual position and how to apply.

Finally, openings for temporary positions occur when school librarians take sabbaticals or leaves of absence. Accepting a temporary position may lead to a permanent position in the district. When interviewing for these positions, it is wise to find out one's options. What is the possibility that this position will be permanent in the immediate future? Do others in the district wish to have a permanent library position? Will the school district accept your resignation if a permanent position opens in another location? The responses to these questions will help the job seeker to determine the possibility for permanent employment after a temporary position closes.

Sample High School Job Listing: School X, located in the urban area surrounding Large City, is looking for a *full-time* librarian. The district administration is well recognized for their significant commitment to create a high level of library services.

The community is very supportive and recently passed a special tax for education. The district funds a full-time library assistant.

A Second Example: Madison School District is looking for a dynamic person who is interested in moving the Sample High School library into the 21st century in terms of technology and collaboration with all teachers, but with emphasis on English, History, and Science teachers in the expansion of research projects and the introduction of currently relevant standards. The Sample School District has an attractive salary schedule and provides 12 years of service credit for salary placement. We will be participating in a Teacher Recruitment Fair at the Large City Convention Center on Saturday, March 15. The position is posted on the district website. Please contact me at humanresources@samplesd.org. Interested applicants will submit their applications following the directions on the website, indicating if they will be available at the Teacher Recruitment Fair. Applicants will then be invited for an interview.

From the beginning until the end of your career, you need to build a personal learning network (PLN) as discussed in Chapter 12. This network can help you find your dream job. Often, a dream job means seeking a dream principal who not only has a vision but who will allow you to spread your wings. A great principal may be open to a major renovation or has been hired to develop a new school and is looking for a role model in the library learning commons under construction. It becomes a matter of excelling where you are planted and keeping your eyes open to new possibilities. Plan to keep your portfolio current. Join networks in your state and have an account on a network of professionals. Getting a credential once and trying to practice for many years is no longer an acceptable professional option. Think of yourself as you do your personal physician who, you hope, is constantly updating knowledge, skills, and practices.

Interviewing for the Position

The preparation for landing the job begins immediately after you have made the appointment. While the school is conducting the interview, an applicant needs to be prepared to interview the school administrator and the staff and look carefully at the facility. Thorough preparation for an interview will help the applicant remain calm during the process.

After reviewing the criteria listed as essential for an application and interview and making any discreet inquiries from those working in the district or neighboring districts, the applicant can formulate a list of intelligent questions to ask about the school district. It is wise to research the district in much the same way the administrators will be checking the applicant. Just as the administrators attempt to determine whether the applicant will fit the district, applicants will want to know if the situation will suit them.

The principal of the school is a key person from whom to gather information. At this interview, you need to ask questions to determine the importance this person gives to having an excellent school library program. It is usually not too difficult to find out a principal is not interested in the library. Ask to be taken for a tour, and see what the principal can point out to you when the door to the library is opened and when you walk through the facility. Ask about the budget and how it is allocated. Ask what nonteaching responsibilities are assigned to the librarian. Are students sent to the library for things other than research (discipline, excused from gym for the day, to take a test)? Ask about the library collection, especially access to electronic resources. Are students provided with technologies or must they depend upon bringing a computing device from home?

Find out about any staff assigned to the library. Are they part-time or full-time with additional assignments such as monitoring the checkout and return of electronic devices?

Are students allowed to volunteer in the library? In what capacity are they assigned: as a club, as a credit opportunity, as a learning experience?

Principals may have some ideas about the atmosphere in a library and their ideas are paramount in understanding what is expected from students. The principal interviewing you may find noise unacceptable. If so, you may need to explain that noise does not mean students are out of control; students make constructive noise, which is not chaos but active learning. Experience, attitude, and abilities to manage a constructive library may come up in the interview, so you should be prepared to explore the possibilities with the interviewers and demonstrate your expertise as a mentor rather than just a disciplinarian.

Applicants should always be on time for an interview. This means making sure of the location of the building, the amount of time it takes to arrive, and how difficult it will be to locate parking. An attempt to be calm and relaxed will fail if unexpected traffic rerouting, missed turns, or lack of parking space delay arrival.

The interview process is designed to find out as much about the applicant as possible. One or more persons will be asking questions. The applicant should listen carefully to the questions and reply to the person who directs the question, not to the entire review panel. Questions should be answered as positively as possible, with mention of personal skills that are appropriate. Although an applicant should appear interested and enthusiastic about the position, it is important to act naturally. Acknowledge when you are unsure about a response rather than attempting a clever guess.

Many books have been written about clothes making the person. This may not be true all the time, but it certainly is true in the job interview. If an applicant really wants the job, this is perhaps not the time to try out the latest high-fashion attire. It is the time to look professional. The interviewers will learn a great deal about applicants: what kind of person they are, their skills, their thoughts on education issues, and perhaps a little of their philosophy of education. Practicing how to interview can help prospective school librarians formulate careful answers quickly.

The interview also gives the interviewee a chance to ask questions about the position, the school district, and the organization of the educational and library programs. An applicant who asks pertinent questions can learn much about a position during the interview. After an interview, it is appropriate to send a letter of thanks. At this time, your interest in the position can be restated.

Coping with Reality

In the present climate, school librarians are being asked to take positions with multischool assignments and these may have very strange configurations. The plan may return the librarian to the situation in the early part of the 20th century when the English teacher was asked to serve as school librarian for one period of the day. Another plan is for the school librarian to be sent from one school to another, sometimes on the lunch hour or one day a week. Such positions carry a heavy load of frustration because you have a vision of making a difference when in fact there is little time to do anything but management tasks or supervise an onsite library support person.

If this is the only position available, try to determine if any change will be available within the year or if the assignment could be changed in any way to increase the time spent in one school, perhaps for four to six weeks in exchange for that same rotation to be made with the other school(s) in the mix. This could allow time to demonstrate the types of collaboration that make the school librarian essential in the building.

Managing a District with Only Aides or Volunteers

Some would argue that taking a position as single librarian in a district that shows little respect for or knowledge of the role of the school library and librarian in the education of students is in some way acknowledging the situation. It certainly outlines a case for probable failure for the new school librarian who may have little experience in the district. The view of administrators about the role of the library in the school is critical. If they assume that the function is largely the management of a collection of books, they may be satisfied if you are a well-organized person doing a great job in a one-faceted program, buying books for the school library. Such views are difficult to change unless you have excellent persuasive powers and have techniques to demonstrate a very different type of role for the library. Such jobs may satisfy some state requirement for administrators but are often dead-end careers.

Getting your license to practice and finding a job opens the door to a career in a school library. The next chapter offers suggestions for those things to do the first week in the school.

Exercises

1. Compare the regulations and competencies for certification in your state with those of an adjoining state or a state in which you might like to apply for certification. Estimate the amount of time it will take to complete those requirements and determine whether you could complete some of them in your present program.
2. Request an application for certification from your state department of education. Carefully read the instructions and confirm the requirements for certification. What information needs to be included? For example, is a physical examination required? What clearances are needed? What fees are assessed, and what method of payment is suggested? Are college transcripts necessary? To whom is the form to be submitted? What is the probable length of time between submission and return of the certificate?
3. Using the job description above, write a one-page letter of application for the position, briefly describing your qualifications for the position.
4. Generate a list of questions you might ask about school district personnel during an interview.
5. Generate a list of questions you might ask the principal during an interview.

Part II
Going to Work

4
Beginning the Job

Graduation diploma, certification credential, and signed contract in hand, the new school librarian begins the job. Although it may be tempting to launch immediately into the daily routine of the school library, a wise approach would be to learn first about the organizational and political structure of the school district and then to focus on the school environment. The more one knows about the situation, the easier it is to fit the school library program into its environment. To attempt to manage a program without understanding administrative practices may cause the school librarian to make unintentional errors.

When a school district has a coordinator or director of library programs, the school district administration believes in the importance of the library program, and the building-level practitioner has a specialist in administration to query with specific questions related to school libraries and their operation. That person may have been present during the interview. When no such person exists, it is less likely that school librarians will meet as a group for in-service sessions or that an advocate is assigned or chosen to speak for library programs to higher administration.

Determining District Administrative Practice

Members of the school district board of education and district-level administrators are the first group to research. School boards are either appointed or elected. Appointed members may be selected by a public official such as the mayor; these members maintain their position as long as the appointing politician wishes them to do so. When elected, members appear on the ballot in bipartisan elections or on a special ballot. Elected school board members serve at the pleasure of the voters of their community, and their decisions may be greatly influenced by community reactions. Individuals sometimes run for office to correct what they perceive as a problem, such as the actions of the current superintendent, the addition of a program to the curriculum, or the withdrawal of a program considered unnecessary or less necessary. The latter category may include programs begun with outside funds and discontinued when the funds are withdrawn or depleted.

School boards are legally responsible for setting policy for the school district. Because state sunshine laws mandate open meetings of public officials, school board meetings are open to the public. School librarians should plan to attend meetings to observe the actions taken, the sides chosen by individual members, and the general attitudes toward certain issues. School board members are powerful individuals in the public education of children.

School board members review graduation requirements for high school students. Although state boards of education establish criteria for curricula within the state, a local school board may increase the requirements. That is, the state may require two semesters of physical education, and the local school board may include the requirement of swimming a prescribed distance.

School boards approve all budget allocations and confirm that monies are being spent as requested and approved. School boards are also responsible for purchasing and selling property owned by the school district. They must agree to the purchase of additional property and the construction of new buildings in places where the school population is growing. In some locations, school board members place a tax on construction of new homes and apartments to ensure funding for the building of schools. It is the school board that must hire architects, approve plans, award jobs to contractors, and see that the building is built as specified. Board members must also agree to the closing of school buildings when enrollments decline, which are frequently contentious announcements.

Finally, the school board is responsible for interviewing and selecting the superintendent, who then proposes the hiring of all administrators, teachers, and staff for board approval. School board members must ensure that state regulations are carried out with regard to certification of employees. This may include ensuring that proper health tests are conducted, police checks are made (some states now require confirmation that a prospective teacher has no arrest record), and all teachers have the appropriate degrees and certificates.

As stated earlier, the superintendent is usually chosen by the school board, although in some locations, this person is elected by community vote. State law may govern the superintendent's length of appointment. Such mandatory contracts provide the superintendent some protection from the whims of the community. Superintendents are responsible for the day-to-day management of the district program; the selection of administrators and teaching staff; the development and implementation of curriculum; and the continuation of the school district program, including maintenance of buildings. Management of the school program requires, among other things, creating, refining, and presenting the school budget for the approval of the school board.

Superintendents choose administrators to work with them. These administrators are assigned to the central office staff and to the building-level programs. Central office staff is responsible for special areas of the school program and assume districtwide responsibility in a particular function (e.g., art coordinator, elementary supervisor, athletic director). Teachers in those functions are first responsible to their building principals and second to the coordinator of the specialized program.

Other positions that have been added to many school districts include the technology coordinator and literacy or reading coaches. In the case of the technology coordinator, this person's assignment includes maintaining external communication links, servers, and computer-related hardware and software in buildings throughout the district. In some cases, additional staff will be assigned to individual buildings, reporting to this administrator the status of equipment in their buildings. Often the building-level assignment belongs to the librarian, and anyone applying for a library position would need to have appropriate education, training, and experience.

In the case of the literacy coach, this person is assigned to helping teachers help their students learn to read through professional development experiences. They also help students with problems learning to read overcome those problems. The applicant for a position within a school district should determine if either of these positions will be a part of the responsibility of the school librarian when no individual is assigned in that role in the school.

When technology coordination and literacy coaching is the librarian's responsibility, learning how many staff members are available to assist from a district level helps determine the speed with which assistance will be given to any single school. Because it is difficult for school boards to fund technology staff or literacy coaches with sufficient personnel to serve individual schools, a librarian with the knowledge and willingness to help may perform both these roles in the school. If this does not interest the applicant, the job should not be accepted.

In the restructuring movement of the 1990s, many central office staff positions were reassigned to a broader area of responsibility encompassing many functions or returned to a building-level position. The removal of the central staff person responsible for the school library program or the reassignment of someone who knows little about this area means that the new librarian will depend on another school librarian in the district to answer questions.

Building administrators include the principal, assistant principal, department heads, and lead teachers. Filling any of these positions may be solely the responsibility of the superintendent. Or, in the case of a department head, the person may be appointed by the principal or elected by the department teachers. Administrators at all levels manage their programs. Who reports to whom is a system worked out in the central office by the superintendent and staff, and the school librarian should be aware of this process to be successful in effecting change. In many high schools, it is important for the school librarian to be considered head of the library "department" in order to be considered for inclusion on curriculum committees and for other leadership roles.

In school districts, teachers may be selected by a district personnel office, the building principal, or the superintendent. Teaching areas may be determined by certification, and curriculum is specified by the state with local modifications. Choices of textbooks may be dictated by a state or local list, but the classroom teacher determines methods of teaching, choice of primary use of one textbook from the prescribed list, or the use of alternate materials. Nevertheless, assigned the authority by the school board, superintendents are ultimately responsible for the total curriculum.

Superintendents must assure the school board that any national or state requirements are met. Recent changes have involved the movement to increase testing of students, supposedly to show educational progress. These types of "outside" influences affect both state and local curriculum, and the superintendent is responsible to the school board to see that such changes are met.

Sometimes superintendents respond to teacher and administrator suggestions for improvements or requirements beyond state requirements. That is, teachers may consider it important for students to have additional writing experiences or insist that students pass a basic online experience. These activities will then be required by the school district with the approval of the school board. At times, one district's "add-ons" can be added to the state's requirements, as it is happening in some states that students are being required to complete an online experience before they graduate.

The superintendent must be aware of trends in education so the district can offer the best possible education to all students. This is not an easy task, and most superintendents appreciate the quiet assistance of an information professional to make sure they are kept aware of new trends in education. Doing such a volunteer task can make the school librarian indispensable.

Another responsibility of the superintendent is to see that facilities are maintained. Daily tasks in individual school buildings are the responsibility of the principal, but any major changes must be approved by the superintendent, who makes recommendations to the school board. If a school library is too small to provide adequate services, the principal must bring proposals for renovation or new construction to the attention of the superintendent.

The superintendent also develops and presents the school budget in such a way that the school board will accept it. How the budget is divided directly affects the school library. Some superintendents divide the budget into a per-pupil allocation, with additional money given to special areas. That is, instructional funds are allocated with a certain number of dollars provided for each student in a given grade or subject area for newly adopted textbooks (if they are provided by the district) and a supplemental amount awarded for additional instructional materials. Art departments and school library programs receive an amount based on the number of pupils in the building.

With restructuring and site-based management, buildings often receive a lump sum to be allocated by the principal or building committee or by whatever mechanism the restructuring or site-based management committee has chosen. When a district employs site-based management, the school librarian investigates thoroughly the funding devoted to library services to confirm that the program will be supported and can grow.

The School Librarian in the School

School librarians bring to any new position all their background experiences, their observations of other school librarians, their reading and learning in their educational program, and their perception of what makes a good library program. Sometimes, many of the elements are in place in the selected position. At other times, the librarian may accept a position that is less desirable because of other circumstances, such as family needs or preferred location. In any case, the school librarian's own goals and objectives should be developed the first week. These goals and objectives may be refined in the first months on the job, but the initial projects to be planned will be evident from the first week in the school, and objectives must be set if any plans are to succeed.

School librarians just beginning in a new job should try to learn as much as possible about what has gone before, and as soon as possible about the current processes in place to choose the best strategy for implementing a plan. This is not to propose that all that has gone before has not been done in the most efficient, effective, or successful manner, but a newly hired school librarian has a unique opportunity to decide exactly what changes to make and in what order. Ignorance of past procedures might innocently create problems that would impede the progress of other program changes. In fact, some procedures may not be problems at all. Remember the proverb, "If it isn't broken, don't try to fix it." The review helps determine whether something is, in fact, broken or more broken than another procedure.

How up-to-date was the former school librarian? One way to discover this is to study the librarian's use of social media. Do both the school and school library have websites? How often are both websites updated, and who does this? If the librarian has been collaborating with other teachers, will they be posting their homework assignments on the library website?

Beginning the job requires as much knowledge as possible about the facility itself, the human factors, and the collection factors. Each of these will be discussed in the context of what a school librarian who is new to a building should try to accomplish in the first few days on the job.

Facility Factors

No matter who preceded you in your new job, spend your first days sprucing up the physical facilities of the library in a way that announces to the students and teachers that they are welcome! You can do much without any money to make the place much more inviting.

Look around. What impressions do visitors get when they walk through the door? Are they greeted by rows of bookshelves and negative signage? Are back rooms filled with "junk," making them unusable? Find volunteers, your family or friends, or a few students in the school to make suggestions and even come in for a day or two and help. You need to make a statement that there is something new and exciting going on and everyone can help make it happen!

Put up posters around the room and change that negative signage. Look for a box of new books that haven't been shelved yet. Clear a space near the door for a suggestion wall with half of it asking for favorite or original poetry on sticky notes. Feature the principal and/or one or two teachers on a bulletin board, including their hobbies and favorite books. One of your bulletin boards should feature hot topics.

Moving some of the furniture around changes any environment; and you need spaces to accommodate individuals, small groups, and large groups. Should the library be rearranged immediately? This depends on how tolerable any problem might be versus how a bad situation might influence the first weeks on the job. Time is a factor. If a single day is available before students arrive, there might not be time to rearrange. Conversely, changing a library can modify the attitudes of those who used the facility in the past. If the librarian feels that an attitude adjustment is needed, then, by all means, a rearrangement should be carried out to see if it will help solve some of the problems.

A new school librarian who has learned about a trend similar to the present emphasis being placed on a learning commons may wish to implement this immediately, which would mean a great reorganization of the facility. It might be prudent to put this on a brief temporary hold until co-workers and administrators can be shown the concept and buy-in can be achieved from the teaching staff. It will require a careful decision to decide how much change can be made in the facility in a short time and with the desire to build a flexible setting for new uses of the library space.

Get rid of that tattered, ugly rug that doesn't invite children to sit for story time. Create a corner with graphic novels or picture books close by, or if you are considering adding a makerspace to your library, put three computers together and put up a sign for a Virtual Makerspace with a second sign asking for donations of Legos to improve your makerspace corner.

Create your library website with candid shots of students reading and computing with a paperback in their pocket. Plan to change that picture every day. Put up a sign trying to recruit students to volunteer in the library. You will need a Tech Squad to assist with technology. This will be discussed more fully in Chapter 11.

Locate as many members of your advisory committee as possible. This is discussed in Chapter 10. The teacher who stops by to say hello and the students who have been volunteering to help you are likely candidates because they are obviously interested in what is going on in the library.

As you begin this process, you will have ideas of ways to improve your library. A facelift can happen more quickly if you are persistent. Your goal is to have the news get around that something new and fresh is happening; that the library is more than just a place with books and other resources, a place to have a lesson on this or that. It is a place to create, enjoy, help, imagine, think, study, make, do, perform, and collaborate in the physical space. It is going to become much more.

The new librarian should locate not only the technology in the library as soon as possible but also must learn if this responsibility extends beyond the library. Library responsibility for equipment may include items stored in locations away from the library, and an inventory of equipment and its probable location should be available in the school office, if not in the librarian's desk or file. When this equipment expands to the computers located in classrooms and connected to the library for access, this record becomes crucial. When projectors are not mounted in the ceiling of classrooms, are projectors assigned to teachers, or must they sign out a projector when it is needed? Teachers will be using equipment as soon as classes begin. Some may need to preview materials before school officially opens. Locating the equipment and assessing its state of repair are essential.

If your school does not have wireless access, you need to discuss this immediately with the school's technician. If you are the school's technician, your goal is to build all the evidence to convince the principal and teachers of the need, the cost, and the potential to move students and learning into a virtual world. Wireless networks and mobile computing devices make spaces more flexible. Locate and put signage on those outlets throughout the library so students can charge their devices.

Digital Resources

In the age of Wikipedia and the Google search engine, students and teachers may indicate that they are completely satisfied with what they get when they search for information. While school librarians know differently, you will need to compete directly with your own set of digital resources. While this was a topic to discuss during the job interview, check out access as soon as possible and begin to make digital resources both ubiquitous and trusted.

Start with what is already available:

- Subscription databases paid by the school and/or district
- Databases available from the public library
- Databases from statewide contracts

How do teachers and students get access? Are the databases available only in the library or are they available throughout the school and even from the students' homes? Does the system actually work? How and where do students and teachers go to do the searching? Is it available on the online public access catalog (OPAC) and from the library website? Can these resources be accessed on whatever devices the students and teachers own, both computers and mobile phones? What about passwords?

What should you do if your system is broken or nonexistent? Help might be available from other school librarians in the district or from district personnel. Connect with the public librarians to learn out how to help students and teachers access their resources and other statewide resources. Increasing access to these will require a squad of students to help both teachers and students as you begin publicity about these expanded resources. The bottom line will be the amount of usage these resources get and even more importantly, what is starting to happen to the quality of inquiry and the products produced by the students. In Chapter 6 you will learn how to assess whether better information results in higher quality products and students' deeper content understanding. Digital resources are not inexpensive. They must earn their keep in terms of quality teaching and learning. School librarians are held responsible for demonstrating this impact if they wish to keep their databases and even increase the number available.

The Online Public Access Catalog (OPAC)

Your new library is likely to have an automated cataloging system but it may not be one that is familiar or one you have experienced using. If it is unfamiliar, find someone, perhaps another librarian in the district, who can introduce it to you. Once online, check to see if it is current and up-to-date as a catalog of owned resources. If not, it will need to be repaired, but it is not the most important task to begin. First of all, spending time cataloging, an unknown activity and one they do not understand, will send the wrong message to teachers and students who need the school librarian's leadership in many other and more valuable endeavors and other initiatives that will pay huge dividends in teaching and learning. Rather, just input new items and catch up in your off hours or as "homework" just like every other teacher does on nights and weekends. As time passes and the OPAC remains a challenge, begin gathering the information needed, including the probable costs, to convince your principal to get a better system,

Human Factors

Reviewing human factors requires a first look at staff in the school library and then at administrators, teachers, and students. As stated in Chapter 3, the school librarian should discuss the numbers, if any, of professional and clerical staff during the job interview. When job descriptions for these persons are not available during the initial interview, the school librarian should attempt to locate these as soon as possible. If no descriptions are available, these must be developed in a way that covers the services and tasks, maximizes staff activities, and permits each person to feel self-worth. This can be accomplished only when school librarians can match tasks to human competencies.

Finding Out about Library Staff

Many school libraries are one-person operations or may be shared positions between two or more schools. In others, a newly hired school librarian may find there are two library professionals or, in the case of a learning commons, the staff may include any from a wide array of specialists in the school for technology integration and reading. Special teachers for the gifted or special education, art, music, and makerspace coordinators are all candidates for the staff. The guidance counselors may welcome a warm atmosphere to help students away from the principal's office.

With a larger staff, the new librarian should meet with other professionals at the first opportunity to discuss their roles in the process of collaboration. Initial meetings can help determine the perceptions of duties of all staff so that plans for the immediate future are in place by the end of the first week.

A key meeting should be scheduled with the tech director to find out if the school has a wireless connection. If the school is not wireless, investigate the possibilities of wireless with the tech director and the use of mobile computers, networks, filters, possibilities for multimedia, and use of software such as the Google Suite (formerly Google Apps for Education). A school librarian's expertise and knowledge of technology and applications as well as experience using it with students and teachers will help demonstrate its value in teaching and learning. This expertise will help the connection with any tech staff at the central office if not onsite at your school. They often are anxious to demonstrate technology benefits, and you can be their substitute in your school.

Finding Out about Building Administrators

Certainly the school librarian needs to assess the principal's perception of library programs in general as well as the program offered in the school. An easy way to discover some things about administrators is to listen in the teachers' lounge. Knowing a principal's interests can be useful when you need to get this administrator's attention. The librarian can discover all principals' perceptions of library programs by asking them to complete a questionnaire revised from one published in the National Association of Secondary School Principals (NASSP) *Bulletin* (see Appendix B). This simple questionnaire can be completed by other school personnel as well, and reviewing the responses will help the school librarian learn which perceptions must be modified or overcome.

Finding Out about Teachers

The modified NASSP *Bulletin* questionnaire can also be used to determine attitudes of teachers. Perceptions of principals may be compared with those of teachers to check similarities and differences.

As will be discussed later, some teachers are beginning to use management systems to teach and are even creating and publishing their own e-books to use as textbooks, and it may become the school librarian's responsibility to help teachers understand how to create books for their classes and to share knowledge about the copyright issues that must be reviewed.

Records may be in place to show if any collaborative units have been used in the past. These will make the job of working with teachers much easier because you will have instant allies, especially when teaching to the test has become the only mode of instruction. Knowing the resources used, the plan for presenting the unit of instruction, the roles and responsibilities of the teacher and librarian, and the method of evaluating the unit outline of previous work can be used as a model for working with other teachers.

To respond to teachers' needs, the librarian must learn about their teaching methods as well as the curriculum. Some teachers may use library resources themselves frequently, and some may use them incorrectly. If this is known, changes can be tactfully suggested. If teachers never use library resources, the librarian can suggest appropriate resources to use with a unit. School librarians must learn about teachers, but they must help teachers learn about the school library and the services offered. When teachers are unaware of how the library resources can support teaching and learning, the school librarian must begin work to change this as quickly as possible.

What type of assignments do teachers make? Do they make assignments that are busywork and boring to their students? This will not be easy to discover immediately, but it will become apparent as you talk with students when they visit the library. Helping teachers improve their assignments is the beginning of collaboration. This is not always the perception that teachers have of the role of the school librarian.

Teachers often have the perception of the role of the library as their time to get rid of students; the library time is the teachers' preparation period or an extension of study hall rather than an extension of the classroom. If this is true, the school librarian must plan a sales program to develop a completely new image. An in-depth presentation of marketing strategies is provided in Chapter 13. However, if the situation appears to be dire, the school librarian should begin developing an advocacy plan the first week.

Finally, the novice school librarian must try to locate the "gatekeepers." A gatekeeper, in this sense, is that person—teacher, administrator, school secretary, or custodian—who holds information and shares it with an inside group. Gatekeepers often can analyze situations and, based on their experiences, solve problems. The gatekeeper in a school may be able to suggest alternative plans to satisfy teachers when one course of action does not appear to achieve what is desired.

Finding Out about Students

The first step in finding out about students is determining the methods used to admit students to the library. In some situations, admission is by library pass signed by one or more teachers and countersigned by the librarian. Unless very few obstacles are placed before student access and use of the library, most students simply will not bother. Some may argue that a relaxed pass system will fill the library with loafers or escapees from study hall, but this premise should be tested. An analysis of library use for one week will reveal whether students are using the facility for study or recreational reading, whether they are coming from a classroom or study hall, and the types of behavior.

The second step in finding out about students is checking when they are allowed to come to the library. Rigid scheduling of the library may mean that access is severely limited, and students can only attend once a week for 45 minutes. This makes the use of the library something to tolerate rather than to enjoy.

For the third step, the new school librarian chooses between rigid rules and regulations for the library versus expectations for behavior in the library. Rules should be as minimal as possible, and they should be printed so they do not appear to be arbitrary responses to a situation. Regulations may state how many students may come from each classroom for small group study, or other requirements. These rules may also state the disciplinary action that will be taken in case of misuse of the library or the resources there. School librarians should remember that all rules require a response for any infringement of the rule. Often, the monitoring of the penalty is more troublesome than the action that prompted it, making the rule a lose-lose situation. Better a list of expectations for how the library belongs to the users of the library and how what they do in their library affects their colleagues, creating a win-win situation.

After determining the method of access for students, scheduling, and rules and regulations, the fourth step harnesses students to help with technology in the library. The librarian should find out whether students are assigned to the library as a tech team, as aides or work study helpers, or in any other function that might secure student support of the library program. In those first days on the job, students who have worked in the library in the past can help with stress tests of the system in place in the library to check on the capacity and coverage of Internet access not only in the library but also in classrooms and availability at home. Such a view, if taken from the patrons' vantage point, will be helpful in conversations with tech administrators and administration. Certainly, questions about equity as well as digital citizenship including the availability of devices for teachers and students will be central.

Finding out what students working in the library have done in the past helps plan for the future. If the situation is one where no students are returning with an interest in working in the library, recruitment begins the first week. As these students begin to join, librarians must realize that assigning students to dull tasks such as shelving books or reading shelves will not encourage them to remain. Students enjoy helping others use technology, look for answers, and learn how to navigate through new databases. They are very able to prepare new books and other media for the shelf. By assisting in the library, students expand their reference skills, conduct online database searches for teachers, participate in the selection of materials by reading reviews, match materials available to topics needed, and help other students learn how to conduct electronic searches, as well as help them choose from the available resources those that are most pertinent to their needs. A very able and trustworthy student or two can help keep the library website up to date and perhaps launch a Facebook or Tumblr presence for your school library. This will help computer-adept students build experiences and prepare for their lives after school.

In such a busy and creative physical space, your teachers can expect "busy" noise. Planning techniques to encourage collaborative behaviors will come immediately to the forefront. School librarians create zones of quiet, moderate noise and have private spaces where collaborative production can happen without disturbing others. Students and teachers learn the difference between constructive noise, a positive atmosphere, and chaos. Often a person who succeeds in a busy, noisy environment is the person who provides so many interesting opportunities to do, experience, create, and participate, that students immediately get busy rather than become bored and destructive. They learn to appreciate a very different place in the school where they take ownership of their own learning and creativity as well as their behavior.

Finding Out about Parents and Caregivers

The area where the school is located is an indication of the economic condition of parents in that school. In a school located in a community with large homes and two or more cars parked in the driveway, parents may take a great deal of interest in their children. They help children with homework, monitor their progress carefully, and support decisions by teachers and administrators. They observe their children in special events at the school, and they may volunteer to help in the school.

In other neighborhoods, no cars in the driveway may indicate both parents are working during the day. If parents feel they have limited English, or for any other reason, they may feel less able to help in the school on a regular basis. While it would take much more time for you to involve them, that could build yet another advocate group for the school library.

High-rise unkempt apartment buildings trigger the knowledge that low-income parents and caregivers may not be as attentive to students who may be absent from school, may move often, and will be less likely to finish high school. The new school librarian in this school needs to look for all the ways to make the visit to the library a win-win situation for all.

If a school has an active parent association, the librarian may be able to call on parents to assist in the library. The first week on the job, the librarian finds out whether parents have assisted in the library in past years and, if so, how to communicate with these parents. Although working with volunteers is covered more thoroughly in Chapter 10, the librarian should find out as soon as possible whether parent or other adult volunteers are available.

In schools where parents are less able to participate in the education of their children, the school librarian encourages tutors from a local high school or college to help. If students need a place to go after school, check with the public library to see what is offered there so you can direct students to this place of both safety and perhaps homework help.

Some parents may be in situations where they feel threatened, such as those defined as "undocumented." Special attention is needed to help students from these homes reach their full potential, particularly to understand what they need to do to continue in school through high school and what is available after graduation.

Collection Factors

The collection development policy will be discussed more fully in Chapter 9. During your search for other information in the first week, if a collection development policy for the school or the district is there, set it aside to review as soon as possible. If no policy is there, make a note to begin this process before making purchases.

The new school librarian needs to find out as much as possible about the resources available to match the curriculum. While finding out about teachers and their subject areas, the librarian should seek information about their teaching methods. By matching teachers' needs to the materials available in support of the curriculum, gaps in the collection can be determined, and the possibilities for co-teaching can be determined.

Locating Curricular Resources

A first question should be, "Does the library have a website?" Then find out, "Does the library have a social media presence for students to work together on combined projects such as are found in a learning commons approach?" The school library website may have links to databases, outside resources, and a variety of information to help the school librarian understand what students expect to find when they are searching. While you are looking, jot a note to find out as soon as possible if the librarian is totally responsible for maintaining the library website and perhaps even the school's website.

Do teachers and students have online access to the holdings of nearby libraries, and what is the process for borrowing resources? When accessing the Internet for resources, the addresses for resources are added to any bibliographies. Student aides may review the URLs each semester to delete those no longer available. When the actual units are being taught, links to these URLs are placed on the library website to speed student access to appropriate sites rather than have them try to navigate the sheer volume of commercial search engines. When learning about electronic access to resources, find out if there is a limit to the numbers of students who can search at a given time.

If you have been fortunate enough to arrive at a school where collaboration or co-teaching is a standard approach, you will find teachers who respond to the enthusiasm of their students and especially those students who love working with technology. When this happens, the ever-increasing catalog of technologies available to move students from solo learning into group work allows for exciting educational experiences. The inexpensive storage capacity of cloud computing moves control of student information away from the control of local schools and school districts into something that requires more bandwidth and accessibility but allows students to share their work within their classroom, their school, their school district, and all points on the globe. A major concern has been Internet safety.

When Google decided to help create a world that would be safe and free for students, they developed a set of tools for learning. Google Suite provides the framework and the applications for school librarians to share with their teachers. This provides an internal email system for the school, a calendar for individuals and groups within the school, and even a calendar for all school events. Google Suite allows for collaborating on Word documents and spreadsheets as well as survey forms and the ability to create presentations. Students can create their own home pages.

If your new school is less forward thinking, you must develop and get your principal's approval for a training schedule to bring teachers into the real world of technology. It is one of the better ways to increase student learning.

Once materials on the shelf and online as well as the materials created by students for their classes have been identified, decisions must be made about their distribution to patrons. If a written policy exists, the circulation procedures should be reviewed. When no policy exists or if the policy has been in place for so long it no longer covers the newer sources of information, the librarian develops rules for circulation.

Circulation of Materials and Equipment

Two major areas of circulation are of primary interest for print materials: the circulation period and the policy for overdue materials and fines. The two-week circulation period has long been a standard. However, just because it has always been done that way does not mean that the policy should be continued. A great deal of time is usually spent reminding students that a book is overdue after two weeks. Some of this effort might be saved if the loan period were lengthened to three or four weeks or even a semester. A newly arrived school librarian might make this transition. Placing materials to be used by entire classes on reserve to limit circulation is more appropriate than using a two-week loan period.

Fines are always controversial. These authors feel that fines are one of the worst possible public relations devices for any school librarian. The image of the library becomes punitive. Rather than teaching responsibility, a prime excuse for collecting fines, it promotes clipping pages or sneaking items through the detection system. In some instances, the librarian cannot use the funds collected; rather, they go into the district's general fund and are used for other purposes. Even if the money collected from overdue charges is used for the library, the cost to the library's image outweighs any advantage. To keep materials past deadline when other students need them is poor citizenship, and this behavior is not absolved by payment of a fine. Again, a school librarian new to the building may be able to reassess the process and begin the school year with a new, less restrictive and punitive policy.

The variety of potential uses of computers in school libraries increases the need for students to use them for longer periods of time. Collecting data about time wasted by students waiting to use a computer will be the greatest incentive to a school's going 1:1, which translates as one computer for each student. As wireless systems are installed, the cost of technology gets lower and lower, and cell phones get ever larger screens, these problems will be overcome. Students who are allowed to use their phones and other mobile devices are able to access the Internet working independently. However, when the students' only access to the Internet and online resources is at their school library, accommodation is needed for those students "without." The school library must provide access and the school librarian needs to locate places where students can connect after school. This may be the public library or a commercial business.

When Students Arrive

Sometimes students are in the building before school actually begins. They are often in pre-school activities such as athletes, cheerleaders, and band members who need to be ready for their first events. Should any of these students wander into the library, you would have an opportunity to see if they are at all interested in joining your Tech Squad or in helping in other ways in the library. An avid reader might be interested in joining the Library Advisory Committee. This is a good time to ask some questions to a student or a group, and this could help you prepare when the rest of the students arrive.

Expectations for behavior in the library should be in place when school opens on the first day. Students themselves can be useful in developing the expected behavior in the library. Because they have not yet had an opportunity to get to know a librarian new to the school, these expectations may need adjusting very soon. Expectations such as "place for quiet study" or "area for group work" may be written on a handout or bookmarks and distributed or prominently displayed at the checkout desk or elsewhere.

Explaining behaviors is as important as explaining the location of materials and outlets to charge equipment.

Kay Bishop and Jenny Cahall suggest that school librarians plan to "maintain a positive and enthusiastic attitude. A positive attitude and enthusiasm are both contagious. School librarians who communicate positively with students and demonstrate a caring attitude and respect will generally have good relationships with students."[1]

First impressions are critical. The novice school librarian must dress like a professional just as teachers in any building should be role models for their students. The professional appearance of the school librarian lends an air of competence and importance to the activities of the library. This is true for all students in every building. A principal visiting a large school district remarked to one author that the teachers in the inner-city schools seemed to wear drab, "serviceable" clothing, as if the students were somehow less deserving of better clothing on their teachers. As she visited schools more distant from the center, the clothing of teachers changed noticeably as they wore "business" dress. The following additional suggestions should be helpful to the new school librarian as students arrive.

- Be visible when students first enter the library.
- Learn students' names as quickly as possible. This shows an interest in and respect for the students' presence in the library.
- Avoid, at all costs, being intimidated by students.
- A positive posture, use of guidelines of expected behavior, and a genuine regard for students as sincere researchers will bring a positive reaction.

Whenever possible, avoid using voice commands. A strident voice in the library will disturb everyone there. Students quickly learn to read messages in body language and eye contact. These silent signals are far preferable to other means of attracting attention.

Address discipline problems immediately. Ignoring a problem will encourage other students to create similar problems. Quickly respond to students when they misbehave so they understand that the consequences for bad behavior are immediate, fair, and positive. Sarcasm or ridicule is as harmful to the giver as to the recipient. Unkind behavior is often returned later, and the librarian will be the recipient.

Establish a reputation for being positive, fair, caring, understanding, and flexible. Students should be the focus of attention. It is not fair to them if the librarian's personal problems become part of the library attitude. It is difficult to hide personal stress and strain, but students may not understand that a curt response is the result of something that happened elsewhere.

Beware of physical contact with students. Most states have laws against physical punishment of students. The librarian should intervene physically only in a situation in which physical harm might come to another pupil. Again, eye contact and a soft voice are far more effective than aggression.

Take care not to punish the whole group for the behavior of some. A private reprimand or a more public but personal acknowledgment of the misbehavior will be as effective. Depriving a group will only make the group angry and may, in fact, draw the group into support of the poor behavior of the few.

Do not return a student to the teacher for misbehavior. By the same token, teachers should not be allowed to send students to the library for misbehavior. If the library is not to be looked upon as a jail, the librarian should show the same courtesy to the concept of the classroom. In an educational psychology class, the instructor pointed out that students misbehave because they want to leave the classroom or, in your case, the library. To send them to the principal or back to the teacher is, in a sense, rewarding them just as the Fox rewarded Brer Rabbit by throwing him into the briar patch.

Should your library be treated as a jail with detention students sent at the end of the day, plan to give them something positive to do. It's a good time to share the newest *Sports Illustrated* or *Seventeen*. That way they will be increasing their reading skills and perhaps increasing their vocabularies.

Finally, be prepared for the students when they enter. "Flying by the seat of your pants" may work occasionally for the veteran librarian, but it is not likely to work for the beginner. Well-developed plans with more activities than could possibly be carried out are preferable to the embarrassment of running out of things to do. As the librarian becomes familiar with the pace, it will be possible to conduct activities with less detailed plans, but in the beginning, your calendar or plan book should be carefully developed.

Having survived the first week on the job, the school librarian must begin to plan for the immediate future, for the remainder of the school year, and for the long-term future of the library program. The following chapters expand the responsibilities.

Exercises

1. If you are unfamiliar with school district organization charts, visit the administration offices of a nearby school district and ask to see the organization chart. Determine who is responsible for the school library program. How many bosses does the school librarian have?
2. If possible, interview a new school librarian after the first week on the job. Compare this person's experiences with those of someone returning to a familiar situation.
3. Review the school library websites in at least five schools and compare them for their ease of access, their clarity, and their links to resources as well as the information given there.
4. Create a generic website for a school library. Establish links to resources you have found that would be useful to students.

Note

1. Kay Bishop and Jenny Cahall, *Positive Classroom Management Skills for School Librarians* (Santa Barbara, CA: Libraries Unlimited, 2012), 1.

5
The Education Program

The major task of a school is to educate its students. In spite of decades of effort, there seems to be a persistent stereotype that the function of the school library is to be a warehouse of books that are circulated and maintained by a librarian. In the age of Google and Wikipedia, many students and teachers turn first to the smart device in their hand and the library, if one happens to be handy, as a last resort. This chapter explores the idea and role of the school library as the center and heart of teaching and learning in the school. While few entering the profession would like to preside over an irrelevant organization, positioning one's self at the center is a challenge that seems to persist across the profession. It requires a willingness to move into a leadership role, one that requires a vision, a plan, and some suggestions for how to implement that plan.

The school librarian is an integral part of the task of educating students, accepting the responsibility of a leading role in the achievement of students. School librarians provide experiences for each and every student during their time in school so they achieve their full potential. In addition, the school librarian helps students understand the path they will follow at their next level of education whether it be to middle school, high school, or another opportunity after they graduate. This begins what was typically the first assignment, to help students learn to read, but expands into guiding curriculum.

Reading

If students are to learn, grow, and enjoy school, they must be able to read and understand text. Knowing how to read goes beyond success in school and becomes a lifelong skill that helps them comprehend and interpret information and develop new understandings. First, our students learn to read, and then they read to learn. This is not a new belief.

A major priority of school library programs has traditionally been the reading program. Henry Cecil and Willard Heaps, in their 1940 *School Library Service in the United States,* credit Governor DeWitt Clinton and

William L. March of New York and Horace Mann of Massachusetts with traveling to Europe to bring back the best ideas for educating children to put into practice in the United States.

> These educational leaders and others of the day realized that the development of intelligent citizens depended not only upon teaching reading but also on providing reading opportunities. It was for the purpose of providing such opportunities that the school district libraries came into being.[1]

Students who understand what they are reading are more likely to grow into lifelong readers. While they are reading, students should be making connections between the text and what they know. Additionally, comprehension includes visualization, meaning students create pictures in their minds of the text. Students should be able to create questions about what they have read, make inferences and predictions based on evidence from the text, and explain how a text is personally meaningful.

Students must be surrounded with a library collection that will be interesting to them and will have a wide variety of books and other materials, including online materials, using a vocabulary that they can read not necessarily easily but with the possibility of achieving meaning as they read. "When we inundate older struggling readers with superficial and lifeless reading and writing tasks that bear no resemblance to the reading and writing they encounter in the real world, we ensure their status as outsiders in the real literate community."[2]

Most elementary teachers read aloud to classes daily. This is excellent modeling and helps students see the joy in reading and learn about new and different authors and types of literature. Librarians can be invaluable in helping teachers choose what to read, particularly helping them find things to read that are new to them and perhaps out of their usual comfort zone such as poetry or nonfiction.

Middle and high school teachers might be encouraged to read briefly to students at the beginning of the class period. It is a good method to help students settle in their seats. Librarians can offer teachers suggestions of quick reads from current news, biographies of persons important to the subject being taught, or anything relative to the course. This can give students something else to consider beyond the immediate assignment. It also shows that all their teachers believe reading is important and enjoy doing it. Perhaps the greatest damage to high school students is that poor readers fail in their classes, and they are at greatest risk of dropping out of high school. Having materials that they can read and use to complete their assignments is critical. They need ready access to good books.

Quantitative dimensions ask us to consider the traditional reading levels of the text by using formulas such as the Flesh-Kinkaid, Dale Chall, or Lexile levels to determine the complexity of the text. Unfortunately, such formulas cannot determine the complexity of the text when taken in context, and most read in context. These formulas strip out the language and rate the text without the context. Neither the difficulty of the concepts in the text nor the complexity of the grammar is rated by the formulas, so the true complexity of the text is not found. A good resource for help in determining the complexity of text and explaining the three-prong approach can be found in two recent books by Rachel Wadham, *Integrating Children's Literature through the Common Core*[3] and *Integrating Young Adult Literature Through the Common Core.*[4] Librarians can and may be required to rate books in their libraries by quantitative levels in some way, perhaps labeling them or giving teachers a relevant list. However, school librarians need to intervene and help teachers and students find things that they can read but that they are also interested in reading. It is known that students can and do successfully read books above their tested reading levels if the content of the book is compelling for them. Previous studies show that children do not choose only "easy" books for their recreational reading. Much of what they choose is at or above their reading level.[5]

Ready Access to a Good Book Helps Improve Reading Skills

When Stephen Krashen revised his landmark publication, *The Power of Reading,*[6] in 2004, he retained this paragraph:

> There is abundant evidence that literacy development can occur without formal instruction. Moreover, this evidence strongly suggests that reading is potent enough to do nearly the entire job alone.[7]

Almost 10 years later, in *Free Voluntary Reading*, Krashen notes once again that:

> the progress made in free voluntary reading over the last decade, since the completion of the second edition of *The Power of Reading* . . . is all good news: Free voluntary reading looks better and better and more powerful than ever. And the alternatives to free reading as a means of developing high levels of literacy look weaker than ever.[8]

Krashen reports the results of "read and test" studies, in which students read text with vocabulary that is unfamiliar to them. They were not told they would be given a vocabulary or spelling test. Rather, they were tested to see whether they learned any of the meanings of unfamiliar words. Acquisition of vocabulary and spelling occurred without skill-building or correction, which shows that literacy development can occur without instruction.[9] Krashen summarizes,

> In-school free reading studies and "out of school" self-reported free voluntary reading studies show that more reading results in better reading comprehension, writing style, vocabulary, spelling, and grammatical development.[10]

To apply these research findings in elementary schools, school librarians must allow as much free voluntary reading time as possible. A case can be made for using the entire time students are assigned to the school library to read and read and read. This research supports the value of having free voluntary reading in schools where students are assigned to the school library during the teacher's planning period.

Rather than attempting to teach some isolated library skill, the librarian can teach reading by allowing students to read. Studies have shown that the amount of reading a student does is directly linked to achieving higher-order independent reading and that increased volume has been positively linked to increased reading comprehension, vocabulary, and writing skills.[11]

In January 1998, the National Center for Education Statistics reported "Long-Term Trends in Student Reading Performance." Their conclusions were as follows:

> Acceptable levels of literacy are achieved by most pupils, in most systems, despite a diversity of reading methods and traditions. In general, however, achievement is greatest when the educational systems are well endowed financially, when teachers are well educated, when students have ready access to good books, when they enjoy reading and do it often, and when their first language is the same as that of the language of the school.[12]

While the financial endowments of school systems and the educational qualifications of teachers fall outside the responsibility of most school librarians, they are responsible for their students having ready access to good books. Research confirms the need for a wide variety of materials to entice interest in reading for students.

The connection between the amount of reading done and reading proficiency has been well known and accepted for a number of years. Less well known but of equal importance has been the finding that more access to reading materials *leads* to more reading, and subsequently higher reading achievement, and can itself explain a great deal of variation in reading scores.[13]

Elley found that the size of the school library was the number one factor distinguishing the reading scores of nine-year-olds between the high- and low-scoring nations, with an impressive effect size of .82. Frequent silent reading time was the next most important variable, with an effect size of .78.[14]

McQuillan closes his book with this paragraph:

> There is now considerable evidence that the amount and quality of students' access to reading materials is substantively related to the amount of reading they engage in, which in turn is the most important determinant of reading achievement. Many students attend schools where the level of print access is abysmal, creating a true crisis in reading performance. . . . I do *not* wish to argue that simply providing books is all that is needed for schools to succeed. . . . But just as we would not ask a doctor to heal without medicine, so we should not ask teachers and schools to teach without the materials to do so.[15]

The challenge for every school librarian at every level is to provide a robust collection of reading materials, print and digital, equitable access for every student, and to encourage and promote free voluntary reading for pleasure, in addition to the intensive work that will be necessary to acquire and integrate the correct materials at the right level of text complexity for each student into their planning for collaborative instruction with teachers in all areas of the curriculum in order to facilitate deep content knowledge and broad understandings.

Commercial Reading Incentive and Software Programs

School librarians are often asked by their administrators to participate in and coordinate reading initiatives. In an effort to increase reading, schools may implement a commercial computerized reading incentive program. Scholastic's *Reading Counts* and Advantage Learning System's *Accelerated Reader* are the two industry leaders of this type of computerized reading program that have proliferated in the past. With these programs, students read from specific books, generally obtained from the core fiction collection of the school library. After reading the book, the students then take a computer test on what they just read. Points are awarded based on the correct number of answers and the length and difficulty of the book. Although both the incentive industry and educators agree that these tests do not measure true comprehension or higher-order thinking skills, it is also established that they do measure basic recall and the amount of text that has been processed.

Disagreement about the effectiveness of these programs is often debated with two major recurring themes: (1) teachers may use points to assign reading grades; and (2) reading is not connected to its misuse of the points and program intrinsic rewards, but instead an external reward is used to coerce reading as a means to get prizes. The literature has articles in favor of and against the use of such external reward systems. Unfortunately, some of the research has been conducted by the developers themselves rather than independent researchers, and it is not surprising that their research reports that the programs are effective.

Commercial incentive programs can become a real problem or a boon to school librarians. On the positive side, libraries will generally require a larger and newer book collection to support the increased demand and use of books. Administrators and parents who support these programs will generally provide funds to implement them. As long as the money is *in addition to* the amount needed to implement a balanced collection development policy, this is a way to grow a school library's collection. Initially, at least, the students will also tend to read a significantly larger number of books and visit the library more often in their quest for points. Teachers are likely to rely more heavily on the school librarian to support the reading program and to realize the importance of increased access opportunities for their students. Difficulties can occur if the collection development policy is ignored when teachers (or parents) insist that only books available from and tested by these programs be added to the collection. Additionally, a school that makes a small initial investment in one of these programs may have very few quizzes. This can cause students to limit their selections to a small number of options, and this will discourage reading choice based on interest. Once a school is firmly entrenched with an incentive program, school librarians may find that students will resist checking out books (even the brand-new fiction) unless a quiz is available because they can't earn credit for reading them.

It is debatable whether extrinsic rewards provide the literacy development that reading alone can do. School librarians can help teachers understand that the score from a computer test taken by their students does not necessarily indicate an understanding of the content of what has been read. Using the computerized reading program as a way of measuring reading practice and time on task may simplify record-keeping and verify that students have actually read books, which is something that self-reported reading logs do not do. Krashen reports: "Despite the popularity of [a reading management program], we must conclude that there is no real evidence supporting it, no real evidence that the additional tests and rewards add anything to the power of simply supplying access to high-quality and interesting reading material and providing time for children to read."[16] School librarians may implement creative reading initiatives that are successful by keeping reading voluntary, linking it to intrinsic rewards, and maintaining a relationship with teachers to support a strong reading instruction program instead of supplanting it.

Sharing Reading and Curriculum Research

No one doubts that the world is welcoming the advent of telecommunications to provide instantaneous access to information, but this merely intensifies the emphasis on reading. To understand most information on a computer screen, one must be able to read and interpret the language of the information. Students must know how to read, and they will learn when they are in schools with strong reading programs. Content area studies cannot be realized until students become competent readers. Reading is basic. Research shows that reading programs are stronger when they are supported with an excellent collection of materials in the school library. This and other research helps teachers learn best practices. School librarians should be aware of the latest research and share it with teachers.

Fisher and Ivey[17] suggested that the traditional practice of assigning all students to read the same book at the same time results in a singularly unenthusiastic approach to the enjoyment of literature. Even high-achieving students take shortcuts just to finish assignments. School librarians can help teachers move away from requiring students to read the same book by providing a list of quality options within a theme that allows for books of increasing text complexity. This will allow teachers to guide students in choosing appropriate-level texts and will allow students choice and keep them engaged.

Because the school library has current and ongoing subscriptions to either hard copy or online professional journals in the professional collection, school librarians should search the education research for results they can share with teachers. Teachers are often pressured to implement the current educational trend. "Keeping teachers informed will help them structure programs using the library."[18] Sharing research creates the opportunity for you, the librarian, to share in the implementation of a reading program, and everyone wins. When librarians work with teachers to improve reading proficiency, they are helping learners use their skills, resources, and tools to inquire, think critically, and gain knowledge.

The Education Program and the Curriculum

The major task of a school is to educate its students; it follows that the number one task of a school librarian is to assist teachers in successfully turning units of curriculum into opportunities for student inquiry that will promote lifelong learning. Unit activities are planned with full knowledge of current teaching methods, an understanding of student learning styles, and knowledge of the curriculum and the types of assignments. The school librarian's goal is to collaboratively plan and co-teach units of instruction that encourage and enable student inquiry to take place. This means managing the library as a classroom with the knowledge that the librarian will sometimes need to go into the classroom to facilitate a co-teaching experience. For a school librarian to meet the teaching needs of teachers and the learning needs of students, the school librarian must understand how to teach and how students learn. School librarians should strive to be excellent teachers themselves, staying abreast of new technologies and new teaching methods and theories. As excellent researchers, they are able to access and share current information with faculty and administration. They will be able to use those new learnings to model the best instruction and provide staff development opportunities for their fellow teachers. They become the learning leaders or specialists in the school. An excellent resource to consider in understanding this role of the school librarian is *Librarians as Learning Specialists* by Harada and Zmuda.[19]

Analyzing Teaching Methods

Despite the efforts of education leaders who suggest the need to use a variety of resources and teaching methods to accommodate students' different learning styles, many teachers still use textbook and lecture as their primary—if not only—teaching method. A colleague of one of the book's authors insists that this tradition is a product of the faculty in schools of education, who teach almost exclusively by textbook and lecture, following a model from their own basic education and higher education faculty. This textbook model does not demonstrate to future teachers how or why to make use of instructional design strategies to incorporate a variety of methods to teach and a variety of library and other materials into lesson plans to reach every student. Moving beyond the textbook encourages teachers and librarians to plan experiences that will help teachers to expand curriculum experiences and encourage individualized and group activities that will meet the needs of students.

Teachers who anticipate student learning through a variety of methods make heavy use of materials beyond the textbook. Planning curriculum-based inquiry projects with teachers to ensure that students can explore a topic of interest or embrace an interesting project and report this learning or problem solution in a meaningful way requires much more time than preparing a lecture and developing a test on the content. Librarians can also promote the idea of the Genius Hour[20] in their schools, which encourages students to make individual inquiries into topics of their choice. Either type of project is coordinated with the library staff to confirm the availability of library space and materials when activities move out of the classroom. Topics are expanded to permit students to conduct their research as individuals and in small groups.

Many teachers are better able to manage classroom-wide assignments than independent study or group projects, but the school librarian can help them manage individual projects and empower students to research topics of their individual choice. School librarians help by suggesting alternatives to "Make a poster" or "Create a PowerPoint" to show what students can use to demonstrate what they have learned. These boring presentations are as boring for the student carrying out the assignment as they will be to the audience who must view this result. The interesting ways to present student findings grow exponentially with new technology applications. It is the responsibility of school librarians to be informed and continually update their knowledge in order to pique student interest.

Librarians can do much to encourage alternative teaching methods and materials for covering the curriculum. *Standards for the 21st-Century Learner* suggests expanding assignments to be done by groups. It states, "Participate and collaborate as members of a social and intellectual network of learners,"[21] and "Share knowledge and participate ethically and productively as members of our democratic society."[22] The school librarian will encourage project- and problem-based learning activities to enhance student interest and learning.

As discussed more thoroughly in Chapter 11, research studies are ambivalent about how successful certain media are for accomplishing tasks that become knowledge and learning. Certainly when media are used incorrectly, it should be no surprise if there is little improvement in learning. However, media provide a different approach to the learning task, and the librarian must be aware of the hard copy and electronic resources in the collection and available online in order to offer teachers a change of pace. For some students, visual or auditory media are the best ways to learn because they do not rely on reading skills. If teachers are to use media, they must be accessible. Teachers can be encouraged to change their teaching methods only if the alternative is perceived to be no more, and preferably less, work than their previous method. Remind them that collaboration and co-teaching means at least two and maybe more teachers will be designing the strategies, teaching and completing the project, and evaluating the results.

Expanding projects requires extensive planning, but the rewards are well worth it. Working closely with teachers, librarians help plan units of work by agreeing on desired student outcomes and designing the unit of study; deciding on appropriate teaching methods; preparing activities related to the unit; helping teach the unit; deciding methods of testing; and, finally, helping score the products and assigning the grades.

If examples are needed to show projects and how they are evaluated, this is explained in *Assessing for Learning: Librarians and Teachers as Partners.*[23] A wide variety of assessment models are also shown in this volume.

Helping Improve Teacher Assignments

Helping teachers improve their assignments will increase learning opportunities and make learning more interesting. It is easy to illustrate a boring assignment. A common use of the library for classroom assignments is the book report. At the elementary level, the assignment may be as unexciting as, "Read a book with at least 100 pages." From the management standpoint, this is simple. It does not take long for the school librarian to spot books with more than 100 pages. The assignment lacks creativity, and this is not lost on students. Offering to help teachers make creative assignments, adding inquiry research activities and creative reporting of what was read, becomes a major opportunity for librarians.

The librarian encourages the use of appropriate and accurate referencing of sources in all projects. This means that the librarian must teach students how to verify and cite correctly information they find in various resources and learn how to use the various software programs and online resources available for students to use as well as monitor and assist students with the process of completing the assignment. Assisting teachers in reading, viewing, or listening to the final projects and sharing responsibility in grading projects are both part of the librarian's curriculum responsibilities. Reviewing student projects allows the librarian to understand when further instruction is needed to help students become more efficient researchers and users of ideas and information.

Understanding the Learner

As accomplished teachers themselves, school librarians must draw on their knowledge of learning theory and child development to participate in designing instruction in collaboration with teachers. Librarians have in-depth knowledge of literature for students of all ages and know just the age when a particular title is best used. They have in-depth knowledge of all types of learning materials accessible from their library and know just the right one for the age group or type of learner in any given instructional situation. The classroom or subject area teacher will know their students and be able to bring that knowledge of their preferred learning modalities to the collaboration discussion. The school librarian will have expert knowledge of what materials are best to use with all types of learners and is invaluable to the planning process. Together the school librarian and teacher make a great team in planning the best learning experience for all students.

Understanding Curriculum

School librarians who have elementary teaching certification or a subject specialty at the secondary level in addition to library certification already know a good deal about curriculum. These persons are highly knowledgeable about the relationship of the curriculum to the classroom. Most preparation programs for school librarians provide some experience in the development of curriculum units in course work and in the practicum setting.

In preparing to participate in curriculum collaborative planning, librarians learn as much as possible about the curriculum in the local school. Begin this process by creating a collection of all textbooks used in the building, both commercially produced in hard copy and e-format and teacher created e-textbooks. In some schools, textbooks are not used in some subject areas and the curriculum may be based on an online program or some type of software program or other media. Make sure that the school library has access to these types of programs as well. Include copies of curriculum guides developed at the building and district levels and at the state department of public instruction. Collect state or national standards for student learning in all subject areas. These also will be useful to teachers who need to know what has been covered in previous grade levels and subject courses and what will be covered in the future. Library staff reviews textbooks and other materials used by teachers to help plan for the semester's probable units of work.

Throughout the year, the librarian expands on the projects reviewed during the first week in the building, determining what each teacher teaches and integrating the method of teaching, the materials needed beyond those provided in the classroom, and the probable use to be made of all types of resources available in the library and online.

One way the librarian can take an active part in curriculum development is by volunteering to serve on textbook or curriculum development committees. The choice of textbook opens the possibility of locating both text and technology to meet new needs. The collaboration process for developing units of instruction begins in advance of the arrival of the textbooks. When hard copy textbooks are replaced by e-books, the technology must be available for all students and some will not have access to readers. This will require purchases and perhaps new policy development if students are to be allowed to check out tablets or other e-readers in order to access the texts.

Librarians also serve on curriculum committees. By serving on these grade level or subject area committees, librarians are better able to collaborate and provide library resources for the unit plans of all teachers. Managing time to participate in these meetings may appear to be difficult or even impossible. However, this is one of the primary roles of the school librarian in the education of students, and it must be given high priority. The need for backup assistance so the librarian can attend meetings and still keep the library open and the instructional program proceeding as usual can be used to justify additional help in the library. The librarian should ask for the services of a substitute teacher when curriculum planning meetings are scheduled for more than one period in the day. Justifying this need emphasizes the importance of co-teaching units of instruction, of working with teachers and curriculum and keeping the library available with a professional replacement when the librarian has responsibilities elsewhere.

In the process of developing curriculum, school librarians take a leadership role because they teach all the students, work with all the teachers, and understand the curriculum throughout the school. By taking the lead, the librarian suggests units that could go across grade levels and across subject areas, making the instructional program an integrated whole rather than separate, segregated components. Students often have difficulty relating to what they have learned before, what they are learning in other classrooms, and how this affects their everyday lives. Ultimately the relationship of what is taught to what is needed for the future may become more apparent to the students who are tasked with the learning; they may be able to design some of the activities to improve learning. They can begin to collaborate with the teacher and librarian team.

Helping teachers provide the kinds of experiences that students will translate into their immediate future and when they are adults is difficult. Faced with the often required, rigid programs tied to test results, teachers are very limited with little opportunity for experimentation with curriculum. The role of the school librarian is one of leadership in helping teachers move beyond the test and into activities that will help students see the relationship of their schoolwork to their futures in the real world. The librarian's in-depth knowledge of what is being taught and what will be taught in each classroom provides opportunities to suggest combining some learning experiences. The big-picture knowledge of all content standards enables the librarian to see overlaps and repeated broad requirements, which can be streamlined and taught as one lesson—thus freeing up instructional time. Students working in makerspaces or participating in schoolwide Genius Hour projects can cross grade levels with an interest in a particular application. Methods for creating this environment in the library are described in *School Library Makerspace*[24] and *Challenge-Based Learning in the School Library Makerspace*.[25] This will be discussed in more detail later in the chapter.

Integration of learning has become a challenge; rote memorization to pass a test should not replace critical thinking, and librarians can help teachers remember the value of critical thinking assignments to help students prepare for lifelong learning. When curriculum is discussed, the librarian should be an aggressive advocate of expanding student learning into real-world experiences such as project- and problem-based learning to place the learning of students into the context of how they will function in the future. One way to assist in this is to make sure students are given opportunities to engage in inquiry learning and help teachers to guide and scaffold research projects for student success as described in *Guided Inquiry*[26] by Kulthau, Maniotes, and Caspari.

The School Librarian as Teacher

The willingness of the librarian to participate in teaching a lesson and reviewing the final products will encourage teachers to plan units of work together. To have someone help make teaching both easier and more effective and assist with the assessment of student progress should be irresistible. Teachers quickly realize that one plus one equals two, and students now have the skills of two teachers focused on their project rather than one. This simple equation should help other teachers recognize how teaching across the curriculum and across grade levels is sharing responsibility. And, while it might take a little extra planning time, the return on the investment in the learning of students seems a small price to pay.

It could be difficult to coordinate the collaboration of teachers who may not, at first, feel comfortable in joint teaching experiences or in setting their students free to learn independently and in small groups. It requires the best efforts of the librarian to lead the teamwork to make this happen. It can begin with jointly teaching the various kinds of literacies.

Teaching All Kinds of Literacy

Long seen as a major role of the librarian has been the responsibility for teaching research skills, "information literacy." The ever-increasing quantities of new information being generated daily dictates the role of the school librarian as responsible for teaching many kinds of literacy to students; the original "information" literacy remains in place but the concept has been divided into specialties such as technology literacy, digital literacy, and health literacy, among others. Reminding teachers that assignments promote information literacy so that all students become information literate means teaching students how to access, evaluate, and use information. This is more than showing students how to find information through the OPAC or online through the resources there. It begins with a student who recognizes the need for information. Students are capable of understanding when they have a need for information.

One author remembers an in-service session in the mid-1960s where the guest speaker suggested that schools in the 21st century would no longer exist. Rather, a child would see a caterpillar in the backyard. Carefully picking it up, the child would move to a central building, where an information specialist would be available to help find out where the caterpillar came from, what it eats, and how long it will live, among other questions. The questions would come because of a need for information, and information specialists would assure that the information located was accurate and complete. Teaching the sources of information would only be necessary *after* the student had developed the research question. These are all part of teaching the research process.

Inquiry Learning

The librarian helps teachers implementing inquiry-based learning with a focus on activities that will help students develop critical thinking skills and prepare them for tasks that they will be doing after they leave school and join the workforce. Many models exist for teaching the research process, but Carol Kuhlthau's six principles of guided inquiry have been thoroughly tested.

1. Children learn by being actively engaged in and reflecting on an experience.

2. Children learn by building on what they already know.

3. Children develop higher-order thinking through guidance at critical points in the learning process.

4. Children have different ways and modes of learning.

5. Children learn through social interaction with others.

6. Children learn through instruction and experience in accord with their cognitive development.[27]

A second component of information literacy is that students can evaluate the information they find. Just as librarians establish the authority of authors and publishers before selecting materials to add to the collection, the student learns to establish the authority of all information presented. Is the information written, collected, photographed, and stored on the Internet accurate and relevant and valid? Students must learn to expect to find all sides of controversial issues, misinformation, be able to distinguish fact and the opinion of the author, and find the sources to correct inaccurate information or to expand into another point of view if information is questionable.

Students who locate information are taught and retaught how to write a research paper. This process begins in the early grades and continues through high school. At the most basic level, students construct an outline of information after they determine the organization of the report. Drafts of the report are shared with other class members so the editing process is two-way. That is, when one student's draft is being evaluated, the student is reviewing a colleague's paper. Current performance evaluation models include the student's oral and written products, again with the student's self-evaluation as well as evaluations of other students' products.

Teaching information literacy is more easily accomplished with the use of Kuhlthau's information search process. The steps include

1. the teacher's initiation of the unit of study

2. the students' selection of a topic

3. exploration to find a focus

4. formulation of a focus for the research

5. collection of information

6. presentation, and

7. assessment with self-reflection process.[28]

When the librarian joins teachers in planning classroom assignments, it is easy to move into the inquiry process.

Assistance with classroom assignments also involves evaluation of student performance. While the current focus is on testing, school librarians can encourage teachers to continue to help individual students and their preparation for the workplace and lifelong learning. The librarian can be actively involved in several ways:

1. Locating the various methods of assessing student progress reported in the literature.

2. Assuring that assessments of student progress include an analysis of their ability to locate and synthesize information from a variety of resources.

3. Working with students and teachers to make judgments about what was learned and, if the presentation was disappointing, what needs to happen for learning to occur.

Planning inquiry-based units of instruction through evaluating student performance brings the school librarian into the classroom environment.

The School Librarian in the Classroom

The role of the librarian in the classroom is one of co-teaching with the teacher. The placement of the librarian, media, and equipment in a location away from the library must be planned in advance. Students who wish to use the library throughout the day will expect to find it open and all reference materials readily available. If the school librarian is in a classroom teaching, additional staffing must be considered so that the school library remains open.

One solution is to use the library as a classroom.

The School Library as Classroom

The library is changed into a classroom for everyone and expanded to include every teacher when it becomes a learning commons for the school. Koechlin, Rosenfeld, and Loertscher describe the learning commons as a "new learning model":

> Schools must develop new relevant learning models in response to
> students who expect to learn in new ways using the technologies
> they use ubiquitously outside of school. The Learning Commons is
> a real world approach to creating such a new collaborative
> learning model for students and teachers.[29]

This library is scheduled to accommodate students engaged in a wide variety of activities planned by a different composition of collaborators. Art, music, physical education, counselors join classroom teachers to work to initiate activities that are collaboratively planned. Once the curriculum, teaching, and student assignments have been determined, students go to work.

Librarians still teach how to find resources in the OPAC or other electronic resources, in book format (reading a table of contents, consulting an index) and online, help students create bibliographies and avoid plagiarism, and, perhaps, discover "truth." The library classroom offers access to library collections around the world, databases, including full text, interactive video, and e-mail communication, among others. Teaching students to discriminate between fact and fiction, truth and falsehoods is becoming an ever-increasing task for the librarian.

Acting as a classroom, the library offers access to the world through social media allowing students to communicate with other students, perhaps practicing their knowledge of another language. They can hold discussions with authors, politicians, journalists, and others through interviews via Skype or another similar source. Establishing these links is one of the activities enabled by the school librarian as a manager of the education program provided in the library.

Makerspaces

A current hot trend for speakers at school library conferences and in the literature is makerspaces. If the library is not a large space, this may mean a small corner with wider use at a time other than the school day. Students move beyond preparing reports or even building a diorama into publishing their own books or building other projects that allow them to use their creative thinking skills. In some schools the activities in the makerspace are curricular related. For instance, if the third grade is studying types of bridges, the makerspace during that time period would feature activities in building various types of bridges and perhaps participating in challenges relating to building such structures.

Many school librarians are developing their makerspaces into places where students are given the opportunity to solve challenges. These challenges may be puzzles, or problems involving constructing vehicles, robots, bridges, or other physical solutions that solve a particular problem. Students may be asked to carry out an experiment or learn to do something they do not know how to do. The librarian is charged with helping students research, seek expert help if necessary, and find the appropriate materials to solve the challenge using critical thinking skills and much perseverance. *Challenge-Based Learning in the School Library Makerspace*[30] was mentioned earlier as a reference to help with this.

Awareness for Teachers and Administrators

The librarian keeps administrators and teachers aware of trends in all areas of education so that they can determine which changes they may be asked to implement. When professional journals come into the library or the monthly new edition of a popular journal is posted online, the librarian suggests articles that administrators and teachers will find of benefit. Ideas gleaned from a review of each table of contents can target information literacy–related activities to match the discussion in the subject area. For the principal, the librarian helps interpret national and state government regulations. Preparing frequent collections of articles on particular subjects or sending electronic links to current hot topics will help administrators make informed decisions.

Improving the Curriculum

School librarians may feel helpless in the face of a rigid curriculum centered around a need for students to score well on statewide testing or to match rigid standards.. However, changes can be made if teachers are willing to collaborate on meaningful assignments. Small pilot programs may be implemented to see whether they result in improved learning for students.

The authors are concerned when noneducational "services" are put into place such as organizing resources rather than using the time to work with teachers and curriculum. It is far more important to work with students on their inquiry research projects than to send them fine notices, and the time expended in both cases may be equal. Helping complete projects at the end of the school year and doing preliminary planning for the next year are far more important than taking an inventory. Weighing these activities to meet management needs against curriculum should show curriculum in the winning column.

The curriculum is the foundation for the school librarian's planning. That foundation is built by knowing what teachers want and need to be able to be effective teachers. Loertscher[31] recommends that this platform be created using a participatory culture. The following has been adapted with permission from an unpublished document he created for a planning committee.

This paper has given the planning committee the opportunity and choice to build within each school a participative culture vs. a prescriptive culture.

The question might arise: Why build a participatory culture when the juggernaut of testing seems to favor, even demand a prescriptive culture? In the [past] era of No Child Left Behind and now Common Core, exact specifications of what every learner is to know and is able to do actually is antithetical to the concept of "library" since the exact texts, concepts, and skills can all be supplied to the learner in a package as now offered by many commercial firms. There is no need to explore beyond the prescribed resources or strategies to meet exacting rubrics and levels of competence. Furthermore, data gathering is present at every step of the way to insure uniformity in learning.

In such a world, the school librarian might have a single set of prescribed content to deliver and guarantee that each learner will meet expectations as a part of the whole school prescriptive culture. Such an approach might lead to an "information literacy" curriculum with a state, national, and international comparison that would demonstrate that every child would have identical skills. Thus, the library becomes one piece in the larger prescriptive framework. Commercial firms can design and supply such a curriculum as a part of the prescribed curriculum and are already doing so. In this world, is there any need for a separate teacher known as the librarian when the classroom teacher can have those skills embedded into whatever curriculum they are delivering?

One of the best arguments for a more participatory culture is the simple fact that the dropout rate of young people is now more than 50 percent in all urban centers. Is this an acceptable rate, and how does this rate compare to what is happening in every state?

Each year, the voices for a participatory culture grow louder and louder. This is evidenced in the many videos and articles being published today.

The idea here is that a library or Learning Commons spans both worlds. It can fit into the prescriptive culture wherever small windows happen to open, but it also provides a major "island" in the school that will appeal to all sorts of learning styles, current technologies, excellence above and beyond minimums, both formal and informal learning. In other words, it is the center where former dropouts can flourish under the mentorship of the librarian, technology specialists, school counselors, gifted and talented specialists, and any other specialists in the school. Further, the idea is that the program of the Learning Commons and its emphasis on collaboratively taught learning experiences *increases* the percentage of those who meet expectations and exceeds those minimums.

As envisioned, the school librarian does not have to make the choice of being either prescriptive or participatory because the library/Learning Commons program encompasses all types of educational paradigms.

Teachers who embrace constructivist principles usually trust their pedagogy because their students meet or exceed test scores delivered by behaviorist and prescriptive teachers.

If the framework is created as participatory, then the school librarian has a broad range of choices under which to creatively develop the kind of program that works under the local school umbrella and the varying teaching styles of the faculty. To prescribe a rigid framework, in this writer's opinion, is to ignore the real world of information and technology as it now exists and that is unlikely to remain the same.

It is a charge worth leading.[32]

The charge above is one to create a learning environment in a new type of library or learning commons with many new avenues for teachers to work together. However, the most creative librarian can plan the most helpful implementation of the curriculum and have yet another hurdle to cross. Even with sufficient staff, quantities of materials, and a pleasant facility, enticing users into the library remains a major management task.

Exercises

1. Visit an elementary classroom teacher and talk about how he or she has been working with students to improve their reading. Try to determine how the school librarian might work with this teacher and that plan.
2. Choose a middle or high school teacher and discuss the concept of text complexity with that teacher. Create a bibliography of books of varying levels of text complexity to use in helping students choose a book to read on an assigned theme.
3. Plan an integrated curricular lesson that will teach reading skills, inquiry skills, and required content area curricular content.

4. Create a 15-minute presentation to explain information literacy to a group of teachers or parents and the community.
5. If you have access to a school, ask the librarian if a teacher has made an assignment that needs to be modified and plan those modifications.
6. Plan to visit a school if possible that houses a school library makerspace. Make notes about the activities available for students. Are the activities applicable to curriculum? In what way?

Notes

1. Henry L. Cecil and Willard A. Heaps, *School Library Service in the United States: An Interpretative Survey* (New York: H. W. Wilson, 1940), 41. Reprinted in Melvin M. Bowie, *Historic Documents of School Libraries* (Englewood, CO: Hi Willow Research and Publishing, 1986).

2. Douglas Fisher and Gay Ivey, "Evaluating the Interventions for Struggling Adolescent Readers," *Journal of Adolescent & Adult Literacy* 50 (November 2006): 182.

3. Rachel Wadham, *Integrating Children's Literature through the Common Core* (Libraries Unlimited, 2015).

4. Rachel Waldham, *Integrating Young Adult Literature through the Common Core* (Libraries Unlimited, 2013).

5. Stephen D. Krashen, Sy-Ying Lee, and Christy Lao, *Comprehensible and Compelling* (Santa Barbara, CA: Libraries Unlimited, 2017), 46.

6. Stephen Krashen, *The Power of Reading,* 2nd ed. (Englewood, CO: Libraries Unlimited, 2004).

7. Ibid., 20.

8. Stephen Krashen, *Free Voluntary Reading* (Santa Barbara, CA: Libraries Unlimited, 2011).

9. Ibid., 13.

10. Ibid., 17.

11. R. L. Allington, *What Really Matters for Struggling Readers: Designing Research-Based Programs,* 3rd ed. (Boston, MA: Pearson, 2012); W. G. Brozo, G. Shel, and K. Topping, "Engagement in Reading: Lessons Learned from Three PISA Countries," *Journal of Adolescent & Adult Literacy* 51(4) (2007): 304–315; J. Cipielewski and K. E. Stanovich, "Predicting Growth in Reading Ability from Children's Exposure to Print," *Journal of Experimental Child Psychology* 54(1) (1992): 74–89; S. D. Krashen, *The Power of Reading: Insights from the Research* (Englewood, CO: Libraries Unlimited, 1993).

12. National Center for Education Statistics, *NAEP Facts,* U.S. Department of Education, Office of Education Research and Improvement, *NAEP Facts* vol. 3, no. 1 (January 1998).

13. Krashen, *Power of Reading,* op. cit., 13.

14. Warwick B. Elley, "Lifting Literacy Levels in Developing Countries: Some Implications from an IEA Study," in *Promoting Reading in Developing Countries: Views on Making Reading Materials Accessible to Increase Literacy Levels,* ed. V. Greaney (Newark, DE: International Reading Association, 1996), xxi–xxii.

15. Jeff McQuillan, *The Literacy Crisis: False Claims, Real Solutions* (Portsmouth, NH: Heinemann), 86.

16. Krashen, *Power of Reading,* 121.

17. Douglas Fisher and Gay Ivey, "Farewell to 'A Farewell to Arms': Deemphasizing the Whole-Class Novel," *Phi Delta Kappan* 88 (March 2007): 494–97.

18. Anne DiPardo and Pat Schnack, "Partners in Reading, Partners in Life," *Educational Leadership* 60 (March 2003): 56–58.

19. Violet Harada and Alison Zmuda, *Librarians as Learning Specialists* (Santa Barbara, CA: Libraries Unlimited, 2008).

20. Elizabeth Rush, *Bringing the "Genius Hour" to Your School Library: Implementing a School Wide Passion Project Program* (Santa Barbara, CA: Libraries Unlimited, 2017).

21. American Association of School Librarians, *Standards for the 21st-Century Learner* (Chicago: American Library Association, 2007), 6.

22. Ibid., 3.

23. Violet H. Harada and Joan M. Yoshina, *Assessing for Learning: Librarians and Teachers as Partners*, 2nd ed. (Santa Barbara, CA: Libraries Unlimited, 2010).

24. Leslie Preddy, *School Library Makerspace* (Santa Barbara, CA: Libraries Unlimited, 2013).

25. Collene Graves, Aaron Graves, and Diana L. Redina, *Challenge-Based Learning in the School Library Makerspace* (Santa Barbara, CA: Libraries Unlimited, 2017).

26. Carol C. Kuhlthau, Leslie K. Maniotes, and Ann K. Caspari, *Guided Inquiry: Learning in the 21st Century* (Westport, CT: Libraries Unlimited, 2007).

27. Carol C. Kuhlthau, *Seeking Meaning: A Process Approach to Delivery and Information Service* (Norwood, NJ: Ablex, 1993), 25.

28. Ibid., 17–18.

29. Carol Koechlin, Esther Rosenfeld, and David V. Loertscher, *Building a Learning Commons: A Guide for School Administrators and Learning Leadership Teams* (Salt Lake City, UT: Hi Willow Research and Publishing, 2010), 2.

30. Graves, Graves, and Redina, op. cit.

31. David V. Loertscher, unpublished paper, June 2013.

32. Ibid.

6
Assessment and Evaluation

School library educator David V. Loertscher has often asked his audience these two questions:

1. If you had 10 cents for each time you had helped a teacher with a curricular unit, what could you buy: a new suede jacket or an ice cream cone?

2. If you were arrested for contributing to a student's learning, would there be enough evidence to convict you?

The response is usually a smile; both are actually thoughtful questions. They turn attention to how school librarians meet the dual goals of helping teachers and contributing to student learning. Successes point out the value of the library program and the importance of the school librarian in the school. Failures identify the need for improvement. It's a matter of assessment and evaluation. This chapter defines these and explains some places to look for guidance in the process. It describes ways to evaluate the degree that a library guarantees access to information, the components of the library that are the responsibility of the school librarian, and ends with ways to assess the value of the library in the education of students.

Measurement, according to Brian Kenney, former editor of *School Library Journal,* is the key to the survival of the position of school librarian:

> Neither better relations with our colleagues nor more preaching about the importance of information literacy will save our jobs. Data—that measurement of a library program's impact on student learning—isn't something we traditionally collect, or even know how to collect, but if we are to survive, it's the information we desperately need.[1]

Evaluation has many definitions. According to one dictionary, to evaluate means "to ascertain or fix the value or worth of; to examine and judge, appraise."[2] Determining the worth of a project, product, service, person, or program to fix a value to it can be threatening. The judging process is frightening because it may reveal that what was thought to be helpful is, in fact, not helpful at all. From early years, children are tested and retested for scholastic achievement, experiences that are often anxiety provoking. This tension is not easily outgrown, and adults are seldom secure in what they perceive to be a test atmosphere. The same is true when the outcome of the evaluation is to fix a value to a program or a service. It becomes more complex when one tries to assess learning.

The difference between assessment and evaluation is subtle. Assessment uses the word "evaluation" in its definition. It is "the evaluation or estimate of the nature, quality, or ability of someone or something."[3] Assessment is an estimate of "someone or something" while evaluation itself becomes a judgment, an appraisal. Assessment is only valid when it is documented.

A less threatening approach might seem to be analyzing a program through *measurement* rather than evaluation, particularly when evaluation is viewed as measurement to assign a rank order score from high to low, good to bad, or A to F. Top programs receive A's, and a less effective program earns a B. Just as in assigning grades to scores on a classroom test, cutoff levels on any scale appear to be arbitrary. Students regret missing an A by one point or, when numerical standards are given to collections, no school librarian would enjoy having their library collection described inadequate because it had only 19,999 books while 20,000 books are considered adequate. This means school librarians must see that evaluation of the library, whenever possible, is more than measurement alone but testing in the context of quality rather than any arbitrary numerical quantity, not a test score. However, so many things are judged on a numerical score that this must be acknowledged.

Evaluation of the school library program and its components is undertaken for one or many reasons. The school librarian may choose to test a single program facet. School district administrators may wish to compare all programs or any part of their library program at the local level, or they may wish to receive approval by a regional accrediting agency. The most important evaluation results, especially if school library programs are to continue to exist and be managed by a certified school librarian, mean gathering statistics showing student learning gains through research and teaching in the school library. In each of these cases, a different approach may be necessary to provide the proper responses to evaluation. This is never an easy approach, especially when the evaluation is only counting numbers.

One major problem with any numerical test is that most elements of the school library program are not easily quantified. Many quantity measures are not real measures of a program. For instance, circulation statistics reveal only what materials have moved out of the library. They do not tell the amount of use or, for that matter, whether there was any use at all. Results must be documented.

Documentation is the result of careful evaluations of many aspects of the program, and it can involve counting things, especially if the assessment is based upon some standards imposed by state law or evaluated by regional accrediting agencies. However, your evaluation is more than what you have in your collection or the number of times you offer special programs; school librarians also must assess student learning, which is much different and much more difficult than counting items. The most important aspect of evaluation and assessment is to show your worth to your administrators, your teachers, your parents, the school district, and your local community. But what kind of data do you need for your evaluation?

Quantitative and Qualitative Measures

To choose between data to collect will mean choosing whether the questions to be asked will gather data that is either quantitative or qualitative. Connaway and Radford explain this data in the following way:

> Quantitative research methods "use measurements and statistics to transform empirical data into numbers and to develop mathematical models that quantify behavior." Qualitative research methods "focus on observing events from the perspective of those involved and attempt to understand why individuals behave as they do."[4]

Simply said, quantitative evaluation collects numbers while qualitative evaluation collects answers to questions. Both have their pros and cons.

A major problem with quantitative evaluation is that few yardsticks exist against which to measure. Administrators place too much emphasis on counting things with little regard for their quality. The necessity of providing a certain number of books per pupil may result in neglect of the weeding process. Collections may meet an arbitrary numerical count but be out of date, in poor condition, or of no value to the current curriculum.

Quantitative measures may result in a one-dimensional perspective. School librarians develop and distribute a checklist asking students and teachers to indicate which services they are receiving. A wide variety of services may be offered, but such a survey will yield inaccurate results if most students and teachers are unaware that these services exist or if many services are offered that are not requested by teachers or students. It will not matter whether a service is available if no one makes use of that service. Although quantitative measures are often less helpful, some output measures are useful in describing the library program.

Counting output will certainly confirm library use. Output includes the number of teachers and students who come into the library each day, an estimate of the number of materials that circulate, the percentage of the student body using the library at least once a month, and other similar statistics. The better measure is the relationship of quantity to quality, although one may lead to the next.

Because quantity measures are specific and have little cause-and-effect value, they do not test a program adequately. Quality measures are much more significant but much more difficult to determine. A beginning is to measure what is against what should be and calculate the discrepancy; in some instances, this can be translated into an actual dollar amount. Although this sounds as if it is a quantity count, it is not. The "*what is*" is a quantitative count of professional and staff time allocation to tasks, equipment, materials available. The "*what should be*" outlines what is needed to provide quality for teachers and students and begins the process of determining how to make up the difference.

When students become frustrated finding data in the library, you can document this and create a chart with "what is" available (see Table 6.1). Then, finding resources in books or databases provides the evidence needed to improve the collection.

What happens next extends to the qualitative assessment. Qualitative evaluation is more difficult to collect simply because it is not easily quantifiable. The analysis can be very subjective and often open to charges of bias. However, this data will usually provide more in-depth thinking about issues

Table 6.1 Databases for Holocaust Unit

What Is	What Should Be	Available on American Memory (free)	Need to Add	Cost
1	3	Yes	1	$–

than a checklist to fill in numbers or a survey, even when the survey has a scale for the answers. Both of these will be explained further when the components of the library are measured. All evaluation relies upon what you want or need to measure.

Deciding What to Measure

If no one has suggested that any assessment is needed, then what you choose to assess will define the questions you and only you want to answer. How much do book talks in the library increase not just circulation but a genuine increase in reading for pleasure? Does creating a graphic novel corner in the library draw more readers? These answers help the librarian decide if an activity was successful and to continue the activity, to do more selling of the activity in the hopes of success, or to replace that activity with a different one.

Another approach is to gather information to match standards. How effective standards are to the improvement of school libraries depends upon who creates the standards. Regional accrediting agencies publish guidelines for components within the school, and the library is a part of this process. When an accrediting agency review is on the horizon, "standards" may become mandatory and the statistics required before the visit may involve counting the collection or other reports of library activities.

National associations such as the American Association of School Librarians (AASL) create and publish standards for libraries but their impact is only as great as school librarians make them. If no school librarian shares them with the school community, it is less likely they will be seen. However, these are developed by knowledgeable school librarians, and AASL provides information for exactly how to share them with the administrators, teachers, and parents. These can be applied to school libraries and the degree to which they are met is reported to the school and community.

Sometimes standards are mandatory by state law and districts must report compliance. They often outline minimum requirements that are within easy reach of school library programs. If not, local officials might demand that state funding be supplied to meet state-imposed standards, and this is never politically popular.

In a very few states, the standard is that professionally trained school librarians are required by law in every school; students are served by a librarian rather than a library aide or a volunteer. This is a yes/no evaluation. "Yes," the school has a librarian or "no," it does not. Because the salary factor of education is a large part of any budget, it is very difficult to get state legislators to pass standards specifying one professional personnel in every building. However, research has shown over and over that having a professional running the school library affects student achievement, making it an essential standard.

Moving beyond trying to find out if an idea was successful or completing the forms for a regional accreditation visit moves the librarian into a wider approach to assessment and evaluation. Planning these research projects may move you out of your comfort zone, but the end results will help chart the future of the library. Serious evaluation moves beyond standards.

Assessment and Evaluation beyond Standards

Perspectives of program evaluation exist:

1.   to find out what is right
2.   to find out what is wrong, and
3.   to use as an awareness device.

All of these perspectives are useful. Once these evaluations are begun, the process may center on looking at programs, services, and activities as they are impacted by facility, staff, and collection, while the larger need is to determine the role of the library in the learning of students and in the degree that the program offers access to information and how information is used. It's a stepping-up process from very little success to major success. Let's begin with finding out what is right and what is wrong.

Finding Out What Is Right or Wrong

Certainly, school librarians need to learn what is wrong so that simple adjustments, more in-depth changes, or alternatives can be put into place, or the activity can even be halted altogether. Finding out what is right is satisfying because it confirms that proper decisions have been made, adequate procedures are in place, and the program is running smoothly in those areas. Evaluation is not threatening when it confirms accomplishment or provides constructive plans for improvement. It should not be considered threatening if, by analyzing what is wrong, corrections can be implemented.

Asking teachers and students what they like about the library indicates the successes. Asking them what they would like to change about the library can point out what might be altered or even stopped to make improvements. Usually those answers are qualitative. However, they can begin as quantitative, but if you survey students and teachers on a 1–10 scale where you can count the answers, these scores can become qualitative as shown in Table 6.2. It becomes a more qualitative study when you have interviews or hold focus groups to respond to queries, yet the easiest scores to tabulate and report are quantitative answers, as was discussed in the difference between quantitative and qualitative assessment above.

Table 6.2   Ranking for Services

Low					High	Services
0	1	2	3	4	5	Individual students may come to the library when necessary.
0	1	2	3	4	5	The librarian regularly provides information about new resources to teachers.
0	1	2	3	4	5	Wireless access is available throughout the school.
0	1	2	3	4	5	Instruction in the library is tied directly to the curriculum unit being co-taught.

If no one acknowledges a service, it may point out that teachers and students don't recognize that the service is available for them. This leads to using evaluation as an awareness device.

Evaluation as an Awareness Device

Evaluation serves as an awareness device for teachers and administrators and is particularly useful for those who have misunderstood the purpose of the library program. Most school personnel base their expectations on models they observed when they were in elementary and high school, in teacher training programs, and in student teaching or practicum experience. These librarians who served as role models in previous teaching and learning situations may have been mediocre to excellent.

After graduation, teachers and administrators added to their perceptions when they accepted positions in schools and observed the library program and its relationship to their classes. Although some of these experiences may have provided excellent models, many did not. An effective evaluation designed with teacher and administrator input can raise their awareness and expectations. Generating a list of services currently offered as well as some potential services to add can inform administrators and teachers of opportunities available in the library. When the language of the questions is in something other than library jargon, it should be easier to get good answers and promote understanding.

Reporting back informs teachers who haven't been using a service that it is highly chosen by other teachers; this should cause some interest in exactly what that service is. On the other hand, a service that is recognized but not considered important can be either discarded or, for something like "organizing the collection," this "service" should be done outside of school hours.

Evaluation as a Management Device

School library managers need to know the success and failure of the basic aspects of their programs: facility, staff, resources, and services or programs. Testing these is described using both quantitative and qualitative measures. They are also measured against their support of the curriculum. The library is integrated into curriculum offerings, but how well is this happening? Resources are tailored to meet the needs of teachers and students, and these needs change as the curriculum changes, as grade levels are shifted among buildings, and as teachers are replaced. Do the current resources support the curriculum? The different types of learners in the school affect the collection, just as the teaching methods impact programs. How well are you supporting teaching and learning?

Methods to evaluate your program are described here and others will need to be located. If your evaluation can be patterned on an existing model and applied directly, you can begin immediately. It might be adapted by the library staff with assistance from other building-level or central administrative staff. Measuring devices may be created from scratch if other models do not seem to fit, but this requires knowledge of research methodology and experience that many school librarians were not introduced to during their college programs. In this case, help may be available in the school district or in a nearby university. Documents are available that show measuring techniques, and a list of these resources is found in Appendix C. A search of the recent literature will point to new ideas and methods to supplement what is found in this text.

Appraising the Facility

Management of the facility is discussed in Chapter 8. Evaluating space has to do with the more important element, the ambiance of the library and just how inviting it is for users. Students and teachers may be asked to make suggestions for improving the ambiance of the library with a survey or focus groups to get opinions. In so doing, they may take responsibility for helping raise funds to make simple or even more comprehensive adjustments. A quantitative analysis is simply counting the number of students who are in the library and at what times they come. Learning what they do in the library is also helpful. Students who are only reading books, many of which they bring to the library, or texting friends aren't seeking access to information. If they need to work in small groups, that will become apparent in how they arrange themselves in the space. This usage points out a lack of co-teaching that must be increased.

Space in the library is evaluated for the probable use by individual students, groups, or classes at all hours of the day. As the need for shelving books diminishes, space is opened up for different activities. What can be done in these spaces to open the library for small group learning spaces, makerspaces, and even a performance area? It is a moment to consider modifying the present library facility or building a learning commons in the school.

Gathering the information support for a plan to change the school library into a new configuration such as a learning commons for the school collects evidence of the need for such a renovation. Having students and teachers participating in gathering the testimony ensures their support and may lessen the time it takes to gather buy-in by the administration. Documented need for a larger and a differently arranged facility will support remodeling the present library or even building an entirely new facility.

Appraising Staff Performance

Performance appraisal is easy in the world of sports, where the height of the basketball player and the weight of the football player are easily determined facts. Success is calculated by baskets scored, rebounds made, yards gained, or number of tackles or passes completed. The ultimate test for the team is not the score for the individual players but that season's number of wins and losses and invitations to end-of-season tournaments.

Such statistics are not readily available for library staff, and the calculation of wins and losses is arbitrary most of the time. Asking teachers or students to determine wins and losses is difficult because the qualities that appeal to one student or teacher may not appeal to another. Frances Henne's basic rule for staff performance bears repeating:

> For some students, and in certain schools this may be many
> students, the only library skill that they should have to acquire
> is an awareness, imprinted indelibly and happily upon them,
> that the library is a friendly place where the librarians are eager
> to help.[5]

The score for "friendly place" and "librarians eager to help" may be determined in part by the numbers of students who seek the advice and counsel of the librarian, not only for curriculum needs and help in gaining access to information but also for matters that go beyond the scope of the classroom such as help for middle school students to learn about study opportunities in high school. High school librarians focus on helping students learn about educational opportunities after graduation and ways to finance these opportunities. The numbers of students who ask their librarians these types of questions depends upon their analysis of the librarian's willingness to listen, their compatibility with students. An especially important statistic that remains difficult to gather is the number of students who do continue their education after graduation. Schools gather the numbers of students who attend community colleges and universities, but few look at other training opportunities. An even more difficult statistic to gather would be the numbers of students who complete their training or education after high school and become successful members of their communities.

Friendly staff personalities are even more difficult to score. Interpersonal relationships, though identified, are not easy to describe in terms of quantity or quality. Communication patterns among library staff and users of the library can best be determined if someone spends time observing such patterns, and this method is seldom possible to implement. Another measurement is to ask students and teachers to describe what they like best about the library. If a student likes the librarian best, this would indicate rapport between the student and the librarian. Conversely, if the response to a question about what students like least about the library elicits the same response (the librarian), one would evaluate this as lack of rapport. In-between measures on the scale are much more difficult to determine or analyze.

In some states, evaluation of all teaching staff is mandated and a state-approved form is provided. The activities expected of all staff should be the baseline for appraisal of that person's success or failure. Expectations should be written as job descriptions and discussed with each individual when they are hired. Most librarians lament the fact that the items on state-mandated forms do not apply to their unique assignments, and their evaluation by this mechanism is both inaccurate and incomplete. While it is not possible to match performance to previously determined job expectations, school librarians should meet with their principals early in the school year to discuss evaluation criteria.

Clerical staff should also be measured on preestablished performance criteria. These criteria are related to their job descriptions, and evaluation may be based on a districtwide process. If not, the school librarian must maintain documentation of the staff member's work falling below the established standard if changes in behavior are to be expected.

Another measure of performance is the ability of the library personnel to provide information for the library's clientele. If materials are well organized and access to electronic information is well taught, if teachers and students are given correct and pertinent information in an efficient manner and with a minimum of difficulty, the staff is performing well. If these same teachers and students are reluctant to ask for assistance, if they are consistently provided with little information or allow students to use misinformation, performance of the staff is considerably below adequate achievement levels.

Staff may be evaluated on how many services they offer as well as on how well they deliver their services. Mary Virginia Gaver verified the assumption that size of staff can affect the number and quality of services offered.[6] It was later confirmed in a study by Keith Curry Lance and colleagues when they replicated a national study that showed the number of staff in the school library affected the achievement of students.[7] This was shown to be true in a statewide replication study in Colorado and many other states.[8]

If the number of staff is large enough to offer a wide variety of services and they do not, one would investigate why not. Similarly, it is not practical to attempt to offer a wide variety of services with limited staff. Librarians would not be exercising good judgment by trying to offer many services but offering no service well.

The principal may define quality as how quiet the library is, control of the behavior of students in the library, and the number of books lost during the school year. Although these items may seem helpful in the evaluation of the librarian, it is unfortunate if these are the only criteria for performance appraisal.

Appraising Resources

School library resources are growing smaller in physical size because newer technologies provide online resources and e-books. Although analysis of the library collection should be done yearly, this is impractical in most situations. Rather, part of the collection may be analyzed each year. Certainly, each item in the collection should be reviewed at least every five years. Several measures are useful for evaluating the collection. Some are simple, and others are more time consuming.

Resources can be matched to curriculum areas. When materials needed by teachers and students to carry out assignments are missing from the collection, replacements need to be located and ordered. The availability of information on various websites takes time to locate, but provides immediate help for students. Students need to learn how to confirm the accuracy in what they find in books, the media, and on the Internet. Materials are also needed for students who prefer to read a hard copy book about a topic of interest being studied rather than reading an e-book or locating shorter bits of information online. Even though it may be small, determining the percentage of students still preferring hard cover resources helps define the resources needed. It will certainly indicate whether the use of online information makes the purchase of print materials a smaller part of the budget.

Records should also be maintained for materials, if any, that are borrowed from outside the school district or used online at the local public library. Collecting statistics on materials used from other locations will help in budget requests for future years. It should also highlight the need for the school librarian to collaborate with the public librarian and others providing resources to school students.

The reference collection of any library today is almost totally online. The speed of searching for information sends most to their cell phone or a computer. How many students are using their cell phones to find quick facts? Having resources for students to check what they find online will be helpful to judge relevance and accuracy. Some attention is still needed in checking for relevance. It should still be measured by asking teachers and students whether the print materials or online resources they used were relevant to their needs. This does not mean an item should be discarded because it did not meet a need for one assignment. However, an item lacking relevance for the topic it covered under all circumstances should be discarded. When documenting use of a database and it seems students aren't using it, try to determine why not. If it isn't helpful, it should not be renewed; and if more useful information is available elsewhere, that resource should be considered for subscription. Perhaps the database is too difficult for most students in the school to read. Is there another database that features curricular readings at different reading levels?

Many school librarians with computerized circulation systems can program the system to tabulate the circulation by each Dewey class number. Then the librarian can analyze use or lack of use of materials in each area. Individual books can be tracked to see how often they circulate. Although neither of these procedures can determine how the materials were actually used, knowing the topics being researched may be helpful. It will indicate whether the item is worth the space it occupies on the shelf.

Actual use can be identified in many ways. Teachers and students can be interviewed concerning their use of materials when they return them. Students can also be asked to keep a log of materials they select to note how they use them. They might also be willing to record materials secured from other sources. The usefulness of all materials should be assessed at the completion of a unit of work; a citation count, long a favorite in academic research, can be applied to students' research papers. Citations can then be checked against the library holdings to see whether materials and databases are available in the collection or students chose items from other libraries; if a bibliography is generated for the unit, if a database is bookmarked with relevant items, or URLs placed on a website. If a collection is pulled to be placed on reserve or for use in one classroom, teachers and students can be asked to indicate use and to evaluate the quality of items provided on the bibliography or in the classroom collection. If, in doing an analysis of citations, it is obvious that most students cite a URL, a completely different picture evolves.

At a time when print collections are being reduced, collections can be checked to see how many print materials have not circulated in the past three years. Are the research assignments being fulfilled with online resources? If these materials remain relevant and useful, why have they not been located and used by students or teachers? If they do not appear relevant or useful, they should be reviewed to determine whether they would be more appropriate at a different grade level or in a different building. Materials cease being relevant when curriculum changes; if it is unlikely that curriculum will be returned in the foreseeable future, those should be discarded. If they are not being used, are unlikely candidates for use in the near future, or are unused because they are out-of-date or in poor condition, they should be discarded and all records removed. No collection, no matter how large, can be judged high quality when it is cluttered with out-of-date, worn, unused, or irrelevant materials.

Services and Program Appraisal

Public librarians working with children and teens are constantly considering programming for their patrons. The school librarian has a different primary role. A school librarian's checklist of services would have curriculum planning, co-teaching, and access to information as high priorities. However, school librarians do plan programming and the success of these programs should be assessed. It may be as simple as evaluating book talking in classrooms. That may be evaluated by the increase in circulation of the book presented and other books related to the theme of the book talk.

Drawing students into the library with a contest requires only a number count of participants. Providing bulletin boards and showcases for exhibits of student work can also increase attendance, a number tabulation. Observation will be the best means to track whether students use resources while they are in the library.

Getting students to help in the library has always been an objective of school librarians, particularly when they are the only person in the library. Evaluating their service to the school involves the work they are accomplishing, leaving the librarian free to do the types of collaboration with teachers and teaching students. Student helpers' contribution to the school library program is reported to teachers and principal because they are opening time for the librarian to co-teach.

Organizing a tech squad of students to help troubleshoot technology issues and even help other students find information is a service to be documented, too. Qualitative assessment includes the numbers of satisfied customers using the service. Another assessment to gather might be the changes in interpersonal behavior with students who are seen as helping and not just the nerds in the school.

Administrator's Program Appraisal

Principals and superintendents should understand the complete program of the library and its relationship to teaching and learning. These administrators should have a simple means of evaluating this contribution to student learning, effective teaching, and the relationship to the school's curriculum. However, many administrators seldom have any instruction or experience that would allow them to understand the role of the librarian, so the school librarian should plan a session to inform the principal using students and a teacher sharing a co-teaching activity that was planned, presented, and evaluated. Getting students and teachers to join guarantees the principal's attendance and will be a powerful example of what should be. Documented changes in the principal's attitude may be difficult to gather, but any change will be encouraging.

When it is time to make program cuts in any school setting, the principal must believe in the necessity of the school library program. This is not something that is accomplished in one day, but rather something that goes on constantly. If program appraisal is essential for any reason whatsoever, it is to convince principals and superintendents of the worth of the library in terms of student achievement and the provision of access to information. Ongoing evaluation with regular reports of results is the key. It may seem that evaluation is more difficult and more time-consuming than a school librarian can afford, especially with the other facets of the program that demand attention. However, when program evaluation is the road to survival, its importance is better understood.

Evaluation to Assess Value

Simply saying that the school library program is essential to the learning environment in the school is not enough. Library programs are scrutinized by program appraisal methods to begin to test their value, to analyze which components are meeting the needs of the school. Do services meet the objectives established by the library advisory committee? Those objectives must stress the importance of the library to provide access to information, and measuring progress toward these objectives is the first step. For example, if a program objective is to provide access to online database searching for research papers, the evaluation should not be a simple yes or no answer: "Yes, online database searching has been added to library services." A better value statement tells how many searches were made for how many students, the number of students trained to do their own searching, the average length of time for each search, and the number of *relevant* citations found. Data should be collected to see which subscription databases are more popular because their continued purchase affects the budget. If students cannot find appropriate information in the library, what do they need? Is it more instruction in searching or different resources? If data collection resources in the library have not been able to provide this information, teachers and students need to be asked in a visit to the classroom, a survey, or by some other means.

What about those students who think that they only need to use Google to find what they need? Access to information must not only be relevant, but most important it must be accurate. Helping students learn to assess the information they are finding in any resource is a critical measure of access to information. This process will be evaluated with units the teacher and librarian co-teach. Students as individuals or working in groups are asked about the accuracy of statements in their papers. Helping students learn to verify facts is teaching them one of the more valuable skills they need in their lives. This will be very difficult to do in any formal evaluation, but asking students how they confirmed their accuracy will gather some information.

The importance placed on the role of the librarian and the concept of the library program must be assessed in relation to its location in the community. If students and teachers have access to a wide variety of information sources in other locations such as public and academic libraries, are they making heavy use of these locations? If yes, they may need a totally different type of collection and service program in the school, and the school librarian needs to work with the other information centers' staffs. Relationships among nearby information agencies and the use of these outside sources should be part of the evaluation process while determining exactly what percentage of students do not have easy access away from the school.

When the school library is the only source of information, including access to online resources, for most students, a different concept may prevail. Access in the school is critical, and information about the numbers of students who have no access away from school needs to be assessed, although the assessment needs to be done very quietly so no attention is drawn to students with no access.

School staff and students are necessary in the evaluation of all components of the library, and they must understand the evaluation process for an accurate study to be conducted. All must view it as a self-evaluation that requires responding with accurate and well-considered answers. Again, it is impossible to improve a school library if the library staff does not recognize the flaws. The counterpoint is that successes should be confirmed rather than assumed.

Methods for testing must be designed with care to determine exactly who will be queried, which items measured, and what procedures used to acquire the needed information. Careful consideration must be given to the choice of statistical methods used to tabulate and analyze the responses. Furthermore, individual components of any library program should not be measured in isolation.

Assessing Student Learning

Students nationwide, for the past few years, have been tested and retested supposedly to assess student learning when in fact, it is merely testing the capability of a student to regurgitate facts at the appropriate moment. Very little of the testing at the present time evaluates if education is adding any value.

The statistics gathered in the many studies by Lance and colleagues have shown the importance of the school library and its staff in the achievement of student learning.[9] Studies continue to be replicated in other states; and even though such statewide analyses are significant from a wider perspective, they have not had the attention that was hoped for. The results might not be applicable to the next state over. Even within states with studies, these results did not seem to resonate. At this point school librarians should be directing their research efforts to showing how they and the school library are providing access to information to improve student learning.

Students who are searching for answers to their questions, both those assigned by teachers and those that are more personal in their daily lives, must have access to enough information to find answers and to test the validity of the answers they find in their research. This begins with a joint review by teacher and librarian of student bibliographies matching the variety and quality of resources used and an analysis of the accuracy in presentation of content in their papers.

Students who seem to have trouble finding answers should be asked where they have been searching, what they have found, and what seems to be missing. With all the information on the Internet, it is not difficult to launch a search for a term, but it is very difficult to choose between the myriad of responses that appear and to determine those that aren't biased or totally inaccurate. If little access to information is available, then checking validity becomes problematic. It takes the assistance of a school librarian to show students where to look for additional information from both print and electronic resources to confirm or disavow what students are reporting. Checking with students as they are conducting research, checking bibliographies turned in with assignments, consulting with students working in groups as they look for information builds documentation of the progress with students as they check for validity. As bibliographies improve and as students begin to identify misinformation, the need for a school librarian, the information professional, in the school increases. This type of statistics gathering would be of interest to a faculty member in a university who might not need to collect additional information, but merely review the online papers submitted to teachers to check for accuracy.

Lance and colleagues have shown how to conduct impact studies at the state level, but few studies are undertaken at the school level—where the focus is on individual students. Harada and Yoshina explain that assessment is different from evaluation because assessment is "an ongoing activity that provides critical *formative* information about what the student is learning and how that learning is taking place."[10] Learners who are involved in their own assessment are learning in the process. These authors discuss assessing authentic learning and information literacy and how they are related to the content standards. It would be difficult to discount if this research was conducted in your school.

The critical point is that school librarians must seize the opportunity to show how what is being taught as a part of research projects reinforces and enhances classroom learning. Notes can be taken of changes in student engagement in both the classroom and the library. When students approach an assignment with enthusiasm, it is obvious. When the quality of output increases, it is obvious. The bottom line is that teachers need to see how the classroom-library partnership targets their own goals and priorities.[11]

Harada and Yoshina explain and share assessment tools such as check-lists, rubrics, rating scales, assessment conferences, logs, personal corre-spondence, graphic organizers, and student portfolios. They also provide elementary and high school examples. As soon as possible, school librarians should begin working with teachers to assess student learning; results should be reported so the impact on student learning can be demonstrated.

The school librarian is equally essential in helping teachers and admin-istrators locate appropriate information for their needs whether a new teaching method, a new way to solve a problem, or, in the case of some teach-ers, some help on their coursework when they are seeking an advanced degree. Keeping administrators and teachers informed of new resources that would be helpful to them demonstrates access to information. Keeping a record of these "hints" is yet another way to record access to information. When teachers return to find additional information, it is a success and an even greater success when the teacher is a "new" user of library resources.

Impact studies are definitely needed for evaluation and assessment in the immediate future to test the value of the expenditures being used to purchase new technology. Confirming the value of the choices between the different types, the equipment and software and their successful use with students and teachers is critical to future purchases. Some of this is pre-sented in Chapter 11.

Many resources are available to help plan and carry out evaluation studies. These will be cited in the annotated bibliography in Appendix C.

After the First Year

Evaluation is a process of deciding what to tell, whom to tell, and why to tell. One evaluation measure that can be useful is to use the application for AASL's application for the School Library Program of the Year Award. The criteria for this award are a tried and proven way to look at a complete program and the statistics to gather. Sometimes one set of statistics can be used for two purposes. When large numbers of students use the library for assignments, these numbers can be used in a positive report showing library success, and such reports are made regularly to administrators and teach-ers. When students cannot find materials because the collection is out of date and students need access to computers and iPads for online searching, the same statistics become part of a failure report that is shared with teach-ers, administrators, and parents. By the middle of the librarian's second se-mester on the job, the year's goals and objectives should be under scrutiny for their success to date. The degree of accomplishment may be high, and this should appear in the annual report to the principal. If accomplishments have been much lower than expected, a careful analysis of the reasons should be made so needs for the next year may be stated. This analysis be-comes the blueprint for the second year and into the future.

The Continuing Need for More Research

School librarians have been fortunate to have doctoral students con-ducting research on school libraries. They have also been fortunate to have researchers such as Keith Curry Lance to carry out funded research proj-ects. Lance has continued his studies and others have used his model so that research is available. But this is not enough. The need for more research is critical to support the value of school libraries in schools today. One way to continue this is for school librarians to contact faculty in colleges and universities for whom research and publication is important to their success. If they are given the opportunity to use a school or a school district to conduct research, they will welcome the chance. They can help set up the research methodology, create the questions for a survey, report the related research in the literature, and analyze the data they collect, thus adding to the body of research about school libraries.

Don't overlook what can be designed by one or more school librarians within a district. School librarians who are able to carry out simple action research projects can also report those findings in the literature or at conferences. Having a knowledgeable person to help make sure the research is well designed and a statistician to help with analyzing the data collected can perhaps alleviate any concerns that might arise when an action research study is carried out in a building by the librarian, but this adds to the body of research, too. What is discovered during the research can benefit all.

Assessment and evaluation are essential to note successes and provide an opportunity to fix or improve challenges. The next chapter addresses the business side of management.

Exercises

1. Meet with one or more school librarians to find out what program evaluations they have conducted in the past year and to whom they reported their findings. If no evaluation has been conducted recently, volunteer to help design and implement an evaluation project to test one component of the library program. Prepare a written report of the data analysis that will be suitable for a presentation at a school board meeting.
2. Conduct a simple study of the numbers of staff in school libraries and the budgets for purchasing new materials and equipment in your immediate region. Report your comparison of these centers and your school on any rankings by the state for all districts and student performance.
3. Discuss with a school principal the appraisal process being applied to the school library, staff, and services in that school.
4. Locate one or two articles to share with your principal on the role of the principal in evaluating the school library. Describe how you would share these articles with your principal when you first begin your job.
5. Decide on a service you would provide to students in your school and decide what quantitative measures and what qualitative measures you would use to determine its degree of success.

Notes

1. Brian Kenney, "Getting It Together," *School Library Journal* 53 (July 2007): 9.
2. *American Heritage Dictionary of the English Language* (Boston: American Heritage and Houghton Mifflin, 1969), 453.
3. *The New Oxford American Dictionary* (New York: Oxford University Press, 2005), 95.

4. Lynn Silipigni Connaway and Marie L. Radford, *Research Methods in Library and Information Science*, 6th ed. (Santa Barbara, CA: Libraries Unlimited, 2017), 3.

5. Frances Henne, "Learning to Learn in School Libraries," *School Libraries* 15 (May 1966): 17.

6. Mary Virginia Gaver, *Services of Secondary School Media Centers* (Chicago: American Library Association, 1971), 39.

7. James C. Baughman, *School Libraries and MCAS Scores: Preliminary Edition* (Boston: Graduate School of Library and Information Science, 2000); Keith C. Lance, Marcia J. Rodney, and Christine Hamilton-Pennell, *How School Librarians Help Kids Achieve Standards: The Second Colorado Study* (San Jose, CA: Hi Willow Research and Publishing, 2000); Keith C. Lance, Marcia J. Rodney, and Christine Hamilton-Pennell, *Impact of School Library Media Centers on Academic Achievement* (Castle Rock, CO: Hi Willow Research and Publishing, 1993); Keith C. Lance, Marcia J. Rodney, and Christine Hamilton-Pennell, *Information Empowered: The School Librarian as an Agent of Academic Achievement in Alaska Schools* (Juneau: Alaska State Library, 2000); Keith C. Lance, Marcia J. Rodney, and Christine Hamilton-Pennell, *Measuring Up to Standards: The Impact of School Library Programs & Information Literacy in Pennsylvania Schools* (Greensburg: Pennsylvania Citizens for Better Libraries, 2000); Keith C. Lance, Marcia J. Rodney, and Christine Hamilton-Pennell, *Good Schools Have School Librarians: Oregon School Librarians Collaborate to Improve Academic Achievement* (Salem: Oregon Educational Media Association, 2001); Keith C. Lance, Marcia J. Rodney, and Christine Hamilton-Pennell, *How School Libraries Improve Outcomes for Children: The New Mexico Study* (Santa Fe: New Mexico State Library, 2002); Marcia J. Rodney, Keith Curry Lance, and Christine Hamilton-Pennell, *Make the Connection: Quality School Library Media Programs Impact Academic Achievement in Iowa* (Bettendorf, IA: Mississippi Bend Area Education Agency, 2002); Ester Smith, *Texas School Libraries: Standards, Resources, Services and Students' Performance* (Austin, TX: EGS Research & Consulting, 2001).

8. Ibid.

9. Ibid.

10. Violet H. Harada and Joan M. Yoshina, *Assessing Learning: Librarians and Teachers as Partners* (Westport, CT: Libraries Unlimited, 2005), 1.

11. Ibid., 13.

7
The Business Side of Management

The management of the school library is more in the realm of business than in teaching and education. Although school librarians are educators, equally responsible for all parts of the school's curriculum and for the learning of all students in their building, they must also manage a many-faceted operation involving staff, materials, equipment, facility, and furnishings. These are covered in the chapters that follow. However, the library itself is a commodity and the inventory of the library has a very big price tag, as many districts learn when they are opening new schools or when they must rebuild after a disaster. It takes planning and budget to manage this commodity, its inventory, and its upkeep, and this business of management requires different skills to make this all happen. This is a great deal more complex than managing a single classroom and its students. That complexity is often overlooked by administrators who may wonder why a clerk or a volunteer can't replace a school librarian in their school. It begins with a strategic planning process and creating a vision, mission, goals, and objectives.

According to Barbara B. Moran, Robert D. Stueart, and Claudia J. Morner,

> Strategic planning, then, is the systematic outcome of a thinking
> process that enables libraries and information centers to
> organize efforts necessary to carry out major decisions and to
> measure the results of these decisions against the expectations
> through organized systematic feedback and adjustments.[1]

When a district has a director of library programs, a vision, mission, goals, and objectives for the program may be in place; if a district does not have a director of library programs, school librarians must create their own mission, goals, and objectives after they have defined the vision for the library in cooperation with the users: teachers, students, administrators, and parents.

The library program's shared vision grows out of the vision of the school and the school district and should align with both. This is the direction the library program will take for the future, where the library should be going, and as such, it guides the development of the mission statement.

The vision should be translated into a mission statement, a "short, succinct statement focusing on the purpose of the organization, its reason for existence, and what it hopes to accomplish."[2] The library staff and the advisory committee members first discuss the mission statement for the district and their school if it has its own mission statement. They then develop the library's mission as it relates to the school's mission and agree upon this statement. In the best of all possible worlds, the entire school will agree on the mission. Identifying the mission allows the formulation of objectives, policies, and, finally, the procedures and methods to provide services to meet needs.

Developing policy statements, goals, and objectives is the next step in the planning process. The sound library policy statement, if missing at the district level, is developed at the building level. This statement need not be redone each year, but it and the mission statement should be reviewed yearly.

Policy Statement and Needs Assessment

At the theoretical level, planning begins with a policy statement to describe library services. Two books can help in developing a school library policy. *School Media Policy Development,* by Helen Adams,[3] describes the argument for developing policies, the policy development process, and the political process for ensuring acceptance of established policies. In *Policymaking for School Library Media Programs,* Marian Karpisek cites the following eight steps of policy writing:

1.   Research: written manual, district and school policies, climate of the school

2.   First draft: philosophy

3.   Advisory committee consideration

4.   Final draft: rewriting to incorporate advisory committee considerations

5.   Advisory committee review of revisions

6.   Administrative approval

7.   Distribution to faculty and parents

8.   Dissemination to students[4]

Developing policies for exemplary library programs may come up against school practice. If principals use the library as the teacher preparation period in elementary school or for large numbers of students coming from study hall to the library in secondary school, the climate of the school will be different. Changing that schedule will require an acceptable plan for alternatives and full teacher support.

Once the basic policy has been determined, planning becomes the identification of problems to be corrected. In this phase, objectives, policies, procedures, and methods are developed based on the needs of students and teachers. During this part of the planning process, school librarians also work directly with those who will carry out the plans, the library staff, any other teachers who may be assigned to the library area as in a school with a learning commons, and the advisory committee.

The advisory committee acts as an advocacy group speaking for additional resources from its awareness of needs. The librarian uses the advisory committee to test new ideas and interpret the results of any evaluation exercise to the appropriate audience. In a sense, the committee becomes an extension of library staff in recognizing needs. For example, a committee member reports that a new world history textbook is being adopted. As a part of the needs assessment process, the textbook is analyzed to find which topics, when matched to the collection, have print and electronic resources available in the library and then what new materials need to be added to the collection. If new materials are to be ordered and if special databases are not available on a network database and need to be licensed, world history teachers are queried about suggestions for additions to the collection and asked to prioritize the order of purchase to meet budget limitations while allowing some materials to be ordered immediately. Perhaps the history staff is hoping to take advantage of new history-oriented databases or introduce their students to collaborating and working online together with the aid of experts from around the world. This may require additional funds for technology and can be added to the budgetary priority listings.

As teachers in your building are creating e-textbooks or are planning to do so, you will have an entirely different challenge. This will affect both helping teachers learn of available resources and also the need to provide professional development opportunities to remind teachers of copyright as well as help them learn how to create their online materials.

After the needs assessment is conducted, courses of action are reviewed and needed items are prioritized for potential purchase. Needs might be small, such as a change in the placement of furniture to make it easier to handle new configurations such as small group use or to accommodate a makerspace. Needs may be great if the concept of library as learning center is to be implemented. The learning center concept allows students to come into the center to meet in small groups and to create and produce projects. Alternate strategies are determined in case the first course of action is not possible, and the results of each alternative are discussed.

The following returns to our example of a need for more materials in world history. Because students are quick to use social media and the Internet to find information, the most effective strategy to meet the world history need would be the use of databases and resources on the Internet. Using Internet access as a substitute for any print resources requires consideration of the following:

1. Parental concern about open use of the Internet

2. Filtering problems if schools are required to filter the Internet

3. Costs of the purchase of databases

4. Need to teach students how to make careful, relevant selections

5. Number of devices available for searching

6. Ease of downloading that leads to plagiarizing

7. Teaching teachers and students how to use the various databases

8. Licensing of databases to be available to students 24/7 on their mobile devices

9. Consideration of help for students who do not have Internet access away from the school

---

Example 1

One objective determined during the planning process for the new world history curriculum is to provide each student with at least six in-house sources for research papers. The teachers recommend the type of materials to be added and types of access needed to support this curriculum unit. The library staff prepares a purchase list and their cost. The librarian bookmarks websites for use and shares them with teachers, showing them the websites so they are familiar with their content and can help students navigate through the information.

The librarian arranges for preview of potential additions to the collection and schedules teachers to make selections. Orders are initiated and items are processed and shared with teachers and students. Website addresses used in a previous semester must be tested to see whether they remain active resources. The usefulness of every related item, both new and existing, should be assessed and recorded so that future plans can be made to reuse those that worked well. The librarian and teachers will want to know whether the materials have been adequate, relevant, and recent enough for research and whether students were able to complete their assignments.

At each step of solving a problem, alternatives may be reviewed in terms of cost accountability while keeping in mind the focus on program objectives. These follow the needs assessment.

Objectives

Objectives written after a needs assessment process define the library role meeting the needs of users as it relates to the curriculum in the school. The objectives should be clear, and the reasons (basis for their choice) should be recorded. The activities or strategies to meet the objectives will depend on the librarian's level of participation in curriculum planning. It is essential that the librarian accept and seek leadership responsibility in this process, becoming an integral part of classroom planning, participating in the development of all strategies and alternatives and the reasons for final choices. This planning will make it easier to adjust the strategies later if they appear to be failing. The librarian should record this process, perhaps in a log, to help recall successful activities as well as the outcomes of revisions. These successes can be reported to the advisory committee, teachers, or administrators in monthly or yearly status reports. Recording changes or planning to use a previously successful strategy will help anyone who wishes to implement similar plans.

Organizing

In the process of strategic planning, school librarians organize the efforts that are necessary to carry out major decisions. In the organizing process, collaborating with teachers is logical because school librarians have full knowledge of the curriculum, the way teachers teach, the assignments they give and the activities they plan in classrooms, and the library support teachers will require. These activities—whether conducted in the library or elsewhere—impact management because the different forms of instruction and the assignments requiring resources used both in the library and away from the library through its online resources require much more planning and organizing than in the past. School librarians perform a variety of roles, from merely being consulted to collaborating fully with the design and implementation of classroom units of instruction. Organizing teaching for inquiry-based learning units could go across the curriculum and include the entire school. This type of teaching, particularly when it involves many teachers and many curriculum areas, requires the particular organizational skills of the librarian.

While organizing, decisions are made about who should do what work, the activities the work entails, and the facilities available to accomplish the task. What is the nature of the library's involvement in the teaching activities? The librarian and the teachers must agree on work division and work assignment, and activities should be allocated between classrooms and the library in the organizing process. Returning to the example of the world history project, a first activity is selection of new materials, and teachers are asked to review materials for purchase. The librarian sets up a system of preview, and receipt of items and their subsequent distribution to and return from teachers should be automatic. Clerical and professional staff should carry out the process. Again, websites and possible databases are reviewed for their availability, continued relevance, and usefulness.

A next step in organizing is to review the unit to see exactly where activities involve library staff. What will go on in the classroom and what in the library? When will materials such as new databases and information available on the Internet be introduced and linked to the library website?

Example 2

A major goal for school librarians is to ensure the availability of a wireless connection throughout the school and, if at all possible, to homes. If one is not available, at the planning stage, those involved write objectives and investigate the cost and installation of such a system. If the project requires selling to school administrators, cost benefits should be determined. This can be done first by a simple survey to show that students prefer materials online. Then a comparison is made of the price and availability of online resources versus the cost of adding materials in print such as ease of access, search time saved, and even clerical time saved in reshelving print materials. Justifying search time saved acknowledges that student and teacher time is real time with a cost factor, even if students are not paid and teachers are "paid for their time anyway." Many forget that time spent looking for print items is time lost from teaching or learning activities. Having wireless access allows resources to be used at any location in the building by students and teachers. Learning is no longer tied to time and place. Students are encouraged to become anytime, anyplace learners.

Other questions come to the surface. Who will maintain the network once the system is in place, and how will access to terminals be managed? Will students be allowed to bring their own wireless devices (BYOD) to school, and will access be allowed from home? Will the school provide additional mobile wireless devices to students who do not have their own? What would be the cost for the least expensive devices to provide for permanent loan? In overseeing the search process, databases are monitored to see which are used most often and if users are choosing the best databases to answer their questions. Are the library's databases accessible on their mobile devices? Some are not. Finally, during feedback, the librarian completes an analysis to evaluate real time and cost savings in relation to anticipated time and cost savings.

What about access to materials? Are they only available on devices in the library? Should teachers and students have wireless access throughout the school and at home?

As the time to begin the unit grows nearer, those involved must decide how to divide the teaching of the unit, what research skills are required, and what reference sources and materials will be used so that involvement of the library and the library staff can be scheduled. This review continues throughout the unit so that library staff is available whenever needed.

At the beginning, decisions must be made about when and where the assignments will be introduced, how many sessions students might need in the library, how much actual research time will be allocated, and when the assignment will be due. Responsibility for each activity is assigned to the appropriate person or persons. Care is taken to ensure that the activities continue as planned and that the appropriate materials and equipment are available. This stage involves matching the plan books of the teacher and librarian with the library schedule.

Systematic Feedback and Adjustments

To meet the guidelines of Moran's previously noted planning definition, school librarians must constantly evaluate the process, particularly as it applies to student learning. Did the unit work as planned? When, where, and how were the activities performed? Were they performed in accordance with the plans? To answer these questions, those involved will check progress during the unit and hold follow-up sessions. How well did students perform on evaluation exercises? Were sufficient resources available? What activities did teachers and students consider the most successful? Any final reports, comparisons with other units, costs, and projected budget needs are a part of the planning process. Finally, librarian and teachers ask whether the activity met the program goals.

Planning for Extended Projects

Planning for one week at a time is better than no planning at all. However, a school library program can continue to succeed and improve more efficiently if planning extends beyond one school year. For too long, librarians have neglected to set goals and objectives beyond a single semester. Such short-term planning limits the ability to set priorities for major purchases that will continue the progress of the program beyond a single school year. For this reason, school librarians should develop a three- to five-year plan for library operation. In this plan, all components of the library program should be listed with an indication of "what is" and "what should be," taking into account all necessary additions to the program—whether staff, equipment, materials, or facilities. Additions or modifications to the present situation should be proposed somewhere in the first, second, third, or fifth year, with a budget analysis for each activity. A sample five-year plan is shown in Appendix D.

For planning large projects, school librarians can learn from project planners who develop a time line. One simple time line is the Gantt chart, which displays tasks on the left side with the time line across the top or bottom. The time line is flexible, depending on the time allocated for completion of the project. The chart shown in Figure 7.1, on page 95, was developed as a planning chart for a new elementary school's library.

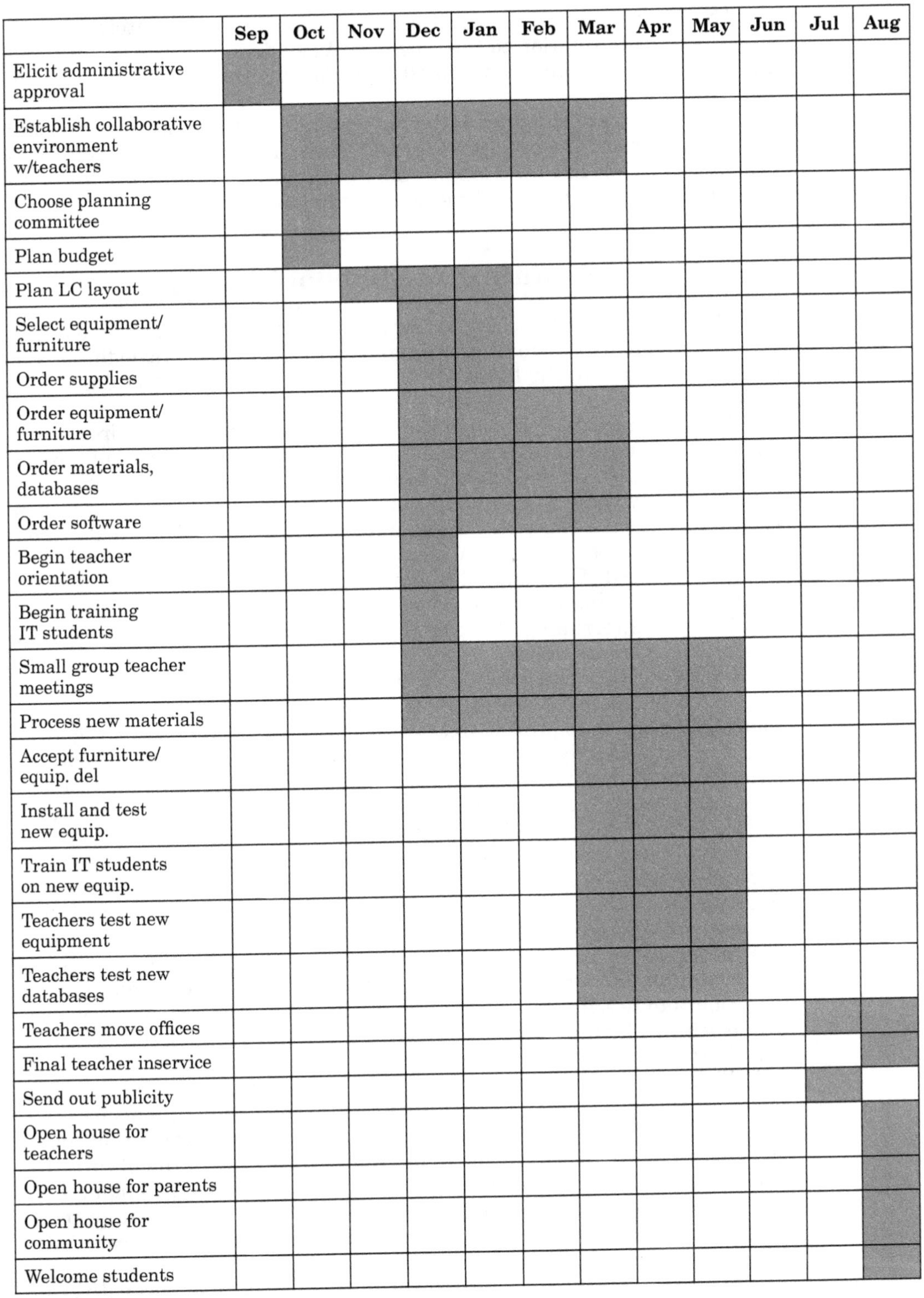

Task	Sep	Oct	Nov	Dec	Jan	Feb	Mar	Apr	May	Jun	Jul	Aug
Elicit administrative approval	■											
Establish collaborative environment w/teachers		■	■	■	■	■	■					
Choose planning committee		■										
Plan budget		■										
Plan LC layout			■	■	■							
Select equipment/ furniture				■	■							
Order supplies				■	■	■						
Order equipment/ furniture				■	■	■	■					
Order materials, databases				■	■	■						
Order software				■	■	■						
Begin teacher orientation				■								
Begin training IT students				■								
Small group teacher meetings				■	■	■	■	■	■			
Process new materials				■	■	■	■	■	■			
Accept furniture/ equip. del							■	■	■			
Install and test new equip.							■	■	■			
Train IT students on new equip.							■	■	■			
Teachers test new equipment							■	■	■			
Teachers test new databases							■	■	■			
Teachers move offices											■	■
Final teacher inservice												■
Send out publicity											■	
Open house for teachers												■
Open house for parents												■
Open house for community												■
Welcome students												■

Figure 7.1 Planning Chart for Opening a New Learning Commons and Virtual Learning Commons Developed Using the Gantt Chart Technique

The Gantt chart is helpful because one can see immediately where a project stands in relation to the schedule. When deadlines are not met, additional resources may be allocated if the opening date appears to be in jeopardy.

The final step of the chart is the turnkey date. At this time, "keys" should be turned over and the project completed. The purpose of such an exercise is to establish a time line for a long-term project. However, the school librarian must also be able to manage time on a day-to-day basis.

Scheduling the School Library

The facility must be scheduled for maximum use by students and teachers: as individuals, as small groups, and as entire classes. Scheduling and monitoring access to the library is a major task requiring careful management of time.

Time management is a particularly difficult skill to acquire in any school, where interruptions are commonplace. The school librarian, just as any other teacher, must plan carefully to allow for these interruptions. In fact, librarians come to expect the unexpected. On any day, a student or small group from a classroom needs information immediately. At the same time, a teacher needs additional time for research because of an event that has just occurred. They enter the library enthusiastically, only to find the librarian conducting a story time with the kindergarten, an activity that should not be interrupted. Working this special need into the day is possible with a little advance notice.

Capturing the "teachable" moment involves the library as often as or more often than any other area of the school. Perhaps this is one of the most compelling reasons to provide free access to the library rather than limiting access because of a rigid schedule of classes. Students and teachers with information needs must have these needs met at the earliest possible moment. Most high schools have full-time staff and large enough libraries to accommodate both full classes and small groups. This is not as often true in elementary schools, and creating a flexible schedule will be a challenge. Sometimes this can be done by seeing two classes from one level in the library at the same time for book exchange and silent reading or listening to a story. If they are studying a topic, book talking some books on that part of the curriculum can encourage research. When this works, a time slot is freed for a different use of the library. Creative thinking with teachers involved can generate other ideas to test flexible scheduling. It will not be easy when the elementary teachers' planning time is built around "special" subjects, such as music, art, physical education, computer literacy, and the library.

When this occurs, an administrator arranges scheduling, and the school librarian can only hope to find additional time slots for spontaneous use of the library and its resources. Many school librarians will argue that unless elementary teachers are scheduled to bring their classes to the library, they will not do so; therefore they do not object to a strictly scheduled plan. If this seems to be the attitude of teachers, a book exchange time must be scheduled regularly so that students who finish their books quickly can return them.

Another typical scenario is that the librarian may be shared with one or more schools and paraprofessionals may be employed to do library story times and book checkout with the students when the librarian is at another location. In these cases, the librarian may be scheduled to do isolated skill instruction on the scheduled day at a facility. This scenario precludes the use of the library as a learning place. As discussed earlier in planning use of the facility, the advisory committee can be helpful in suggesting an appropriate schedule for the library and the librarian that allows for teachable moments to occur and real learning to occur. Any emphasis on teaching students how to do research emphasizes the role of the library and the librarian and should lead teachers in advocating for correct usage.

When a rigid or shared schedule is in place, the librarian must plan activities to help change this use of the library. It will take the endorsement of the advisory committee and detailed, careful, curriculum-related planning with one or more teachers. If a class activity has been planned for a full semester, it may be possible to exclude other classes from the library for their regular schedule for a special culminating event for one class. For example, students in a class focusing on the study of early settlers in the Northeast may build one or two houses in the library for a week's activities, sharing this project with the entire school. This will not be easy to achieve, but if such an event is successful with one class, other teachers will want their students to have a similar opportunity. This can create the attitude among teachers that the library is a research center rather than a free period.

At the secondary level, many students who have no study hall scheduled can come to the library only when their teachers bring an entire class. Other students have so many study halls scheduled that they use the library as a change of scene or social gathering spot. Both situations must be addressed. Students need opportunities to use the library during the day. Homeroom might provide access for those with no study hall scheduled. With the help of teachers, librarians might plan alternative activities for students using the library during study hall. The time it takes to plan such activities would be well spent, especially if the activities could be repeated with other students at other times.

For all students from elementary through high school who come to the library with no apparent reason or assignment, this presents an excellent opportunity to encourage reading because, in this instance, it will allow the students to choose and read whatever interests them. Stephen Krashen reports that free voluntary reading (FVR) is one of the most powerful tools we have in language education, and FVR is the missing ingredient in first language "language arts" as well as in intermediate second and foreign language instruction. It will not, by itself, produce the highest levels of competence; rather, it provides a foundation so that higher levels of proficiency may be reached. When FVR is missing, these advanced levels are extremely difficult to attain.[5]

When free reading and direct, or traditional, instruction are compared directly in method comparison studies, free reading nearly always proves superior on tests of reading comprehension, vocabulary, writing, and grammar.[6] A variety of reading materials—from catalogs from department stores and specialty shops, graphic novels, comic books, paperback light reading, and magazines—can be placed near these reluctant refugees from study halls. Kindles, Nooks, or other e-readers for use in the library on which to browse the e-collection of online magazines and books should tempt reluctant readers. The daily newspaper also provides many possibilities (perhaps multiple day-old copies could be obtained)—a contest to discover the best price for bananas in grocery ads or a tracking of stock market prices for a month, for example. Some librarians have developed daily reference questions for contests. Some companies provide daily calendar quizzes with reference questions. Developing a series of activities that can be used from one year to the next may lessen student boredom and increase the value of the library in their education. This would be a good time to introduce those students to makerspace challenge activities if your library is large enough.

The librarian takes every opportunity to plan classes around the curriculum and often reminds teachers to share their unit plans so that library visits can be built into the unit at appropriate times. Librarians who collaborate with teachers find their libraries heavily used by students who need the resources of the library and the expertise of the librarian to complete their class assignments.

Electronic Calendars and Daily Plan Books

Classroom teachers are expected to maintain a daily plan book to post the goals and objectives of the lessons, activities, and evaluations of progress through the units. The school librarian, also a teacher, maintains a similar record, although the daily plans cover several classrooms rather than one. This plan book is a log of activities being planned, in progress, and being evaluated. It is a record of alternatives when the original plan is being revised. If timing of a unit is off, the plan book shows the new schedule. In this book, the librarian states goals, objectives, and activities and, finally, records progress. Keeping the plans as an electronic calendar makes it easy to record revisions to the daily schedule. When this calendar becomes available on a school's electronic communication system, teachers have immediate knowledge of open periods in the library and can make their preliminary plans with an e-mail message. Note that the plan may list activities of the librarian as well as activities in the school library that may be monitored by someone else. Teachers need to be specific in their emails as to their needs. Do they desire to sign up for the library space, which they will monitor, or do they also need to schedule the librarian's time?

The planning function is complemented by the budget needed to manage a school library. School librarians may not recognize or may forget that they are responsible for managing resources that would be extremely costly to replace. Only the coach with athletic equipment and the band and orchestra directors when their musical instruments are furnished by the school come close to having such inventory to control. These are actual "things" that must be kept working and must not be lost. The value of these is high, and their continued usefulness often depends upon the budget allocated to the school library. This is the true business side of management.

A great deal of this chapter relates to the budgeting process for the school district. School librarians need to learn as much as possible because

- School librarians need to be aware of the actual amounts in the budget for both salaries and materials and equipment.

- Orders for materials must follow procedures and rules and often have dates affecting when these orders are submitted and when they must have been received and invoices paid.

- Business managers often need help because purchases for the library are different from other classrooms within the district.

School district budgets are not secret. Anyone in the community should be able to see a copy of the district budget. However, these are often pages and pages of numbers that may seem very difficult to interpret. If school librarians are not aware of the actual amount budgeted for libraries, they may not receive all the school board intended for them to have. This will be discussed later in the chapter.

Budget

School librarians are given a budget. The size of this budget varies from year to year. The management of a small budget may be more of a challenge to the school librarian as manager than a much larger outlay of funds.

A fundamental responsibility of the school librarian is to be a conscientious steward of financial resources. Regardless of the size of the budget—or whether there is an allocated budget or not—it is the job of the school librarian to be aware of the financial resources that are required to support a library program that is integral to learning and teaching in the school. School library programs expand or disintegrate depending on the amount of money regularly allocated in the school district budget for purchase of needed resources, staffing, technology, and equipment. District administrators plan the district budget and present it to the school board for approval.

Funding for school libraries generally is allocated either throughout the district on a per-pupil basis or is determined at the building level by the principal in each school. In districts that use the per-pupil allocation formula, the per-pupil dollar amount may vary by level—elementary, middle, or high school—and most establish a minimum level of funding so that very small schools (those with student populations of less than 200) are not negatively affected. In addition, special allocations often are made to address unique needs such as schools with very old collections that need updating, schools in which the curriculum is changing significantly, new schools, or schools that require more access to technology because students' resources are limited at home. Per-pupil funding generally results in more equity of library resources and services across schools within a district.

In the 1980s, many school districts moved toward school-based management, and many districts have continued this practice into the new century. Rather than allocating resources to schools based upon a per-pupil formula, funds are given to the principal, who individually or with a school-based committee decides how they are dispersed within the building. In schools in which the principal or the budget committee recognizes the value and importance of the library program to teachers and students, funding is often sufficient to support the program.

Unfortunately, in programs in which the principal and the librarian do not have a good working relationship or those in which the principal has low expectations for the library program, the support is insufficient to meet programmatic needs. Additionally, librarians working in site-based managed schools often cannot depend upon a consistent funding stream, which may make long-range planning difficult. Also, changes in leadership within a school may result in radical changes to budget priorities.

Whatever the model the school district uses, school librarians must understand the model and conform whenever they have input in the budget process or when they are submitting items for purchase. School librarians must always be ready to respond to requests for budget input. They must be able to demonstrate that they have engaged in a planning process to show how the library contributes to meeting the curricular and personal information needs of teachers and students and what funding is needed to adequately support those needs. It is important for the school librarian to be able to demonstrate why supporting the library program is a more cost-effective approach than replicating resources in individual classrooms or departments.

Conflicts arise out of the realities of the school district's financial situation, usually defined by local taxation, and the practical need to provide a wide variety of materials for students and teachers. These conflicts can occur at the district level, when the library budget is distributed from a central library budget, or in each school, if district funds are distributed to individual buildings. Because budget items for the library program are part of the total school district budget, funding requests compete with other units, such as academic requirements, art, athletics, and music programs. Site-managed budgets distributed in the local school will find the librarians' requests competing with the classroom teachers' requests as well as with requests from other programs.

Annual budgets for school districts are prepared early in one fiscal year for the next year's expenditures. Superintendents may request assistance from others who are asked for input, but they are responsible for the final decision on items and amounts. The principal's and superintendent's central office staff are usually included by demand rather than by request. An example of others involved would be negotiators for the teachers' bargaining unit. All of these oversee preparation of the budget to make sure no budget decreases will necessitate personnel reductions and to confirm the inclusion of salary increases and other benefits.

Once the budget is prepared, the superintendent presents it to the local school board for approval. In some states, the state board of education grants final approval. In other states, voters are asked to pass a referendum for funding and budgets can be voted down by the members of the community. The amount of control exercised by local or state boards of education or by the voters in a referendum is in direct proportion to the amount of funds they control. In states where the major portion of education funding comes from state rather than local revenues, state officials maintain closer control over the local budget process than in states where most school funding is locally generated.

Regardless of how money is allocated for school library programs and where decisions are made, it is important for school librarians to understand how budgets are created, how to find the funds allocated for purchases, and how and when to make those purchases. School librarians should locate the persons who can help with questions. In some districts, it will be the district library supervisor. In other districts, it may be a secretary or accountant in the school or the business manager in the central office.

Most states and districts use line-item descriptions. Budget processes as well as numbering vary from state to state.

Each line in the budget represents either the source of the revenue or the amount of funding that is allocated for each category. A school district's revenues can come from local property taxes, the state or federal government, proceeds from bond sales, sale of property, interest from investments or trust funds, grants, and/or rentals from facilities. Each source of revenue has a specific code.

The next pages of the budget include the expenditures. Most school budgets reflect the past year's budgeted and actual expenditures, the current year's budget with anticipated and actual expenditures, and a column to project the next year's budget. For example, in a budget being prepared for 2020, the first two columns would show the budgeted and actual expenditures for

2018. The middle two columns would show the budgeted amount for 2019 and the expenditures against that amount as of the date of budget preparation. The final column would show the anticipated budget for 2020.

The Fiscal Year

School districts' fiscal year usually matches the state government pattern. In some cases, the fiscal year begins on January 1 and ends on December 31. All orders for materials or services to be charged to a particular fiscal year must be placed after January 1 and received and paid for no later than December 31. If the fiscal year is July 1 to June 30, the accounting books will close June 30, and all expenditures not cleared by that date will be charged to the next year's budget.

Business managers often require that all purchase orders be issued in enough time to receive the merchandise, confirm shipment of the appropriate items, and issue payment before the end of the fiscal year. In some cases, no purchase orders are issued within four months of the end of the fiscal year so orders will be completed in ample time before closing the books. School librarians seldom have large budgets, and any loss of funds can be crucial. Items that require longer times for shipment should be ordered as early as possible. If jobbers or publishers send orders in more than one shipment, it is important that all shipments are received before the end of the fiscal year so the invoice can be approved and paid with the current year's fund.

Some distributors will allow "fill up to" or "do not exceed" orders. If these options are available, the school librarian sets an upper expenditure limit for a specific order and the distributor ships as many items as can be purchased with the identified dollar amount. This approach ensures that no money from an order is lost because some items on an order are not available.

The need to handle fiscal matters promptly is one of the reasons fiscal officers sometimes wish to limit the librarian to one or two book orders each year. Limiting orders seriously affects the librarian's ability to provide materials for students and teachers when needs arise. Working closely with business managers and clerical staff can help overcome this problem.

It is wise for the librarian to be as supportive of the fiscal officer as possible. Most librarians are expected to present necessary buying information to the purchasing agent by submitting printed lists, online forms, school or district requisitions, or purchase orders. All forms must be completed accurately, from correct spelling and address for the supplier to correct spelling of author, title, publisher for books, and ISBN or ISSN for periodicals. Accurate item numbers for supplies, accurate model numbers for equipment, and accurate quantities desired, unit item costs, and item totals are essential. Any erroneous information on an order may cause an incorrect shipment or incorrect billing, which will result in additional correspondence from the business office for the return or exchange of items. This costs staff time in the accounting office and may lead the business manager to restrict the librarian's freedom to issue a requisition or purchase order.

Those school librarians who are allowed to order from a vendor using an electronic device may bypass creating orders and submitting them to the business office. This should be treated as the perquisite that it is, and care should be taken to stay within budget limits for materials and to confirm all shipments when they arrive.

As more and more routine ordering is performed electronically, librarians need to be even more attentive to making sure that item numbers and other information is carefully submitted. The ease of ordering does not release the school librarian from writing specifications for purchases.

Acquiring Resources: The Purchasing Process

Many methods exist for acquiring resources for the school library. Although sometimes the library receives gifts, most additions to the collection must be selected, ordered, received, and paid for. A first step in the acquisition process is to select a source for purchasing an item.

Purchasing Materials

In some school districts, purchase orders may be issued to the school librarian and sent by the school office to the vendor. In other places, orders are submitted to a central office to be issued. Items purchased may be shipped directly to the school, or they may be sent to the central office. A document should be available showing exactly how and to whom orders are to be sent and can be created if none exists. The school's office staff should be able to help develop this, or you should ask the principal from whom at the central office you can get this information.

Online purchase of books and other smaller items over the Internet is becoming commonplace. One can order from online bookstores such as Amazon and Barnes and Noble or from jobbers with selection lists such as Follett Book Company's *TitleWave* and have access to the same information you would find in *Books in Print*. Equipment is usually more expensive, and you may want to learn from a salesperson.

A purchase such as laptops for 200 students in a school is a very big order. It may be that a district wishes to have one brand of computer in every school, which could substantially lower the cost of a single item. A consortium may have a procurement list with established prices based upon large quantities. If it is up to individual schools or school districts, most states regulate the way things are purchased.

In many states, selection of a purchase source is based on a bid process when an item costs a specified amount. For example, all items over a designated amount, perhaps $100, must be placed for bid. This means that suppliers bid to provide the material or equipment and the lowest bidder receives the order. This is often true of the jobber chosen to supply library resources.

A jobber is a supplier who buys from a wide variety of manufacturers or publishers, so the librarian sends only one order for most resources. Individual publishers and suppliers may give a better discount, but this means that individual purchase orders must be sent. Business managers often prefer to order from a single source rather than send multiple orders to individual suppliers because of the cost of issuing payment. Once materials and suppliers have been determined, materials are ordered, using the process in place in the school district.

At present, most large school districts order by electronic transmission. A purchase order is returned, often by fax or email attachment, to the librarian to confirm receipt of the electronic order. This replaces the paper copy or multicarbon purchase orders of the past. No matter how materials and equipment are ordered, great care must be taken in completing the ordering process.

As stated earlier, school librarians may now purchase from jobbers who offer electronic ordering, often as simple as check-marking a box. The availability of all titles ordered will be confirmed, and the materials shipped and billed immediately. Many purchasing officers welcome this easy method of ordering. The school librarian sets a total price limit beyond which the jobber should not send further shipments. This ceiling on purchases allows the librarian to maximize quick-order opportunities. When the shipment is received, the original order must be checked against the shipment, any missing items noted, and the jobber notified. This acknowledgment is copied to the business office.

As said at the beginning of the chapter, school district business managers do not always understand the idiosyncrasies of the library world and will welcome assistance with selection and ordering. They may need help in selecting suppliers of materials, especially when the suppliers are not the more familiar sources of other educational items; in writing specifications for equipment; and in confirming that products ordered have been received. This is one way to make friends with those who handle funds for library programs.

Creating rapport with the business manager is as important as making friends with the administrators in the building and with the custodial staff. Remaining friends with these persons is easier if care is taken to make their jobs easier. One excellent way to do this is to notify them as soon as items are received. This enables them to make full or partial payment to the supplier. Otherwise, the supplier continues to send bills to the business manager, and no one likes to receive second or third notice of unpaid bills.

Selecting Equipment

Selecting equipment is a never-ending challenge. The need for electronic equipment continues to grow and, while the costs vary, it is still a costly proposition in most district budgets. The older problem of getting sturdy, longer-lasting equipment that would survive heavy use is not as much a problem as the need to constantly update equipment to accommodate changing software. Multimedia has taken on a much broader definition, as videos and tapes have faded away. Reference books, magazines, and newspapers are no longer only paper and print, and decisions to buy the print copy or the online version also require determining the number of computers available in the library and available from the library for use in classrooms or the home of a teacher or student.

Libraries and classrooms today offer many computers to access information while students are in the building. If schools are financed well, laptops to take home may also be available. This is a double-edged sword when students do not have access to the Internet at home. Certainly when only some students can access information from their personal iPads and cell phones, the need to provide wide access to the library's databases becomes critical for those who do not own these communication devices and do not have the communication links in their homes. As entire cities begin to provide wireless access, this will allow the use of a device that can be checked out from the library.

Selection of equipment is a further responsibility of many school librarians, and some may feel inadequate to make these choices. It is important to keep in mind the user of any equipment as well as the equipment's quality, compatibility, warranty, maintenance, and repair. The first consideration in choosing equipment, as with all items in the library, is the user. If the user is to use the equipment frequently, it must be easy to use and difficult to misuse. This concern will be of less importance as more schools acquire systems that network audiovisual transmission through stacks of projection offerings, playing devices, or online resources that project to a remote classroom, and even less as the quality of streaming video improves. Electronic transmission of instruction to multiple classrooms is currently available in some schools. The need for this type of technology will also fade away as students bring and use their own devices while they are at school.

A major concern is quality of the equipment. Many school librarians consider purchasing less expensive home-use equipment rather than commercial-use machines. This is a false economy because home-use machines are not designed to withstand the rigors of school use.

Warranty for the entire piece or parts of equipment should be considered. If the supplier is reluctant to give any warranty, it is better to look elsewhere. Computers are a particular problem because they are in constant need of upgrading. New software often requires additional memory. Other concerns are the need to purchase and install cards to use computers in a wireless network.

Finally, maintenance is also important. A backup supply of communication devices is needed when students are assigned equipment by the school so that they can exchange one item that isn't working for another that does work.

With all the challenges involved with equipment and with the probable need for your business manager to be able to get the best possible price and equipment, the librarian assists with helping to write specifications. This means reading reviews, talking with other librarians and technicians about their experiences with different equipment, and keeping careful notes to make sure appropriate requirements are in the specifications.

Writing Specifications

Specifications are written to ensure the delivery of materials and equipment to meet the stated need. This is an area where many business managers in districts where no central office staff is available need the help of the school librarian. They will appreciate your assistance and your knowledge of the equipment you need and what is the best for the money, how well this purchase will hold up with wear. For major purchases, the specifications may be a half page or longer. This is not an easy task, but the result will be a better product that will serve the teachers and students well. Your ability to do this will add status to your position and will demonstrate another way the school librarian helps the school.

If this task seems overwhelming, you could ask someone in another school or in another school district to help you. If you are on a professional association list, you might pose a question to that list and use the responses in your request. The list of specifications should include the following items:

1. Provide a clear description of what you want, written so the vendor can understand.

2. Offer as much information as you can about the product you will be purchasing. Any criteria for anticipated performance will ensure the delivery of a quality product rather than one that was lower priced and of lower quality.

3. List any conditions such as "deliver by" or "must provide an in-service session for teachers immediately after product is delivered." This is

especially helpful in purchasing databases because the introduction or orientation is by someone with a great deal of knowledge about the database who can answer questions that will help you when you do a later in-service on the use.

4. Explain how the equipment will be used. If laptops are going to go home with students, the vendor may suggest a carrying case to protect the laptop as it is stuffed in the students' backpacks.

5. Explain the way the equipment may be used. If you are purchasing a three-dimensional copy machine, it may seem to be most useful at the beginning with art classes.

6. Define exactly how you anticipate the item will perform. If the vendor states the database is to be updated daily, this should be a part of the specification.

7. If equipment requires installation, you must specify when it will be delivered, when it will be installed, and when it will be tested. Some description of the quality of workmanship is needed. You may need to specify where it will be installed.

8. The next section will tell who will take delivery of the item.

9. The final statement will tell when the bids for purchase are due and where the bid should be sent. It will also let vendors know when the bids will be opened to see who is going to be granted the purchase order.

When a very large purchase is anticipated, the business manager may have the bids sent to the central office to be opened on a particular day at a specified time.

The final task is checking to see whether the product offered meets specifications. When it does not, the reasons for rejection must be outlined based on how the product did not meet the written specifications. When the shipment is received, it must be carefully checked to see that the specified item(s) was shipped and it meets the specifications described in the bid. In returning an item, its deficiencies must be described in writing because the school district will be rejecting a contract.

Demanding quality products for the library is a very large step in being cost-accountable to the taxpayers or the sponsors of the schools. The section that follows describes cost accountability for the school librarian.

Cost Accountability and the School Librarian

Placing a dollar amount on components of a library program is not an easy task. Determining the costs of services requires estimating labor as well as materials used. Often, the cost of time—whether volunteer, staff, or professional—is overlooked because it is assumed that the librarian and staff member are on the job anyway. However, computing the cost of any service in terms of the time necessary to provide the service divided into the salary of the person conducting the service is an important part of the cost figure. To this must be added the cost of materials, supplies, or equipment used in the project.

Human costs include professional and clerical staff in the library. If the annual salary of the librarian is $60,000 and this person works 180 days per year and seven hours each day, both daily wage and hourly wage are easily calculated. To calculate the daily wage, divide the days worked per year into the yearly salary. This indicates that the librarian earns approximately $333 per day. Calculate the hourly wage by dividing the hours worked per day into the daily rate. This person's hourly wage is approximately $44 per hour. If the librarian spends 30 minutes to catalog and process a new item, the cost for this is $22 in labor, not counting any costs for supplies. It would be difficult to defend this expenditure, because purchasing complete processing from a book jobber is much less. The time saved by ordering books fully processed frees the librarian to spend that time collaborating with teachers or teaching students. The cost for processing an item increases as the librarian moves up the salary scale.

To calculate the cost of equipment use, list the pieces of equipment and their purchase prices. Divide these figures by the number of expected years of service and number of days of possible use and then the days by hours of expected use to arrive at a use-per-hour figure. For example, if a piece of equipment costs $2,700 and its life expectancy is three years of 180 days each year, or 540 days of use, and it is anticipated to be used five hours a day, the anticipated use would be 2,700 hours. The cost of use is $1.00 per hour, not counting any repair or replacement parts if the machine does not operate as anticipated. This figure will not reflect any repairs over the life of the equipment. However, unless a piece of equipment is in constant use, the downtime for nonuse should help cover anticipated additional expenditures for repairs.

Material costs are calculated based on their replacement cost, which rises with inflation. An annual average cost figure for books, even though these are no longer the major purchase item, may be calculated by adding the total of all purchase orders for books submitted in a fiscal year and then dividing by the number of books received. Both of these figures are easy to find on billing statements. Using the average cost of a book multiplied by the number of books that were lost, missing, or stolen from the library can show the replacement cost for a single year.

The approximate cost of a book can be used in another way: to show the total replacement value of the library and the amount of materials and equipment the librarian oversees. If a library has 20,000 items and an item costs an average of $24 to replace, the librarian oversees $480,000 in materials. Adding the cost of replacing equipment greatly increases this amount. Book, media, or equipment estimates can also be used to show students and their parents how valuable the library is to them. That is, if books have an average cost of $24 and 200 books are circulated each day for nine weeks, the value of the books circulated during one grading period is $216,000 (9 weeks × 5 days per week × $24 per book).

Estimating the cost per use of a database can be done in a similar manner. If the subscription for a database is $600 per year for the 180 days, the total cost per day is $3.33 or $0.66 per hour for a five-hour day. If you have multiple workstations and can have 10 students using that same database, your per-pupil cost is $0.06 per pupil. This decreases as students are able to use their own communication devices to search a database.

Librarians in single-person centers are often concerned about the time it takes to complete clerical tasks, reshelve books, or replace paper in printers. When a $44-per-hour person spends an hour shelving books, the cost to the district is very high compared with the $15 per hour for clerical staff to do that job. For some librarians, clerical tasks are somewhat rewarding in that they have a beginning and an end. However, as demonstrated above, when professionals are required to complete clerical tasks because they have no assistance, it is not cost-effective for the school or district. The greater loss, and one even more difficult to calculate, occurs when a professional is not available to collaborate with teachers. A librarian who is preoccupied with clerical tasks cannot help students find, analyze, and evaluate materials or assist teachers in locating materials to meet students' abilities or learning styles. Comparing the costs of time for professionals and clerical staff members can assist in this effort.

Many school administrators may not see developing budget requests as a function of the school librarian. As a result, many librarians have little opportunity to plan a budget or request funds. However, it is a fundamental responsibility of the school librarian to assume a more proactive role and plan for their programs by quantifying the value and cost of services and differentiating among those that are strictly administrative and those that contribute to meeting the mission and goals of the school and are integral to learning and teaching. This process must take into account the present, the immediate future, and long-range plans. Unless librarians engage in long-range financial as well as program planning, carefully detailing the anticipated costs of necessary services, administrators will remain unaware of the costs of providing for the information needs of teachers and students. Needs and objectives must be established and proposed expenditures clarified. Success is more likely if the requests are presented in a structured format not unlike the formal process of project proposal writing.

Writing Proposals to Expand Programs

It is the responsibility of the school district to provide the funds to support the library program. It is not appropriate for the district to expect the school librarian to be responsible for raising funds to build the book collection or provide electronic resources. However, many school librarians consider fundraising options to offer special programs like author visits or reading enrichment programs or to expand specific sections of the collection. One option to use to obtain additional funding is to develop a carefully thought-out and documented proposal. The type of information you collect and the way you explain your needs can be used in both an outside agency or to other individuals from whom you are asking for support. Potential funders include the principal, the school board, parents, a foundation, or a state or federal agency. Whether a funding request remains in the district or is sent to an outside agency, a proposal must be developed.

The remainder of this section discusses writing proposals for the school district or agencies that fund proposals directly related to school library programs. For someone who has never written a proposal for funding, this may seem an overwhelming task. If you know of librarians who have written project proposals, listening to their suggestions will be helpful. Five successful proposal writers have shared their ideas in their book, *Librarian's Handbook for Seeking, Writing and Managing Grants*.[7] It includes everything from how to research possible funding sources through how to manage the grant when you have been successful.

Sometimes school librarians are invited to join other, perhaps larger agencies to develop a broader proposal. For some agencies, collaboration is either encouraged or required. The expertise, experience, or other resources of a co-writers' group can also add value to your proposal.

Most project proposals include the following elements: a statement of needs or goals and objectives, a plan of action or activities and procedures anticipated, a time line, an evaluation plan, information about facilities and other resources available to support the project, and a carefully planned budget with detailed budget notes that explain the anticipated expenditures. Additional items, such as employment opportunity regulations, may be required if the proposal goes beyond the school district. Résumés of staff and consultants for the project also may be expected.

Developing the Statement of Needs

Few individuals are willing to allocate money without a needs statement. As children, we learn to justify additional allowance requests from our parents. As adults, personal budget decisions to make major purchases are based on a needs assessment. School librarians cannot expect additional funding without presenting a strong case of need. Needs are defined in a variety of ways. One approach is to read research studies that address the problem in your school. You can ask for funds to implement a program that that has been demonstrated to address the problem. One example could be the purchase of a test preparation software program that will help students practice taking the PSAT or SAT exams for college admission.

Another effective way is to compare the resources available in your school with a similar school in the district or a nearby district where the student body is similar but achievement levels are higher. The difference in resources available could be suggested as a reason for the difference in achievement levels and would give you the opportunity to test the result of adding materials and equipment for student use.

The process will be much more effective if the input comes from the advisory group rather than the librarian as a single individual who has identified the need. The composition of the group is very important. Funding agencies want to know if those to be served by the project helped identify needs and if those identified needs were used to help set the priorities. Proposal writers should cite the persons involved in the needs assessment process. In this case, administrators, teachers, and parents are most likely to be those who helped establish the needs because they know when students have problems with reading or another area of the curriculum.

Although a librarian can say that the collection is inadequate in particular areas or to support particular programs, the statement is more powerful if teachers review the collection and determine that it is inadequate. Alternatively, students could compose lists of missing or inadequate materials for projects they have researched. It is a good time to have student and teacher input in the process because it is important that the assessment of needs involves those directly or indirectly affected by the proposed project. It would be foolhardy to ask for an expanded collection of art books if the art teacher did not plan to use the books or make assignments that require students to use them. It has strength when the missing information is available on a database that will help students learn they can find information in places other than Google.

To confirm the participation of others in establishing needs, the proposal writer should list all meetings held and who attended, tests that were administered and their results, and any other relevant details. Participation may also be confirmed by letters of support, which are appended to the body of the proposal. Once the need has been established, a goal should be stated and objectives for the project developed.

Preparing Goals and Objectives

A goal is a broad, general statement and is not measurable. Because a goal is such a broad statement, it is not always required for a project proposal. When a goal is required, it should be realistic. Consider requesting additional reading materials as an example of a goal. Trying to overcome reading problems in an elementary school in a single year might be an unrealistic goal. If children are reading below grade level, or not reading at all, a few books and magazines added to the library collection will not alleviate the problem and the goal cannot be met.

Objectives, conversely, must be measurable. They are designed to help address the needs that have been determined, and they should state the precise level of achievement anticipated and the length of time expected to achieve them. Objectives must be an outgrowth of the stated needs. They should describe where the school library program should be at the end of the grant time frame in relation to where the program is currently and who or what is involved in the project. The better the objectives are written, the easier it will be to prepare the evaluation later. An attempt to increase reading scores will need to include the number of students, how much increase will occur, and the time frame. These elements are included in the objective.

Goals and objectives themselves may be evaluated when the proposal is reviewed. Context evaluation is the assessment of goals and objectives to see whether they are written in terms of the intended constituency of the project. For example, this evaluation reviews the number of students who will benefit from the project, for they should be part of the stated objectives. For the reading project, you might choose to work only with third-grade students for one year, and you would suggest that each student would raise reading scores by two years.

Objectives are often confused with activities. Rather than state the expected outcome, novice proposal writers often list the methods to achieve an outcome. These methods are activities rather than stated objectives, and they are a part of the plan of action.

Establishing the Plan of Action

The section of the proposal that states the plan of action, or proposed activities, describes the methods to be employed to meet the stated objectives and alleviate the needs. A general statement of the overall design of the project includes the population to be served, how the population will be selected, and how the project will be managed. But the activities themselves must be directed to the objectives, and the relationship must be clear. Activities designed to achieve the objectives must follow from the objectives. If the relationship between objective and activity is ambiguous, those reading the proposal may reject it. Most funding agencies and school administrators prefer projects with a step-by-step plan of realistic activities to meet the objectives and alleviate the need. The activity for third-graders might be to give them books to read that they will want to read and allow them unlimited access to these books.

When a project planner is unsure that proposed activities will meet objectives in the anticipated time frame, alternative plans of action may be presented. A rationale for each alternative may include a brief statement about why the first plan of action was proposed and how, when, or why it will be decided to use the alternative plan. If providing a large collection of reading materials does not seem to be encouraging their reading, providing more reading opportunities during the school day and asking parents to help children read more at night at home could be an alternative plan of action or even a second activity. Whenever possible, proposal writers should include relevant research supporting their choice from the array of possible activities.

As the project activities are described, a time line for each of the activities may be presented. The time line shows the sequence of separate activities that have gone before, what is in progress, and what will be done. This description enables the reviewers to understand how the activities relate—that is, if and when the initiation of one activity depends on the completion of another, when activities overlap, and the progress necessary for project completion.

Planning for Evaluation

After the activities have been designed, proposal writers must then determine the best methods to evaluate the activities to see whether they are, indeed, meeting stated objectives. To do this, two kinds of evaluation are helpful: formative and summative. Formative evaluation processes occur throughout the life of the project. At each step, an evaluation may be made to see if the activities are accomplishing the planned improvements. If the project does not appear to be successful, an alternate plan of action may be put into place. Progress using the new activity will then be evaluated to see if it demonstrates more success than the previous plan. Formative evaluation further determines whether project progress is within the anticipated time period.

At the close of any project, a final, or summative, evaluation is conducted. At this time, each activity is evaluated to determine the degrees of progress made to meet the stated objectives. Proposal writers must detail the means by which they or their agency will verify for the funding source that the project has accomplished the objectives as stated and the degree to which the objectives have been met. Information to be collected must be described, methods to analyze the information must be outlined, and the degree of success that should be expected must be stated. With this example proposal, the obvious summative evaluation would be a reading test to see whether test scores have increased.

This is often not an easy task, and many proposal writers seek help from persons in tests and measurements offices in colleges and universities and in local or state agencies to help define the evaluation procedures to be used after the project begins. Many funding agencies prefer the summative evaluation to be conducted by an outside evaluator to eliminate or modify the possibility of bias and add validity to the evaluation statements. When seeking project funding from outside agencies, choosing an outside evaluator—especially one highly regarded by the funding agency—may increase the likelihood of the project's approval. Someone not directly related to the project may be better able to measure the degree of success. Certainly the evaluation is one of the most important aspects of project planning and should be given full attention.

Deciding the Dissemination

Many outside funding agencies may ask about how the results of the project, if funded, will be disseminated to the broader world. Even if this is not a specified requirement, the school librarian should be prepared to share the results of any project with all appropriate audiences. Just as government agencies and foundation staffs need to know the degree of success of their investment, they anticipate credit for the contribution they made to the project. For locally funded projects, the school librarian reports project success to the superintendent and principal. They should be given material they can use for publicizing a successful project. It is no virtue to hide project success.

Funding agencies need good publicity to continue awarding money for projects; likewise, the school library is more likely to receive additional funds when successful projects are reported in the news media. Therefore, the librarian must consider carefully how to present information to appropriate audiences beyond the project. It may be letters sent home to parents or full coverage in the news media, both newspapers and television. The school district may have a public relations director to handle this, or the librarian may need to send out press releases to reporters.

Information presented for publication must be well written, accurate, and complete. If photographs of students are submitted, permission for publication must be obtained from parents.

Finally, successful school library projects should be reported to the school library community through articles in professional journals and presentations at conferences and workshops. The librarian must share the outcomes of projects with other professionals so successful activities can be replicated in other school libraries. A list of publications of special interest to school librarians is provided in Appendix E.

School librarians may be reluctant to make presentations. If you are the person in charge of the project, in developing the proposal with all its parts, the needs assessment, preparation of objectives, activities, evaluation, and dissemination, you are the best person to share how this happened and the results of the project. Even if the project didn't meet its objectives, you will have some idea of how things could have been done differently. You need to share your expertise with your colleagues, and your professional associations may be the best place to do this. As you write the proposal, you will need to list all the ways information will be disseminated about the proposal.

Describing Local Resources

Project proposals should also describe the facilities where the project will be conducted. If the school or school district has excellent facilities in place to support project activities, there is a greater chance for success. Conversely, if an elaborate program is described but the school does not have adequate space for it, there is a greater likelihood for failure. Describing facilities and additional resources available, human, material, and electronic, will help the funding agency realize that the school librarian has a better chance of conducting a successful project. If special equipment is needed for the project, the equipment must become part of the project proposal or the method of securing the equipment must be shown in the project narrative and budget as in-kind equipment.

Proposal writers should list all resources that add credibility to what, or who, is being proposed. If a school librarian lacks long experience in the library world, assistance may be available from a district-level administrator. The community may be supporting the school librarian in some unique or special way, and this should be explained. Additional funding may be available for the project from other sources—the community, individuals, or the state department of education. This support should also be cited.

Personnel who work on the project must be listed. If they are available as in-kind contributions to the project, this means their salaries will be paid by the school district and will not be part of the cost charged to the project budget. All personnel to be added must be listed. Job titles, job descriptions, qualifications expected, and length of time assigned to the project must all be described. Résumés should be attached for all persons who are identified as part of the project staff. This includes project director, coordinator, consultants, clerical and technical staff, teachers, and evaluators. These résumés must be brief, and the activities and positions described in their backgrounds should be only those showing skills related directly to the project.

Before submitting a person's name as part of any project staff, proposal writers must secure permission from that individual. Most people are annoyed if their name is submitted without permission. Often, an implication exists that these proposed project consultants or staff have approved the proposal in principle, even if they did not actually participate in writing it. Also, there is the danger of including someone's name in a proposal when that person is writing a proposal in response to the same request for proposals.

When competing for limited funds, the proposal writer should try to find out whether project staff under consideration is known to the funding agency. The agency may be more willing to fund a project if they recognize the capabilities of those directly involved. Also, the funding agency may insist on approval of the categories of persons to be hired, such as researchers, technicians, trainers, or clerical staff. Finally, many funding agencies are reluctant to approve the hiring of new persons for a project if there is no indication of how this staff will be continued after the project is completed. School district administrators may find themselves obligated for any unemployment benefits for furloughed staff unless they can be placed in other positions.

Building the Budget

The final part of project planning, the budget, includes the anticipated costs of the project, item by item. Government agencies provide a form to be completed. If no form is provided, some suggestions of items to be included are found in Appendix F. These items can be used to verify that the information usually required is included in the project budget.

Two budget items that may cause unexpected problems are fringe benefits and overhead. Fringe benefits are part of salary statistics. The percentage figure used to calculate fringe benefits for proposed project personnel will be the same used for all school district salaried staff. Fringe benefits for a district employee are determined by the monthly salary, percentage of time, and length of time of the project. That is, if a school librarian with a $2,000 monthly salary is to be employed half-time for six months, the project would show $1,000 times 6, or $6,000 for the project. If the school district has a fringe benefit package of 27 percent, $1,620 must be added to the project costs.

Overhead percentage may be set by school districts, universities, and private agencies. Overhead is an assessment of the use of staff, equipment, and facilities that will not be specifically included in the proposal budget. Examples of overhead are the preparation of purchase orders, checks for payment, bookkeeping, use of office furniture and equipment, heat and lighting, and computer use. The overhead costs are then added to the total costs for the project. This is sometimes discouraging to a proposal writer when the overhead costs add another charge to the project. It sometimes means cutting other parts of the project that seemed essential in order to submit a proposal that has a reasonable budget.

Some agencies, such as state departments of education, may prohibit assessment of overhead percentages or limit the amount that can be added. This needs to be determined before you begin the project proposal so that it is not an unexpected cost to the planning. If your district has a contract with the agency to which you are submitting the proposal, you will need to put a copy of that contract with your proposal.

If space or equipment is to be rented, those costs must be calculated. Consultant or contracted services also must be listed. Consultants may be paid a per diem amount rather than a salary, in which case fringe benefits need not be calculated. School librarians should keep in mind that telephone charges, mailing costs, duplicating fees, online database searches, and office supplies should be added to the budget if the school budget cannot absorb these additional charges. Finally, if the staff or consultants require travel funds, these must be included.

Additional Considerations

When planning the project, proposal writers should check to see if evaluation points have been assigned to each part of the proposal. The number of points assigned is the highest score that proposal readers can give each part of the proposal. Careful attention must be placed on all parts of a proposal, but special attention should be given to the sections that have been assigned the most points.

Throughout project planning and proposal preparation, school district administrators must indicate their support. It is heartbreaking to complete a project proposal and have the principal or superintendent refuse to send it to the funding agency. It is even more difficult when an agency awards funding and the school board refuses to permit the school district to accept the funds. Not all administrators or school boards welcome funding from an outside source, especially if they perceive that strings are attached. This is especially true when personnel must be added because, as stated earlier, these persons may expect to become permanent employees at the close of the project. A successful project may encourage other administrators to demand similar materials, staff, or services from already overextended district funds. Convincing administrators of the value of the project and the potential benefit to the school building and school district is important. This is better accomplished when the school librarian provides an honest, realistic assessment of the regulations and requirements for the school district at the close of the funding, the probable level of enthusiasm for similar projects in other schools, and the funds required to continue even a small portion of the project.

After preparing the proposal, the writer should reread it to make sure it is written without jargon, to be sure the plan of action is logical and will achieve the objectives, eliminate extraneous words and unnecessary materials, and correct any spelling or grammatical errors. Finally, the proposal should be neatly formatted in an easy-to-read style or in conformity with the format outlined in the request for proposal. Format instructions might include size of font, spacing requirements, number of pages for each section of the proposal, length of abstract, and other details.

Be sure that all necessary documents are included, but do not send materials that are not requested. It would be unfortunate to lose evaluation points because a required item, such as a copy of the district's selection policy, was not sent. Further, some agencies require confirmation that equal employment opportunity requirements are met and other legal regulations are in place.

Most funding agencies are interested in what will happen to the project at the close of the outside funding. If parts of the project will be continued with school district funding, the project may have a better chance for outside funding. If administrators are involved in planning throughout, they can help determine how to continue the project.

Those who are required to sign the proposal must be available to do so. If the proposal requires school board approval, copies must be distributed to members prior to the board meeting, and someone from the proposal preparation team must be ready to answer questions at the meeting. It may not be possible to call a special meeting of the board, so the school librarian must pay attention to the closing dates of all requests for proposal to allow time to secure board approval and all appropriate signatures.

Proposals must be submitted on time. If a deadline exists, this date must be met. Proposals that arrive after the deadline are usually returned unopened.

Writing proposals is a way of life in many situations. In others, it may be a way to get additional funds, expand a program to meet a specific need, add equipment, add materials, or try a different way to provide materials to help teach students.

Most persons who have had one proposal funded are very willing to write another. They have been given an opportunity to improve their school library, test a new method, offer a new service, or provide more materials for students and teachers.

To write a proposal is to enter a competition, and the process is similar to any other competitive endeavor; sometimes you win, sometimes you lose. Sometimes it may seem better to lose. One gains all the applause for the effort to establish needs, develop objectives and plans of action, and write and submit the proposal. It is an opportunity to meet new colleagues and reestablish communication with old acquaintances. Sometimes you win, and then you have to work to see that the project succeeds.[8]

Proposal writing skills may help increase the budget, but just how much increase is needed? Also, a budget for one year is a narrow vision for the school library. The school librarian should plan for the immediate and extended future and that plan is written by as many as can be included in the process and is then shared with the principal.

This chapter anticipates that the school librarian will manage the library using a business approach. This may be a difficult change because librarians have long considered their role as a guide to reading resources and helping students read and enjoy reading. In this current century, applying a business model is the only way to gather the needed resources to provide access to information. The next chapter discusses the library space and housing the contents.

Exercises

1. Review the daily plan book of a school librarian. Estimate the percentage of time spent (1) working with students, (2) planning with teachers, (3) performing administrative tasks, and (4) doing clerical tasks.
2. Using information from a school library, create a five-year plan for improvement in chosen aspects of the entire program.

3. Review the literature published by the National Association of Secondary School Principals or the Association for Supervision and Curriculum Development to see what trends are being proposed there. Make an appointment to discuss these trends and their effect on the school library program with a principal to see what information is needed to help with understanding or implementation and any costs that might be needed.

4. Given the following outline, draw a Gantt chart for closing a school library in two months and transferring the holdings to two other libraries. A suggested procedure is:

Step 1.
Weed the collection.

Step 2.
Review contents for integration into the other two collections.

Step 3.
Pull items from shelves, sorting for the two locations.

Step 4.
Create electronic records to match sorted items.

Step 5.
Pack items.

Step 6.
Unpack items at new locations and shelve.

Step 7.
Check electronic records against items placed on shelves.

Step 8.
Add electronic records into existing OPAC, noting duplications.

5. Locate an active request for proposal for funding for a school and brainstorm ideas that could be written into a project proposal. Then write the proposal for a school librarian who would appreciate having the assistance.

Notes

1. Barbara B. Moran, Robert D. Stueart, and Claudia J. Morner, *Library and Information Center Management,* 8th ed. (Santa Barbara, CA: Libraries Unlimited, 2013), 67.

2. Ibid., 78.

3. Helen R. Adams, *School Media Policy Development: A Practical Process for Small Districts* (Littleton, CO: Libraries Unlimited, 1986).

4. Marian Karpisek, *Policymaking for School Library Media Programs* (Chicago: American Library Association, 1989).

5. Stephen Krashen, *The Power of Reading* (Englewood, CO: Libraries Unlimited, 1993), 1.

6. Ibid., 19.

7. Sylvia D. Hall-Ellis et al., *Librarian's Handbook for Seeking, Writing, and Managing Grants* (Santa Barbara, CA: Libraries Unlimited, 2011).

8. Blanche Woolls, *Grant Proposal Writing: A Handbook for School Library Media Specialists* (Westport, CT: Greenwood, 1986), x.

8
Library Spaces and Contents

School librarians are responsible for the management of the spaces allocated for the library and the contents housed there. The actual inventory is a sizeable investment and management is a major responsibility. School librarians must regularly review the arrangement of the existing center to see that it is responsive to the needs of students and teachers and that it can accommodate maximum use of individuals in small groups and full classes. This review may result in rearranging and reorganizing the library, for example, adding new signage or weeding and shifting the print collection, or remodeling or reconstruction, for instance, removing or rebuilding walls or completely relocating the library to a more appropriate space. This chapter begins with a focus on the facility and then moves to the contents.

The Library Space

Space is arranged in a library to meet the priorities of the program. Space should be comfortable and welcoming. It should enable multiple activities to take place concurrently. It should be flexible and capable of being reconfigured easily to adapt to changing technologies, teaching styles, and student use. The furniture should be appropriate for the student population that uses it.

Although few school librarians may have the opportunity to design a completely new library during their professional careers, many should take the opportunity to reconceptualize and reorganize existing space as often as it becomes necessary. Making changes in the physical space can result in changing students', teachers', and administrators' perceptions about what can and should take place in the library. When the facility is flexible, changes in space are simple and allow for a myriad of different activities. Assessing the functionality and relationship between the space and the program is critically important when the librarian takes a new position and periodically reviews the space as part of the long-range planning process. While it may be unwise for a new librarian to make drastic changes in the library space during the first few weeks, a change in the configuration of some elements of the library may enable the users to think differently and have different expectations about how the space could be used. Often making a change in the arrangement of the library is the only way to change perceptions of what should happen there. However, the first rule is to make the library welcoming.

The school library should make a positive first impression on all visitors, but especially the primary users: students and teachers. The view when the door opens must be one that encourages them to move into the space with a positive attitude. Moving into the library, signage should be positive and both signs and letters must be large enough to be helpful in locating areas and resources.

Other considerations are the location of the library within the building or on the campus. The perceived choice location for most is on the first floor in the center of the building. If the library is in an area away from classrooms, it will be more difficult for students to locate and use it without compelling reasons. If this is the situation, attracting use will be a factor.

Students' use patterns have a definite impact on the library. Students who arrive and leave on buses may have limited time to come to the library before or after school.

Some students may attend classes in one building for part of the day and go to another school for the remainder of the day. In this case, a school population of 2,000 may have only 1,000 in attendance at any given time. In schools using a block schedule instructional program, students attend only four classes within a school day and may spend from 90 to 120 minutes in one class. During these extended periods, teachers may often choose to divide the period so instruction is given in the classroom and students then move to the library for individual research or group work.

Younger students usually attend school for fewer hours, and they tend to be voracious readers. Space must be available to allow teaching, reference, and group work to go on in one area, while, in another, students may come in individually or in small groups throughout the day to browse or check out new reading materials.

Other factors include the composition of students who attend the school. When 75 percent of students continue their educations in higher education institutions when they graduate, it is one type of student body. In another, less than 75 percent of students who start high school will graduate. Some high schools may allow students to leave school in the early afternoon for internships, work study programs, or jobs where they are working to practice a skill or to earn money.

Attendance patterns also vary. If an elementary school serves a large number, the beginning time for older students may be earlier than for younger children and they may have a different dismissal time. Some schools have students who arrive in buses and must go home when the bus is leaving. When and how students arrive at school makes a difference for opening and closing the library; when students come to the library during the school day also affects facilities.

Usage is affected by the reasons students come to the library and the arrangement of spaces. If students are scheduled to allow the teacher preparation period, the size and arrangement of library spaces may or may not allow the use of parts of the library by others.

Age and learning styles of students also affect how the facilities are arranged and the types or sizes of furniture that are needed. Some teachers prefer to teach in classrooms where students are at desks in rows while other teachers have students sitting in groups of four. Some students prefer the more structured environment while other students prefer the opposite. When teachers bring students to the library to teach, they may want a classroom to use or an arrangement that resembles a classroom.

When students come to the library, they should be able to choose the seating option in which they are most comfortable. They may need to work in small groups in a conference room; however, present-day students seem to be able to block off noises around them. Moveable furniture will accommodate this.

The number of library staff and teacher spaces affects the size and arrangement of the library. Librarians are best located where students can not only see them but can approach them immediately. Office or workroom-type space is useful to store equipment such as servers that should not be where they can be damaged.

The library may include a classroom or computer lab that can be used by classroom teachers or for instruction by the library staff members. A separate work space or production area for teachers and students may be part of the library space because this area allows for discussions. Offices for reading teachers, technology support personnel, professional development staff members, curriculum coordinators, and/or literacy coaches may be incorporated in or adjacent to the library space.

The library may be used for teachers and/or staff meetings or for professional development offerings for teachers or meetings of parent groups. While the library space may be used by a variety of groups within the school community, it is critical to remember that the fundamental purpose for the library is to support teaching and learning for all learners.

While keeping in mind the users of the library, the school librarian begins by analyzing the range of activities that will happen in the space. Spaces that are too small and too crowded limit numbers of people and what they can do in the space. The research on school library facilities shows that people who liked their libraries gave such reasons as attractiveness and plenty of space. Dissatisfaction came from lack of space and the feeling that staff had no say in planning new or expanded buildings. Flexibility in the space design is the second most critical consideration. The library should be designed to support the range of activities that can be identified and yet be flexible enough to be easily reconfigured as programs, priorities, teaching practices, and technology change. A list of these activities includes spaces for:

- Full class and small group instruction areas
- Small group collaboration and work spaces
- Individual work space
- Quiet areas
- Storytelling
- Circulation
- Browsing
- Access to online resources
- Access to the online catalog
- Individual viewing or listening

- Group presentations
- Comfortable seating
- Displays
- Shelving for resources
- Work space for library staff
- Office for library staff
- Digital video and audio production
- Makerspace areas or other special collections such as a corner for graphic novels
- Materials for students to facilitate their work, production, creation
- Materials for teachers
- Materials for parents

Using this as a checklist, note those areas that are used regularly versus those used only occasionally. This provides an outline for consideration when rearranging facilities.

Rearranging Facilities

Rearranging facilities can be an exciting challenge. Additional services or the program changes may have been made through applying the checklist or through the planning process. To help determine how space might be reconfigured to better support these services in the existing facility, you can sketch ways to rearrange furniture using the grid and furniture in Figure 8.1. Please note that the tables pictured there are larger, more traditional tables. If you are planning to use smaller tables that can be easily moved, they need not be placed on the grid. For elementary students with smaller chairs, you could fit two within one square of the grid. This graphing of possible configurations will help you preview the possibilities for changes.

Some furniture options help with the planning. When island shelving is on casters, then the options for rearranging space will be expanded. If all shelving is stationary, there will be fewer options for reconfiguring the space. Follow these steps to rearrange a library:

1. Measure the library. Use a tape measure or estimate by measuring one tile (floor or ceiling) and plotting from that estimate.

2. Using a grid, place tables and chairs, allowing sufficient space among all furnishings and the surrounding shelves. The second page of Figure 8.1 provides you with furniture and shelves outlined to scale. Trace in shelves, or cut them out and paste them down. Do not forget the circulation area and the librarian's desk if it is to be readily available. Where is the OPAC? Where will students be able to use their devices to do searches?

3. Ask staff and advisory committee to do this exercise.

4. Indicate doors and partitions, and label the main entrance. If there is a fire escape rather than an exit, indicate that. These are all part of the facilities design.

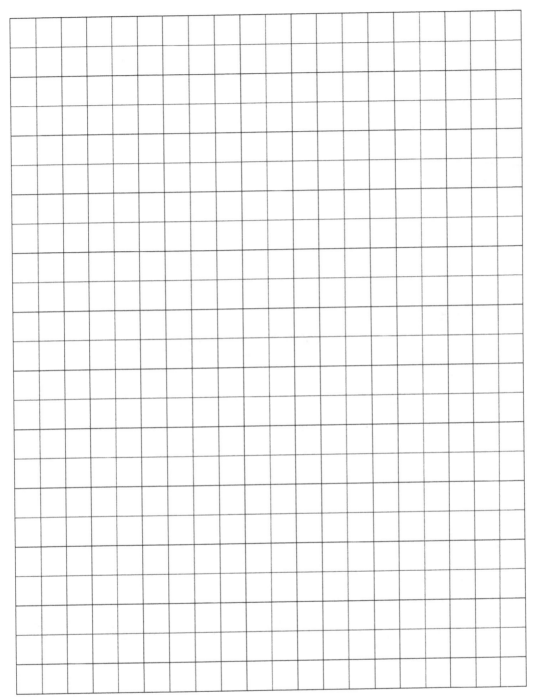

Figure 8.1 Facilities Grid to Scale for Floor Plan and Room Arrangement

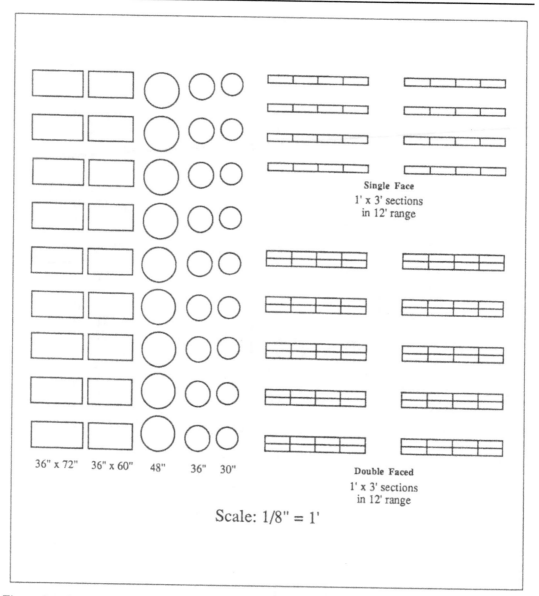

Single Face
1' x 3' sections
in 12' range

36" x 72" 36" x 60" 48" 36" 30"

Double Faced
1' x 3' sections
in 12' range

Scale: 1/8" = 1'

Figure 8.1 *Continued*

Note: Use this grid to outline the library facility. This will provide both a floor plan and a traffic pattern. The grid is to be filled in using a scale of 3/16 inch to 2 feet. That is, each square represents 2 feet. This need not be "architect correct," but it is important that furnishings be placed using approximate size relationships.

5. Review the proposed changes and determine which configuration is best to allow for all of the spaces on the checklist.

6. Determine costs associated with the rearrangement. Is furniture being added? Are more electrical outlets required?

7. Analyze whether the rearrangement satisfies needs or is merely a temporary fix.

If the advisory committee has not been a part of this previously, they need to review the suggestions. Teachers will also be helpful in spotting both better ideas and any problems that may arise.

Plan the rearrangement so that materials are moved only once. If you take all the books off the last shelf and move that shelf, you can begin to restock the first shelf in the empty spaces. Thus, when the next to the last shelf is moved into its permanent placement, you can re-shelve your last group from wherever you put them when you began and it is a simple matter to replace those set aside at the beginning.

Because the ability to make use of laptops and other devices has replaced the reference section, the school librarian provides these communication devices for students to use in the library if they do not have one assigned to them on a permanent basis. Storage for these "loaner" devices is a consideration in planning.

Librarians should keep careful records as facilities are arranged. Before-and-after photos will show an appealing and efficient library made even more appealing and efficient. Teachers and students will forget how the library looked before, and administrators need to be made aware of the alterations. Such modifications should be noted on reports to administrators because they demonstrate this area of management expertise.

Some librarians may be lucky enough to participate in remodeling a facility, which is much more exciting than merely rearranging the facility. It has some of the considerations found in building a new library.

Remodeling the Facility

When remodeling is being planned, the librarian should look carefully at the entire building. It may be better to move the library to a new location than to remodel the existing space. Far too often, the location of stairwells and restrooms impedes expansion. Locate the best place in the building, and help the administration understand how to rearrange what is there so this space can be used for a new library. This will not be easy, but it could make the difference between increasingly crowded spaces where the library is presently located and a better area elsewhere.

Sometimes the transformation of a seemingly impossible situation is fairly easily accomplished. One author is well aware of the transformation of one high school that had two library locations. The fiction library near the office area in the original building had a reading room with a balcony housing back issues of periodicals. When an addition was placed on the building, a new area in another wing of the building was devoted to the library for housing nonfiction books. The librarian walked between these two distant locations to meet students and teachers as they planned activities throughout the day.

The librarian learned that all walls in the new building were temporarily placed and could be easily moved. The next step was to get an estimate on partitioning the former fiction reading room into three classrooms. Within one year, the materials collections had been consolidated in the new wing, an event the district library coordinator had been trying to change since the new building was occupied. A solution of this kind requires only analysis and justification for the change. The three teachers who moved into the three newly created classrooms from the old reading room were the only persons disrupted for the good of all teachers and students.

Remodeling is not always costly. Non-load-bearing walls can often be removed by district or building staff and do not always require the hiring of an architect and a construction crew. Such alterations can be carried out without major expense. However, necessary permits and inspections will still be required.

When more elaborate renovation is necessary, planning and justification are essential. In older schools, electrical outlets tend to be a major problem. Coinciding with the need for adequate outlets is the need for sufficient electricity to support equipment. Rewiring older schools can be expensive. Conferring with someone who has renovated a library to accommodate wireless access can help the librarian plan such remodeling. When costs are high, needs must be documented and detailed enough to convince administrators. However, when placing a wireless network in a school, all staff can benefit.

Librarians need to keep in mind the same considerations when choosing furniture for remodeled facilities. Workstations are needed to accommodate students studying in distance education classes as well as those working on projects. New spaces to house technologies that are checked out to students require a different type of storage space.

When more space is needed, major renovations must be undertaken with care. Earlier it was suggested that non-load-bearing walls would be easy to remove. However, load-bearing walls may support the roof and the weight of the floors above the library, and cannot be moved without being reinforced. Cutting a door through the wall may be considered too expensive for the space gained.

Renovation is often as costly as a new facility. If the renovation is major, an architect is hired before the process begins. Architects sometimes design libraries that are functionally impossible for one person to manage. Sunken circulation desks in the center of the facility, an entire window for one wall making sunlight a challenge to students as well as the collection, balconies in two-story libraries, and multiple entrances and exits are examples of building flaws that need to be addressed in both remodeling and building new facilities.

Form must follow function. It is the responsibility of library staff members working with the architects renovating the space to assist them in understanding how the space is used. Unfortunately, when guidance with usage is not provided, well-meaning architects may be left to make recommendations based upon their experiences in school libraries from when they attended school in the 1980s and 1990s or their familiarity with public or academic libraries, which serve different populations and offer vastly different services.

The areas outlined in the checklist above should be placed in the remodeled facility. In addition, areas that support leisure reading with comfortable chairs will both reinforce the importance of reading and encourage students to come to the library to find materials to respond to their personal interests as well as their curricular needs. Younger children need more areas for group work and storytelling, and high school students are independent learners with different seating requirements. Also, students with particular learning problems may need different spaces, such as quiet areas for those individuals who are easily distracted.

Rows and rows of heavy shelving cannot be easily moved and less and less shelving for books is needed in libraries, so only perimeter shelving should be placed in the renovated library. Rather, island shelving, normally 48–60 inches high and on casters, can greatly facilitate reconfiguring the space to accommodate changing needs. This shelving can be used to separate and define areas, expand or contract specific sections of the print collection, or be pushed against the wall to accommodate a larger group. This would mean adding a small closet room to accommodate a rolling cart with chairs stacked on them much as you would find in a hotel to accommodate conference attendees or a public library with a multi-use room.

While some librarians will want an attached library classroom, others do not. When there is no separate classroom, the placement of tables and chairs to provide a classroom-like setting for teaching and away from the distractions of independent users should accommodate both librarian and teachers who want to teach in the library.

As more and more schools become wireless and also assume the responsibility of providing communication devices for students, storage of these to exchange when one is malfunctioning and at the end of the semester requires a place where these can be locked away when not open for distribution.

School librarians should assess the facility to see if it is functioning as it should and if not, decide what is needed to rearrange space. Others may have the opportunity to participate in remodeling the library. While very few will have the opportunity to plan new facilities, this should be a part of a management book.

Planning New Facilities

When school librarians have the chance to build a new facility, they should visit several sites to review what other librarians consider the strengths and weaknesses of their designs. What works well in one location may not work well in another. What did not work in one location should be avoided if possible in new plans and could be useful for convincing architects to rethink something similar in their plans. Architects tend to have limited opportunities to exercise creativity in designing classrooms, cafeterias, offices, gymnasiums, auditoriums, and band rooms. Thus, many architects see the library as the place to make an artistic statement. Unfortunately, many of those statements create dysfunctional libraries. Collecting ideas is always helpful, and a truly successful idea can be presented to the architect as a suggestion.

The main function of the library is to provide an environment that will encourage and support teaching and learning within its spaces. Enlisting the assistance of teachers and students in planning to meet their future needs creates advocates and supporters who will help define the library and deflect unworkable suggestions by architects. It also builds support for building a new facility for learning and helping find funding for new technologies both present and future.

As teachers and students join in the planning process they are reminded of the library program philosophy and goals. They need to have some descriptions of rearrangement of libraries so that shelves for the fewer and fewer books being purchased do not occupy the central space within the library. They can then be asked to help define the areas of need in the library. The OPAC and computers with access to databases and online references should be near the librarian's reference desk so that students and teachers can be helped quickly. Proximity to a librarian becomes particularly important because software changes so rapidly and also because staff can encourage students to choose a variety of sources rather than depending on a quick Google search.

Some areas may be designated for recreational reading, viewing, and listening, but other areas should be available for quiet study. This is especially needed for students who do not have access to an online connection at home. Schools requiring students to complete online courses must provide the opportunity for students to do their "homework" in the library. Circulation of materials and borrowing and returning materials and equipment tend to be noisy activities and should be located near the entrance. Internet access points may also become noisy when students work in small groups to search or share the information they are finding.

When it is time to meet with the architects, they will be interested in the philosophy of service for the library. This is the time to discuss the placement of the library in the building. Although most teachers feel that their programs are central to the school, the library should be quickly accessible from all classrooms.

Architects need to know the number of students and teachers to be served, the numbers of materials and equipment to be housed, and the areas needed for specific activities such as a room separate from the reading room for computers or spaces that can be darkened as required. Electrical outlets are needed for all equipment. Also needed are conference rooms for small group work, some storage, work space, and other special spaces.

The seating areas, storage areas, shelving to house collections, and production room should be fully described. A separate classroom may be a priority if the library has more than one person on the staff who will be teaching a large group of students. In addition, the architect may need to be reminded of such factors as climate control, acoustics, carpeting, moveable walls, moveable shelving, ceiling treatment, windows, doors, communication lines, and safety.

Current information available online reduces the need for reference book shelving and storage areas for magazines while increasing the need for wireless transmission throughout the school. Moveable walls between areas make it easier to rearrange areas of the library as new uses are determined and former uses become obsolete.

Architects do not want detailed floor plans. Yet, they may wish to see the relationship of one area to another. That is, if the conference rooms need to be where the librarian can oversee them, this must be specified. If there are noisy areas such as a circulation desk, their relationship to quiet reading areas must be made clear. The architects must know of special needs such as an area for a 3D printer, sinks for students to clean up from a makerspace area, cabinets, carpeting, electrical outlets, and plumbing.

Architects design, draw blueprints, and return with the plans for further review. It is important to understand what is shown in the blueprint. A square in the middle of the plan probably indicates a load-bearing pillar. If it is placed directly in front of the circulation desk, rearrangement of the area may be necessary. Care must be taken to see that no blind spots are built into the furniture arrangement. Shelving arranged so students can hide may cause discipline problems. Architects need to have reasons why an attempt to beautify with balconies or exotic entrances or large glass walls looking out onto a sunny courtyard are not workable in a school library.

Strange lighting fixtures that do not emit enough light and melt when higher wattage bulbs are placed in them may show the aesthetic competency of the architect, but they won't be useful. Another architect built two bridges for middle school students to connect open classrooms on the second floor across the reading room to a platform and then steps down to the first floor. Reading room tables and chairs were directly under these two bridges. One can imagine how many objects were dropped onto heads below before these entrances were closed, forcing students into a corridor and down stairs outside the library to enter the first floor door.

It is sometimes impossible to convince an architect to make changes. If the situation is very bad, the librarian should list the problems and the probable outcome if changes are not made. With logical justification, the superintendent should intervene with the school board and the architect.

The school board approves construction plans. When bids for building are far higher than anticipated, cuts must be made from the original design. It is imperative that the school librarian review the proposed alterations to make sure they are made in appropriate areas of the library.

While the spaces needed are listed in the checklist earlier in the chapter, other considerations for planning the new facility include the following:

1. Select shelving with backing, especially for elementary schools. It is all too easy to push books and boxes through double-faced shelving, especially if these are on wheels for easy rearrangement or down behind single-faced shelving that has no backing.

2. Select adjustable shelving to accommodate picture books or outsized books. A three-foot shelf, when full, will hold approximately 30 books of average size, 18 reference books, or 60 picture books (with dividers).

3. In spite of the prediction that the three-dimensional book is dead, select sufficient shelving to hold the present collection and anticipated additions for the next 10 to 15 years. It is difficult—often impossible—to match paint, wood, or even type of shelf with the same manufacturer after the initial order. If bids are let for new shelving and a different manufacturer is chosen, the problem is intensified. If a learning commons is being created, all bookshelves not on the perimeter should be on casters for easy moving. The casters are good for an elementary school whether or not they use the learning commons approach.

4. Select sufficient electrical voltages for present and anticipated use. Sufficient outlets in planning a new facility are mandatory, though state codes may not require enough. The new library may resemble a renovated one if additional conduits must be strung outside walls because the architect was not aware of the numbers of outlets needed.

5. Make sure communication links to the outside are available. This may mean including wiring for telecommunications links, and the cost of this may make using a wireless network more appealing. Today any new library should be wireless from the start.

6. Check carefully the source of shelving and furnishings. Many times, bids are let for educational rather than library furniture. One author remembers a slanting-top picture book table order for an elementary school that was custom-built by the company furnishing the entire building. The legs were too tall for six-year-olds, but the carpenters installing the furniture were reluctant to cut the legs to the proper size because this is difficult to do after the furniture leaves the factory. Be sure to include furniture appropriate for the new technologies.

7. Confirm that partitions are temporary rather than permanent.

The library, as a facility, provides the space for materials, equipment, and services and houses the staff as well. Consideration of office spaces includes allowing a view of activities in the school library. Often, the librarian's main station is a reference desk in the center of the room so teachers and students can ask questions and solicit help quickly when needed. Few librarians have the freedom to close themselves in an office during the school day to work on a project.

Building a new facility provides an opportunity for the librarian to remind teachers and administrators of educational trends that should be considered in planning the new school. One trend in the 21st century is the learning commons.

Loertscher et al.[1] describe five different components of their learning commons: the open commons, the experimental learning center, the virtual learning commons, the virtual open commons, and the virtual experimental learning center. The first is an extension of the classroom, but it has an "expert" bar similar to that area in a technical equipment store, where students and other adults, perhaps even volunteers, respond to technical questions. The experimental learning center is for everyone to try out new trends and ideas and is "the heart of professional development and school improvement initiatives."[2] The virtual learning commons is for students to carry out projects or work on online learning assignments they are taking from an online learning course. The virtual experimental learning center "provides the glue that makes collaboration and school improvement work."[3] These, when put together, build the school's learning center.

A large library staff will allow, and even require, more enclosed spaces as other teaching staff members are moved into a learning commons. The guidance counselor will need an enclosed office to speak with students. The positive in this plan is that students need not sit on chairs outside the counselor's office with little to do but wait. They will have the entire library to browse while they are waiting.

The term "learning commons" or "information commons" has been adopted by a number of school districts and universities to describe a welcoming space in which multiple activities can go on as individuals, small groups, and full classes of students take part in a wide range of activities simultaneously. While the terminology may be new, the concept of a collaborative space that can support many approaches to teaching and learning has been the expectation of a library facility for many years. As defined by David Loertscher, co-author of *The New Learning Commons Where Learners Win! Reinventing School Libraries and Computer Labs*,[4] the learning commons is "the center of social, cultural and learning in the school."[5]

If the school library has been transformed into a learning commons, these spaces will be a part of the planning. However, if they are to be placed in an existing facility, the arrangement of that facility must be flexible.

Moving a School Library

When school populations decline or shift from one area to another or schools close, school librarians are assigned the task of closing libraries. This involves sending collections, furniture, and equipment to a central warehouse or distributing them among other schools.

If the contents are to go to other schools in the district, the librarian plans the shift after taking a careful inventory at each library, the closing library and the receiving library or libraries. Equal distribution may not be a case of "one for School A," "one for School B," "one for School C." Redistribution should be made on the basis of need and existing collections.

Collections, furniture, and equipment should be carefully scrutinized and the old, irrelevant, and broken removed. Certainly the librarian will analyze the materials collection for duplication at other schools. It may be preferable to keep materials in a central location where other librarians can pick only titles of use in their collections rather than to send cartons of unneeded materials to another school.

If remodeling is in progress during the school year, much of the collection may be boxed and stored. Librarians must decide before closing the library at the end of the previous year which important items and equipment will be needed while the collection is stored and move them to a classroom or another accessible area. The most used materials should be kept from storage. Equipment can be reassigned to storage areas or classrooms throughout the building. Again, this process takes careful needs assessment and planning.

Housing the Collection

Traditionally, the library collection has been housed on shelves under the jurisdiction of the librarian. That is, materials have been in a room called the library, locked at the end of the school day and opened the next morning. As the librarian increases the integration of the library, classroom collections for reading move regularly from library to classroom. As classrooms and homes are connected electronically to library resources, this information center becomes truly without walls. Shelving to house the collection is decreased when electronic resources replace three-dimensional materials. The concept of the library is no longer a room with ranks of shelving and tables interspersed throughout.

Some libraries are undergoing a rebirth, sometimes called a learning commons. In these situations the information and materials found there change dramatically. Other teachers bring their resources into this common area; as makerspaces are added, access to hard copy materials declines. Although librarians need to formulate a plan for keeping track of hard copy materials so that they can be located quickly when requested, semipermanent loan to classrooms expands their use. With expanding access to online resources, the concern that students need information available on the shelves of the library is less critical. Although the online capability of access to information may lessen the librarian's tasks for circulating hard copies, it increases the work to make sure that users can find appropriate and useful information in these oceans of information available electronically.

This chapter has detailed the new library spaces needed as libraries are rearranged and their contents change. The next chapter covers the management of the resources found in a library.

Exercises

1. Visit one or more school libraries. Analyze the ambiance when first opening the door. What draws the user into the library? What is less welcoming? Note the signage in the library. Is it positive or negative? How does it help the users find their way in the library and help them locate places they need to go to find both resources and places to study?

2. Review the location of a library within an existing school. Make recommendations for ways to increase the size of the library to accommodate new uses. Are sufficient spaces allocated for the storage of computers for students to check out and return?
3. Visit a library and determine if the present furniture allows for ease of rearranging for different uses. If not, what needs to be done?
4. Using graph paper, draw the floor plan of an existing school library. See if this center can be easily rearranged to provide better access, quiet versus noisy areas, and any other improvements you would suggest.
5. Outline a talk you would give to teachers and administrators to enlist their help in creating more open spaces such as a learning commons in the building. If you were to ask other teachers to speak in support, whom would you ask and why?

Notes

1. David V. Loertscher, Carol Koechlin, and Sandi Zwann, *The New Learning Commons Where Learners Win! Reinventing School Libraries and Computer Labs* (Salt Lake City, Utah: Hi Willow Research and Publishing, 2008).

2. Ibid., p. 14.

3. Ibid., p. 17.

4. David V. Loertscher, Carol Koechlin, and Sandi Zwaan, *The New Learning Commons: Where Learners Win! Reinventing School Libraries and Computer Labs,* 2nd ed. (Salt Lake City, UT: Learning Commons Press, 2011).

5. Ibid.

9
Information Resource Management

One of the traditional responsibilities of information professionals in all types of libraries is identifying, evaluating, acquiring, and organizing information resources to meet the needs of their patrons. This chapter suggests the need for reviewing or even writing a collection development policy, covers the traditional responsibilities, and discusses new challenges facing school librarians today. Protecting the students' rights to information and protecting their privacy and the privacy of all users of the school's materials remain obligations for the library staff. These philosophical issues include the ethical use of information. The chapter ends with building and maintaining the collection, organizing it for distribution, and selecting materials for the collection.

In the past, these resources were primarily in print and nonprint formats; however, the expansion of resources made possible by advances in technology now makes information available to users in libraries, schools, offices, and homes and requires new approaches to managing information. Library users now expect to have information available to them beyond the walls of the physical space and accessible 24/7.

These expectations for access to information and the opportunities for providing it greatly increase the responsibilities of school librarians to make sure that library patrons have equal access, a challenge constantly increasing in a wireless world where not all students have appropriate equipment or access to electronic resources through the Internet. Making sure all students have access to information is more difficult now than at any other time in the history of school librarianship. The divide between students who have devices and access to information at home and those who, at best, have only a cell phone, continues to place some students at an unfair advantage.

School librarians need to be prepared to undertake the process of making this equal. When the cell phone is the only device, show students how to access the library's information. Then if the school isn't wireless, begin with building a wireless school. Suggest ways to help raise funds to provide each student with a device to access information that can be placed on the library

131

website and in databases available in the school's collection. Access to information is the highest priority if students are going to become effective citizens in a democracy.

Working with the wired public library, students with access are able to use both their library and their resources when they have their own devices. Adults who travel often park near a public library to use their wireless to read email. Students can have this opportunity introduced as an option for online access when schools are closed.

The explosion of information available electronically has made collection development more challenging. Technology has exponentially increased the information and the access to information available, and it has made the process of identifying, evaluating, and disseminating appropriate resources more challenging. The importance of the school librarian's responsibility for helping students, teachers, parents, and administrators to effectively seek, evaluate, synthesize, and use the information that they find online as well as in print resources has never been greater. The responsibility of the school librarian to assist both young people and adults in determining whether online information is accurate, reliable, and authentic cannot be overstated.

In addition, new questions must be addressed, such as the most appropriate and cost-effective formats for various parts of the collection. Should all resources in the sciences be electronic? Are any reference books still needed other than the Internet? Is there a need for print journals when most periodical resources used by students are available in databases? If primarily electronic resources are purchased, what does this decision mean for hardware purchases and maintenance? What ramifications must be considered when a decision is made to purchase primarily electronic resources in communities where few families have access to broadband connectivity in their homes? How is physical and intellectual access to information provided when computer hardware is not regularly updated and kept in good repair and/or computer networks are not reliable? When is it desirable to use funds to participate in collaborative purchasing of a collection of electronic databases, and when is it best to limit individual resources that more closely support the curriculum of the individual school? How does the school librarian ensure that students do not choose to plagiarize information from the Internet or electronic resources when it is so easy to "cut and paste" other people's intellectual property? Many of these issues can be addressed through the creation and use of a collection development policy.

Creating a Collection Development Policy

Selection policies should be reviewed by and approved by the school board; if they are, that is noted in the policy for anyone to read. Many school districts will have a fully developed collection policy, which was created by library staff members within their district and approved by their school board. This policy generally is included in a Policies and Procedures Manual available in each school. When considering accepting a job in a new district, it is wise to inquire about the availability of such a guidebook. If one is in place, as soon as possible it should be reviewed to see if the content is still valid or if it needs to be updated. Should the district have no guidebook for its library collections and none seems to be available in your school, a first step is to create such a policy. Regardless of whether the school board approves your statement, preparing allows one to document priorities and methods of selecting materials and to have it available if questions arise.

School librarians who have had materials questioned will admit that the experience is usually very frightening. Most school libraries have a single person in charge, and that person feels very isolated when a parent, community member, or fellow teacher questions the availability of a certain item for students. Having a selection policy for the complaining person to read as well as implementing the procedure they are asked to follow should allow time to notify the principal. The principal may need to be reminded that the superintendent should also be told that a resource in the library is being questioned and by whom.

Librarians, with the help of their advisory committee, should develop a policy that conforms to the American Library Association's (ALA) Intellectual Freedom Policy (B.2.1). This policy statement, shown in the accompanying box, was jointly developed by the Intellectual Freedom Committee and the American Association of School Librarians.

ALA Intellectual Freedom Policy Statements

B.2.1 Library Bill of Rights

The American Library Association affirms that all libraries are forums for information and ideas, and that the following basic policies should guide their services.

1. Books and other library resources should be provided for the interest, information, and enlightenment of all people of the community the library serves. Materials should not be excluded because of the origin, background, or views of those contributing to their creation.
2. Libraries should provide materials and information presenting all points of view on current and historical issues. Materials should not be proscribed or removed because of partisan or doctrinal disapproval.
3. Libraries should challenge censorship in the fulfillment of their responsibility to provide information and enlightenment.
4. Libraries should cooperate with all persons and groups concerned with resisting abridgment of free expression and free access to ideas.
5. A person's right to use a library should not be denied or abridged because of origin, age, background, or views.
6. Libraries which make exhibit spaces and meeting rooms available to the public they serve should make such facilities available on an equitable basis, regardless of the beliefs or affiliations of individuals or groups requesting their use.
7. Adopted June 18, 1948. Amended February 2, 1961, June 27, 1967, and January 23, 1980, by the ALA Council.

B.2.1.1 Challenged Resources

"Libraries: An American Value" states, "We protect the right of individuals to express their opinions about library resources and services." The American Library Association declares as a matter of firm principle that it is the responsibility of every library to have a clearly defined written policy for collection development that includes a procedure for review of challenged resources. Collection development applies to print and media resources or formats in the physical collection. It also applies to digital resources such as databases, e-books and other downloadable and streaming media. Adopted 1971, amended 1990, 2014.

B.2.1.2   Expurgation of Library Materials

The act of expurgation denies access to the complete work and the entire spectrum of ideas that the work is intended to express. This is censorship. Expurgation based on the premise that certain portions of a work may be harmful to minors is equally a violation of the Library Bill of Rights. Adopted 1973, revised 1990, 2008, 2014.

B.2.1.3   Access to Resources and Services in the School Library Media Program

Members of the school community involved in the collection development process employ educational criteria to select resources unfettered by their personal, political, social, or religious views. Students and educators served by the school library have access to resources and services free of constraints resulting from personal, partisan, or doctrinal disapproval. School librarians resist efforts by individuals or groups to define what is appropriate for all students or teachers to read, view, hear, or access regardless of technology, formats or method of delivery. Adopted 1986, amended 1990, 2000, 2005, 2008, 2014.

Source: Printed from the *ALA Handbook of Organization* published annually and used with permission from the American Library Association.

Selection policies are essential because they explain the process followed and the priorities established before any material is purchased or accepted as a gift and placed in the library collection. The policy communicates the selection steps followed, which is useful when items in the collection are questioned by other teachers, parents, or community members.

A collection development policy includes much more than the process for selecting materials. It also generally includes:

- information about the mission and goals of the school district and often its priorities and how these statements are reflected in the library program

- an overview of the types of materials that are included in building-level collections and a description of the types of materials that are excluded

- guidelines for selecting materials

- a description of the acquisition process

- information about donations

- policies and procedures for weeding collections

- statements regarding protections for intellectual freedom including censorship and the process for reconsideration of materials

- policies regarding the ethical use of information

- information about the circulation of materials

- information about preservation and archiving materials

- when and by whom the policy is reviewed and updated

If the district or building in which a school librarian is working does not have such a set of policies and procedures, it is a worthwhile but time-consuming job to develop such a manual. Both the Montana State Library and the Arizona State Library have excellent guides to help both school and public librarians develop their collection development policy at msl.mt.gov /Library_Development/Standards/Documents/CollectionManagement Guidelines.pdf and https://www.azlibrary.gov/libdev/continuing-education /cdt/policies#five.

The collection development policy has several components: goals and objectives, materials to be included or excluded, selection guidelines, the acquisition process, policy for donations, circulation of materials, and weeding the collection. The first includes the goals and objectives.

Goals and Objectives

The goals and objectives of the Collection Development Policy must clearly relate to the mission, goals, and priorities of the district or school for which the document is developed. The mission and goals are overarching statements and demonstrate the purpose of the library collection in the district. The objectives or priorities generally are short-term and measurable. Usually, there is a direct relationship between the objectives and priorities of the district or school and its library program. These objectives and priorities are also reflected in allocating the budget and the decisions about how funds are expended.

Materials to Be Included or Excluded

Types of materials to include or exclude may include textbooks. Will they be circulated or available as part of a reference collection? Will the collection include materials for parents? Is there to be a collection of professional books for teachers? All these decisions are described in relation to the goals and objectives of the district and the library program and the established priorities.

Materials to be excluded could refer to your guidelines for weeding the collection. If you added a brief statement about periodicals because of the availability of issues online, you might have less of a problem with the offering of a collection of *National Geographic* from someone weeding their house.

Selection Guidelines

Selection guidelines provide the "rules" for selecting materials. What criteria are in place to match an item for its possibility to be added to the library's collection? These criteria become the framework to refer persons who are questioning any item found in the library collection. This policy may also cite the selection aids used in choosing materials. These will be discussed later in the chapter.

Acquisitions Processes

The method for the purchase of materials and equipment for the school library varies from school to school, district to district, and state by state. While a building-level librarian is probably not in a position to set the acquisitions process, reporting it in the policy book will help anyone not familiar with the process to understand how it works. The purchase process is discussed in the chapter on budget.

Policies on Donations

Often, well-meaning parents or other community members will clean out their garages, basements, or attics and decide that the books or magazines that they no longer want to keep can be donated to the library program. In some cases, these will be worthwhile to have in the library, but in other instances, they need to be discarded. Any donation can be matched to the selection guidelines to see if it meets the criteria for addition to the library collection. If not, your policy should state what will be the process for taking care of these items so your prospective donors are aware of what may happen to their gift. In some cases, they may choose to rethink their gift.

Circulation of Resources

What items may circulate, the number of items and the length of time they circulate are all a part of the selection policy. When the school takes responsibility for providing devices for students, these may be stored and circulated in the library. Are items checked out for two weeks or a semester? What happens when items are lost or broken? How many items may a student check out of the library?

Decisions about placing limits on the number of items that can be checked out at one time by any user, student, teacher, or another person must be carefully made. In an age in which so many resources are available online, many teachers and students may believe that there are few reasons to actually visit the physical library. Placing arbitrary limits on the number of items that may be circulated may reinforce this belief.

Teachers are usually granted an extended period, and if your students are expected to take ownership of their library, they should be allowed to use the information found there until someone needs it or until the end of the semester. Checking resources out for a full semester makes them exercise responsibility to bring it back when someone else does need it. It halts the need to send overdue notices, which must be sent only to the student in such a way that neither teacher nor parent knows what the student has overdue. It is an extraordinary way to teach both how to share with others and civic responsibility for peers.

Limiting the number of books that can be circulated by elementary students who are just learning to read and for students in higher grades who wish to check out books to read for pleasure is particularly troubling. As students take part in more outside activities such as sports, clubs, and music classes, they have even less time for recreational reading. As many obstacles as possible must be removed, including eliminating fines and extending circulation periods.

In addition to the concerns a librarian should have in limiting access to information available in collections, charging fines for overdue materials is also a very bad public relations event. These materials are purchased with funds from taxes the community pays and should be as accessible as possible. To charge fines for overdue books from a student on free breakfast and lunch makes an uncomfortable choice for that student, who becomes reluctant to take materials from the library if the book becomes overdue after two weeks or something happens to the book. For the more affluent students, it often appears that they can, if they are willing to pay the fine, keep something even if someone else has requested it. They consider that as long as they are willing to pay the "rent" on the item, they should be left alone.

Weeding Collections

Materials in disrepair and materials that are outdated, irrelevant, and inaccurate need to be removed from the collection. This should be a part of your selection policy to show to anyone if they object when you are discarding materials. Many teachers, parents, and even administrators are aghast when they think something is going to be discarded. To have the reasons for these discards in place will help them understand the process.

In deciding upon de-selection of your collection, considerations for retention or discard of materials seems in some cases more common sense than a formal process. Reference books especially must be reviewed from two points of view. Hard copies of encyclopedias, if they are used, need to be replaced every five years. The expense of doing this must be compared to the ease of locating information on an electronic copy. Most reference books that are available in electronic copy are preferable to buying a book because of the speed of access.

It would be difficult to try to justify keeping newspaper files unless it is the local newspaper, which is, hopefully, indexed. Most magazines are available in full text on databases. Any librarian who does not have this technology for their students should begin plans for implementation immediately.

Equipment can be evaluated with two criteria: use and repair record. Equipment that is no longer used because of lack of appropriate software should be removed. Any equipment should also be removed when repair costs exceed replacement costs. Keeping a repair record for each piece of equipment is essential to help in determining the reliability of the company manufacturing the equipment. A simple method is to make notations of the date of purchase and type of equipment. Each time the equipment fails to function, a record is made of the malfunction.

A final caution concerns the destination of withdrawn items. If the reason for withdrawal is a change in grade level or curriculum, the librarian may wish to relocate these items to another library. If they are old, in poor condition, or contain out-of-date information, they should be destroyed. Less fortunate school librarians in poorly funded schools will not find them useful even if their collections were destroyed by hurricanes or fires or they are managing a library in a developing nation. Useless to one is useless to all.

When the school librarian has a well-developed collection policy and adheres to its guidelines, it might seem that no one would ever object to any item in the library collection. However, far too many people think they should have a say in what other people's children should be able to read, and they create a challenge. In some cases this is an orchestrated effort on the part of groups. No matter why or where, it is best to be prepared to withstand a challenge.

What to Do in Case of a Challenge

While what to do in case of a challenge need not be in the actual policy manual, it should be in the folder with the selection manual in a convenient desk drawer. This procedure must be carefully described and cover as many contingencies as can be predicted.

It begins with asking the person with the complaint if they have read the entire document. They need to be given the grievance form and the selection policy to read. While the person(s) are doing this, a message is taken or sent to the principal that someone is in the library with a complaint about an item in the library collection. As stated earlier in the chapter, this message should remind the principal that the superintendent's office needs to know about the complaint.

When the complaint is from a parent, try to get to the basic reason for the complaint. It may be something other than what appears on the surface. A parent who objects to a book on a list given to students to be read over the summer may be objecting to the assignment if that student is expected to work over the summer to save for college tuition. On the other hand, some books are called into question at times by organizations and people are sent to the school to lodge the complaint. When this happens, these persons are prepared to do battle.

Sometimes a fellow teacher may question the choice of something in the library. This is especially troubling because librarians and teachers work side-by-side to teach students. These are treated as any other person with a complaint following the same process. Teachers may also suggest the purchase of a book for the library that you question. This is an interesting situation. A long-ago study of censorship in school libraries found that the greatest censorship was exercised by the school librarian who allowed personal bias to prevail in choices. Reviews of books by other school librarians can offer some assistance in these cases; these are discussed later in the chapter. Another source is the service offered by ALA.

The ALA's Office of Intellectual Freedom has staff trained to answer inquiries from a school librarian who has censorship problems. This office will respond quickly to any question and will even accept collect calls when a school librarian feels beleaguered. Further, state library and school library associations have intellectual freedom committees whose members can offer assistance both when selections are questioned and in developing a selection policy when none exists. Your policy statement is your basis for protecting the privacy and intellectual freedom rights of your students.

Protections for Privacy/Intellectual Freedom

Students have the right to have their use of school library materials protected. However, electronic methods for recording use permit the recognition of persons who had checked out any items. Sharing this information beyond the library staff who must keep inventory records is interpreted as a violation of individual privacy. The ALA policy on confidentiality is found in the accompanying box.

Policy 52.4 Confidentiality of Library Records

The ethical responsibilities of librarians, as well as statutes in most states and the District of Columbia, protect the privacy of library users. Confidentiality extends to "information sought or received, and materials consulted, borrowed, acquired," and includes database search records, reference interviews, circulation records, interlibrary loan records, and other personally identifiable uses of library materials, facilities, or services.

The American Library Association recognizes that law enforcement agencies and officers may occasionally believe that library records contain information which may be helpful to the investigation of criminal activity. If there is a reasonable basis to believe such records are necessary to the progress of an investigation or prosecution, the American judicial system provides the mechanism for seeking release of such confidential records: the issuance of a court order, following a showing of good cause based on specific facts, by a court of competent jurisdiction.

The American Library Association strongly recommends that the responsible officers of each library, cooperative system, and consortium in the United States: 1) Formally adopt a policy which specifically recognizes its circulation records and other records identifying the names of library users with specific materials to be confidential. 2) Advise all librarians and library employees that such records shall not be made available to any agency of state, federal, or local government except pursuant to such process, order, or subpoena as may be authorized under the authority of, and pursuant to, federal, state, or local law relating to civil, criminal, or administrative discovery procedures or legislative investigatory power. 3) Resist the issuance or enforcement of any such process, order, or subpoena until such time as a proper showing of good cause has been made in a court of competent jurisdiction.

Source: This information is published annually in the American Library Association's *Handbook of Organization*. Printed with permission from the American Library Association.

Libraries whose record-keeping systems reveal the names of users would be in violation of the confidentiality of library record laws adopted in many states. Efforts must be made within the reasonable constraints of budgets and school management procedures to eliminate records of use as soon as reasonably possible. With or without specific legislation, school librarians are urged to include statements in their collection development policies to respect the rights of children and youth by adhering to the tenets expressed in the Confidentiality of Library Records Interpretation of the Library Bill of Rights and the ALA Code of Ethics shown in this chapter.

Defending the Right to Access Information

A major problem for school librarians has been the necessity to try to filter information from the Internet, thus limiting access to information. Defending the collection—whether print, electronic, or transmitted—is a continuing obligation of the school librarian, but that role has changed with the introduction of electronic sources. On-site materials are carefully selected to meet the needs of teachers and students in the school. One, two, or more persons lodging complaints about items are not allowed to prohibit use by others in the school. Parents may request that their child not be allowed to read, listen to, or view materials on evolution or holidays, for example, but the materials remain in the collection. With a selection policy in place and a procedure to follow in case of complaint, the school librarian's response to pressures is more organized and less stressful.

This issue became more complex as a result of the passage of the Child Internet Protection Act (CIPA) in 2001. CIPA is a federal law enacted by Congress to address concerns about access to offensive content over the Internet on school and library computers. CIPA imposes certain types of requirements on any school or library that receives funding for Internet access or internal connections from the E-rate program—a program that makes certain communications technology more affordable for eligible schools and libraries. In early 2001, the FCC issued rules implementing CIPA.

What CIPA Requires

Schools and libraries subject to CIPA may not receive the discounts offered by the E-rate program unless they certify that they have an Internet safety policy that includes technology protection measures. The protection measures must block or filter Internet access to pictures that are: (a) obscene; (b) child pornography; or (c) harmful to minors (for computers that are accessed by minors). Before adopting this Internet safety policy, schools and libraries must provide reasonable notice and hold at least one public hearing or meeting to address the proposal.

Schools and libraries subject to CIPA are required to adopt and implement an Internet safety policy addressing: (a) access by minors to inappropriate matter on the Internet; (b) the safety and security of minors when using electronic mail, chat rooms, and other forms of direct electronic communications; (c) unauthorized access, including so-called "hacking," and other unlawful activities by minors online; (d) unauthorized disclosure, use, and dissemination of personal information regarding minors; and (e) measures restricting minors' access to materials harmful to them.

Schools and libraries are required to certify that they have their safety policies and technology in place before receiving E-rate funding. CIPA does not affect E-rate funding for schools and libraries receiving discounts only for telecommunications, such as telephone service.

An authorized person may disable the blocking or filtering measure during use by an adult to enable access for bona fide research or other lawful purposes. CIPA does not require the tracking of Internet use by minors or adults. For more information, see the CIPA website at http://www.fcc.gov/guides/childrens-internet-protection-act.

Teachers and students must learn how to make use of information found on the Internet if they are going to be informed members of present-day society. Prohibiting student use of the Internet, a valuable resource, is unthinkable. Although requirements of filtering software may appear to answer a major concern of some parents and others in local communities, they do not, and the installation of a filtering system does not solve the problem. Filtering programs miss the problems inherent in using such as a solution; they delete text containing specified terms, regardless of the context or content. While others prohibit access to specific websites, they fail to stop access to any new website that appears, and new websites appear every minute. Filters do not ensure limited access. Clever students can find pornographic sites through their own ability to maneuver software. The best approach is to establish parent and student agreements for Internet use. Students are given a password for their privilege, and they understand and agree to the regulations that are in place so they can keep their password.

School librarians who review appropriate websites for use with specific units of instruction may also bookmark these sites. This saves students from unnecessary wasted search time and perhaps even finding inaccurate information because the site has already been "selected" for the library collection.

All of these methods for finding information must be factored into the need to protect the copyright of the school library's collection. This often has unexpected challenges.

Policies Regarding the Ethical Use of Information

School librarians are dedicated to preserving the rights of the school community for access to information. This carries with it the need to spend an equal amount of effort on preserving the rights of the authors and creators, producers, and publishers of the information purchased for the library collection. This means the development of policies to explain the protection of the copyright law and how to monitor these policies.

Copyright

Copyright is a legal concept that safeguards the intellectual work of a creator. Copyright law is difficult to understand for most people except copyright lawmakers, lawyers who defend creators and abusers, and judges who make the final decisions in court cases. It is very difficult for school librarians to have enough accurate information to convince administrators, teachers, and students that, as a law, it must be obeyed. Principals want to save limited funds by encouraging mass copying of copyright-protected workbooks.

Teachers want to use materials brought from a workshop or borrowed from another teacher, carefully ignoring the "copied with permission for X event" statement on the bottom of each sheet. Students who violate copyright may be caught under school rules for plagiarizing as well as for violating copyright.

Librarians in academic, public, and school libraries are the first line of defense for the free flow of information. To continue this flow, the creators, authors, illustrators, editors, publishers, and producers of that information must be protected so they will be willing to continue writing, illustrating, editing, publishing, and producing. This will become more difficult as more information becomes available online.

The ease with which online information may be shared with a very large audience worldwide, downloaded, and reused makes it very vulnerable. For the school librarian to begin controlling this, it is imperative that one keep current about what is legal and what isn't. One-time use of material for classroom instruction is legal because schools are considered nonprofit users for educational purposes, the doctrine of fair use. Considering fair use also means considering loss of revenue for authors and producers, truly a never-ending circle. To have updated information means staying current on copyright changes and not getting lost outside the circle.

Because few educators including school librarians truly understand the copyright law, this is an opportunity for the librarian to take a leading role. Reading in the educational and library literature, attending conferences when copyright is a part of the programming, and making an effort to understand the law and any changes are just the beginning. School librarians must also explain any changes and point out any violations to colleagues, and this is never easy. Working with teachers and administrators to keep them informed helps remind them of the correct use of materials.

Reminding the administrator about the probability that when lawsuits for copyright infringement are filed, they will name the principal, the superintendent, and the school board—a situation most will not relish—may be an adequate warning. Post notices about copyright on all hardware that would enable copyright infringement. Finally, make sure that you are following correct procedures with the use of any material or information at your fingertips, that you yourself are not violating copyright.

New problems have surfaced with the Internet. This resource is so new that intellectual property laws to deal with it are just being written and tested. People can download websites onto their hard drives to be viewed at a later time. Using a downloaded website to show to teachers as a sample website before they create their own is a questionable practice, because you haven't asked permission to use the website. Because it is no longer necessary to put a copyright notice on a website for it to be covered by the law, it must be assumed that this material is under copyright protection.

Another problem area may be in establishing links from the library's website to other materials available online. School librarians need to be very cautious about what part, if any, of the information in that link is actually on the library's website. Such actions may result in creating a derivative work, especially if it isn't identified as someone else's and appears to be the intellectual property of the library staff.

Preservation and Archival Functions

Another component of the school library policy manual deals with preservation and archival functions. As items become more and more digitized, the need for physical storage space within the library is not as critical. The ability to store online information continues to expand. Students and teachers carry flash drives with as much information stored there as one used to need a mainframe computer to hold. Data curation is the managing of all kinds of data as long as it has interest for school library users for their use as scholars and for their education. For those teachers and students who wish to preserve the school's yearbook, it can be digitized. It is probable that the original information was created in a digital format and preserving it is merely copying that to store on a CD. Pictures of one year's activities in a school may also be preserved in digital form for the future. The repository for these should be the school library.

Building and Maintaining the Resource Collection

Collection management of the on-site collection includes the organization and circulation of materials. Organization is the first consideration since materials must be identified in some way for students and teachers to be able to locate them.

Organizing Information

Any collection must be organized in such a way that it provides for ease of access if users are going to find what they need. For book materials, commercial cataloging and processing is available, and the best choice for a given situation should be based on full information. Options for cataloging materials range from original cataloging and inputting electronic records to receiving cataloging from a bibliographic utility (usually very expensive), the district center, or from the jobber who fills the order.

The school librarian should always keep in mind that the purpose of organizing the collection is to provide access to the contents for users. Often, cataloging and classification courses are taught in library and information science programs with a major emphasis on such details as the number of spaces after a punctuation mark; thus, the process becomes more important than the product. Although the organization of a collection should be consistent with the national standards for cataloging rules and subject headings, particularly if the library is part of a consortium or a district with many schools, these must be adjusted to the situation.

The most efficient method is to purchase materials with electronic records shipped with the order and bar codes in place on the item. These records can then be downloaded into the OPAC often downloaded directly from the jobber. Books and other materials may come already bar-coded for immediate placement in circulation.

Another source for cataloging and processing services is from school districts or intermediate units with centralized processing centers. Materials are ordered centrally, shipped to the processing center where records are entered into the district's database, and then sent to individual buildings.

In states where statewide networks are in place, updates to the machine-readable database are a regular part of school library management. New materials are recorded for transmission to those responsible for the update, and the library records are in place.

A current discussion is being held on the placement of materials in genre collections, possibly to encourage more recreational reading. One could decide that was an easy way to go, but some would argue that a student who discovers a different book next to a favorite genre author on the fiction shelf, and reads it, moves away from being stuck in a particular genre and reading all those and nothing else. Those who have done this are very emphatic about the value of turning away from the Dewey Decimal Classification System to what seems a user-friendly system in one school. The lack of continuity for students moving from one school to another even in the district or from one school to the public library system could be troublesome for some students.

Selecting Materials

Selection of resources in libraries is often covered in library and information science programs in one or more courses. School librarians may have taken children's and youth literature in one or two courses and they may have discussed materials to support the curriculum in another course. However, before discussing the selection of resources, a high-priority activity for the library staff, school librarians need to understand they are not totally responsible. Rather, some of these choices belong to library users, including administrators, teachers, students, and, whenever possible, parents. School librarians who select a collection with little or no input from users may find that the resulting range of materials is too narrow. At other times, it is even more helpful to be able to consult with a technology-savvy teacher, parent, or student before choosing a new technology.

While providing a core or basic collection is the first step in collection development, more important is selecting the remaining materials that must be chosen to fit the school's curriculum. Guides to building a core collection include *Children's Catalog, Middle and Junior High School Catalog,* and *Senior High Core Collection,* which are published in hardbound volumes. These volumes contain carefully selected entries of book titles and are helpful to school librarians not only in establishing a core collection but in reviewing materials for retention or discard. These tools represent research and professional experience by experts in the school library field. However, the standard selection tools may not be as useful for selection after selecting the core because many of the materials listed are out of print.

Meeting curriculum needs is a major criterion for placing items in the collection. Librarians can begin to address this task by carefully reviewing the textbooks and review journals in the curriculum area used by each teacher, finding out the length of time any unit is taught and to how many students, and discovering what teaching method is used, and finding out what the research assignments are likely to be.

A bibliography of materials in the collection can be obtained by searching the online catalog for specific subject headings. If the resulting bibliography does not appear to have relevant titles or titles at the ability or interest level of the students in the course, additional materials must be purchased. As a temporary measure, materials may be requested from other libraries in the area.

Current review periodicals such as *Booklist, Bulletin for the Center of Children's Books, School Library Journal,* and *School Library Connections* review new publications. Follett's *TitleWave* lists books with full bibliographic information, cost, and ISBN. This program also provides reviews from periodical sources. One can ask to have lists created by subject, grade level, and places where the item is reviewed. Since all reviews in *Booklist* are for recommended titles, asking for resources that have been cited in that periodical gives a choice of only recommended resources. Testimonials and reviews are featured to help with selection in a way that was not dreamed of in the past. School librarians may also rely on bibliographies provided by professional associations, if these are current.

Several methods are available to encourage teachers and others to make selections. Teachers may need to be shown potential items for the collection, or they may be shown reviews of materials in a review journal. They can be asked to share suggestions in their subject area journals to fit topics they will be teaching. They could also be shown how to use an online service that reviews books.

As stated earlier, students can be encouraged to suggest titles for inclusion in the collection. Preparing a justification for purchase of an item seen or read in another library or in a bookstore can help develop students' writing skills. Students might also enjoy reading reviews of new materials in *Booklist, School Library Journal,* and *School Library Connections* and completing an order form for titles that appeal to them. If students are assigned to the library for work-study or as aides, the librarian should seek their opinions in the selection process and make review of materials part of each person's assignment. All involved in selection should be reminded of the selection policy criteria.

Databases have become expensive additions compared to a single book. These are items that really need some preview by teachers so they will be used. Vendors offer access through licenses for their databases. Sometimes these licenses are offered through the state department of education for all schools and the state library for all public libraries. In other states, this is a responsibility of each individual school or the school district. License agreements for multiuse become pertinent if they are limited to a small number of users rather than being assigned to multiusers. Teachers and students must understand the license they are using so that they do not abuse this.

Online references should have full-text and image files of current information that can be downloaded, and users can manipulate these for research reports; however, this makes it very easy for a student to copy rather than create. Efforts to reduce plagiarism become a part of managing this resource. Helping teachers plan those research assignments that build the research process for students to create products that reflect their work is an important role for the school librarian. The ease of cutting and pasting and even taking a paper written and posted on the Internet can be appealing. Carefully developed assignments to build critical thinking skills will make it very difficult for any student to plagiarize.

Software to check papers for plagiarism is needed, and students should be taught how to check their papers for plagiarism. Some teachers expect this to be done by the student, and the result is turned in with the assignment.

Relevance of Materials

The relevance of materials has always been a key component in choosing information to place in the library collection. This "relevance" describes the content as useful to meet the curriculum of the school and match their age and ability levels. It has become even more important when students go first to Google. Teaching careful choices for their assignments can be demonstrated when hard copy books and excellent databases on relevant topics are available for them to use. As discussed earlier in the chapter, all materials should meet the criteria of the library selection policy.

Selecting Information from the Internet

The Internet, a worldwide communication network, offers both electronic mail and the World Wide Web (WWW) to locate information as discussed below. With email, students and teachers can communicate with other educational institutions, professional association lists, nationally available email lists such as LM_NET, classrooms, and individuals, querying colleagues for answers to questions. One caution is that responses may have files attached to the message that can carry viruses to school servers. Many school districts build firewalls to protect the traffic. If firewalls are not in place, administrators, teachers, and students need to use care in opening attachments and should not do so if the message is not expected.

Access to the Internet provides entrance to the WWW. Created in 1990, information from the WWW can be searched, read, selected, stored, and edited. It permits hyperlinks to more and more distant databases in an ever-expanding realm. Some of these links are not readily available. Scheeren has written a book to introduce these resources and describe information available on the "hidden Web," which is accessible to those who know of its existence.[1]

School librarians create webpages for the library and then link other locations on the WWW to their home pages. This greatly expanded access to information requires a new facet to collection development. It also allows students to find better websites to search for their topics rather than just surfing, which may lead them to be overwhelmed by the amount of information they find with their search engine.

Information located on the Internet does not resemble the information that librarians have traditionally anticipated as a part of the selection process. It is not something that will be purchased, processed, and stored for future use on a shelf. However, information from the Internet, available to students and teachers, becomes a part of the library collection. How to choose the best from the Internet and how to keep what is not appropriate from coming into the library is a major discussion among all types of librarians and their communities.

One of the most important tasks for the librarian is to help students and teachers find the best resources to meet their need. Search engines allow students to locate much more information than they could imagine, and they have no quality control for relevance or accuracy. When selecting websites for students, make these websites available on the system just as you would select books or magazines and bookmark these resources. Lists of excellent websites are available from the ALA's divisions. The American Association of School Librarians (AASL) publishes Best Websites for Teaching and Learning. These provide a great deal of access for students from a world that is already overloaded with information: good and bad, accurate and inaccurate, relevant and irrelevant, useful and useless. Attaching appropriate URL addresses to the library home page at the time students are studying a particular topic is similar to placing all the books on a topic on reserve at the beginning of a unit of instruction.

For all use of the Internet, an acceptable use policy, created by the library advisory committee and agreed to by students and parents, can help librarians with this new and very important part of their daily activities. Remembering that clever students can locate information even though filters exist, librarians and teachers are less vulnerable if they and their students and parents have agreed that library and other school-owned computers are available for research rather than random surfing or playing games. The Internet is certainly an exciting new resource, and restricting access limits this potential reference.

Helping library users find accurate information on the Internet will be a challenge. These authors are less concerned with a student's locating pornography because pornography is instantly recognizable. While a librarian seeing computer screens can recognize pornography and filters may point to something seemingly pornographic, they neither identify nor block incorrect facts. Misinformation that may be on the Internet is not so readily recognized; students and teachers may have extremely biased information and inaccurate facts or statistics and be unaware. Explaining that information from the Internet needs to be confirmed in other sources is a beginning.

Selection of materials is done carefully to ensure the best items are available. When resources in the library are no longer useful, they need to be de-selected or weeded from the collection not on the shelves and in the database collection.

De-selection of Materials (Weeding)

As stated earlier in discussing creating a policy statement, weeding is the discarding of materials that are of little value to students and teachers. This is perhaps as important as selecting additional materials for a collection. This may be a temporary loss of value due to a change in focus, or it may be a permanent loss due to curriculum change. Items may be removed due to age, lack of relevance, or wear and tear. A smaller, more attractive collection of relevant, up-to-date materials on the shelves, particularly when hard cover materials are less likely to be of interest, is more important to students and teachers. Many school librarians find themselves able to reduce shelf space to create a learning commons when unused materials are weeded.

If state standards require a certain number of materials in the collection or if the school administration insists that a large number of materials be kept, a separate list could be maintained for these useless materials. They would still be listed as part of the collection but stored out of sight until they can be discarded. In some states software and databases may be counted as equivalency for materials.

Several factors justify collection reevaluation and de-selection.

1. Changes in the curriculum revise the focus of the collection.

2. Materials must be repaired or replaced if in poor condition.

3. The library shelves should appear attractive and inviting to users.

4. Items counted as holdings should represent useful resources.

5. Students and teachers should have access to the best possible collection of materials.

6. Lack of use of print materials because of the availability of online resources reduces the need for hard copies. Hard copies also age yearly, and if they are no longer useful, consider deselecting.

7. Age of material and accuracy.

De-selection is a continual process. For hard copy items, each item is reviewed as it circulates. Students and teachers can judge whether the material was helpful to them and, if not, why not. The staff should conduct a thorough evaluation of the entire collection at least once every three years.

The school librarian is responsible for reviewing the collection for compliance with the selection policy. As with the selection process, de-selection must be regulated by the selection policy, not by personal bias.

In general, four categories of materials are taken from the shelves: (1) materials to be stored until needed, although this category needs very careful consideration, (2) materials to be sent to another school library for younger or older students, (3) materials in need of repair or replacement, and (4) materials to be discarded. Materials to be stored are of good quality and accurate but treat topics temporarily not being taught, are unlikely to become dated, are attractive, and are at the appropriate level for students in the building.

Materials judged to be below or above the reading levels of students in the building, or those that treat subject areas shifted to another grade level, may be sent to another building. Retaining titles that might be useful in the future is usually not a good plan. It would be easier for the receiving school to return the materials if the situation is reversed.

Materials in need of repair or replacement should be carefully evaluated. Consider carefully if the information in this book is only available there or if it might be located online. Books may be sent to a bindery if the paper is of good quality and the information is important. In-house repair of materials must be reviewed to see that the costs of labor and materials do not exceed the cost of rebinding an item.

Finally, materials must be evaluated for retention or withdrawal. Old, worn-out materials must be discarded. Out-of-date materials should be removed unless they have great historical value. Duplicate titles may be reassessed if demand for the item has slackened. Biographies not linked to curriculum or of persons unknown to the present generation should not be retained.

Outdated materials may be almost anything in science and technology with a copyright date more than five years old. In fact, to answer one of the questions at the beginning of this section, consideration might be given to purchasing only electronic science resources. Psychology, history, business, and education become dated in 10 years. In fiction, certain authors and topics may lose their appeal to an age group. An author read by high school students 15 years ago may be devoured by elementary students today.

This chapter has presented the responsibility of the school librarian to provide access to information as well as manage the information resources in the school library. The next chapter explains the need for managing personnel.

Exercises

1. Determine whether your state has a law related to confidentiality of records. Compare this to another state's law and decide which law would be more difficult to follow.
2. Ask one or more schools how they maintain confidentiality of records.
3. Outline a talk you would present to your principal, teachers, and parents concerning your response to the requirements for confidentiality of records in your school.
4. Investigate the strengths and weaknesses of the filtering systems offered to school and public libraries.
5. Prepare a presentation for your teachers concerning ways to overcome plagiarism in student papers.
6. Interview two or more school librarians to see whether they have had any censorship questions and, if so, how they responded.
7. If you can locate the selection policies from two school districts, compare them against what you have read in this chapter.

Note

1. William O. Scheeren, *The Hidden Web: A Sourcebook* (Santa Barbara, CA: Libraries Unlimited, 2012).

10
Managing Personnel

The title of this chapter is "Managing Personnel," and it may seem that "managing" is too strong for someone who will be "working collaboratively" with peers and students. However, a degree of management goes with working with others and this skill is sometimes overlooked. Traditional practice taught in many preparation programs focuses on selecting materials, organizing collections, and using new technologies, among others, rather than "managing." In fact, many students resist the thought that they need to learn how to manage. Nevertheless, managing people is one of the most important factors in a successful library program.

The librarian must have the ability to manage and communicate with persons using the library and assume responsibility for management of library staff when it exists and any volunteers available to help in the library. Management is needed when working with teachers and students who use the library. The successful school librarian possesses the management skills needed to interact with everyone in the school as well as parents and others throughout the wider community. These skills help create a community of users participating in learning in the library and eliminate the need for authoritarian postures. Thus, the librarian becomes a colleague of all rather than someone writing and inflicting rules and regulations.

Many school librarians are single managers of their library; they have no paid staff to manage. Because of this prospect, education programs for school librarians often provide only skeletal instruction in management skills such as interpersonal skills for communication with those in the school (administrators, teachers, and students) and how to handle students who misbehave. However, every school librarian should have a variety of people collaborating in the library. The secret here is, from the first day in a new school, to help everyone understand that this is not yours, but their library, and it is up to everyone to ensure that their library is readily available for use and its facility and resources are not only the best available but coming to the library is a learning experience for all.

This begins with the principal who may have been responsible for hiring the school librarian. The concept of the library as a learning center should be a part of the interview process. A brief description of the library either orally or in a handout is given to teachers who will be at the school at least one day before the students arrive. As the parents and other caregivers are asked if they can volunteer some of their time in the library, they are told exactly what this will include, from helping open boxes of new books and checking the invoice to serving as an artist in residence in schools with irregular visits from an art teacher.

Finally, at the earliest opportunity the community is approached to see who can volunteer to help in many ways including sharing their knowledge and expertise with students. A good way to start this process is to enlist an advisory committee.

The Library Advisory Committee

A library advisory committee is made up of members of the school community who are assigned by the principal, volunteer, or are asked by the school librarian. It should include representatives of the teachers, the students, and perhaps a parent. If membership is chosen by the librarian, those selected should be a mix of advocates and perhaps one or two for whom such an assignment may be an educational experience.

Classroom teachers may need to be reminded that the library is there to provide access to information for their classrooms and for the entire school. When they are asked to help develop the mission, policies, goals, and objectives for the library, they begin to understand the librarian's challenges. Funding requests for resources is no longer interpreted as support for the librarian only, but to enhance student learning.

If students from elementary school through high school are to believe the library is truly theirs, then they need to have one or two on the advisory committee. They will be able to present the student view of suggested resources including electronic resources and make some suggestions for rules in the library that may inhibit use. They will also be able to analyze any rules for usage of the library from the standpoint of student access. They may be able to help solve problems in some way other than creating a rule that must be enforced.

Having a parent involved brings that point of view about resources needed and things that would be helpful for their children. They and other members of the advisory group can be useful advocates of the library program and their efforts can in no way be construed as serving a vested interest.

An advisory group meets regularly, as frequently as is practical but seldom more than once a month. They will have a clear purpose or charge, and all members must understand their roles. They will want to have an active assignment so they consider their membership worthwhile. School librarians, in consultation with the principal, set the parameters for the group. Advisory committee members should help establish the purpose of the group. All of this is much more easily accomplished when the principal is an active part of the advisory group.

The advisory committee might be interested in many areas of the library program. Members could help with reviewing the mission statement as it flows from the school's mission and in establishing the year's objectives after analyzing the information needs of library users. When these objectives have a relationship to financial support, the advisory group should help plan for budgetary expenditures. This takes some pressure off the librarian when requests far exceed resources. Once an advisory committee has been formed, you can begin the initial step in planning how to manage by analyzing your leadership style.

Analyzing Your Leadership Style

All school librarians need to be leaders, but they will not all have the same leadership style. Self-analysis of your style determines how you will be most comfortable in situations where you need to lead. Not all situations require the same type of leadership, but you need to know when and how to move out of your comfort zone. Sometimes the older sibling in a family is an autocratic leader making decisions autonomously because this person's parents expected that older child would help with younger children. Authoritarian conduct is useful in a crisis situation where there is no time to gather agreement. If a student is in danger, a direct order to lessen the danger is essential. The key is an honest appraisal; not what you would like to be, but how you really feel about handling situations. If you are only comfortable when you are doing all the planning and determining what needs to happen to carry out those plans, you are definitely authoritarian. If most of the time you feel it is more productive to have others participate in the process, you are more likely a democratic manager. However, in all cases, you must lead or the process will become chaotic. Leaderless groups accomplish nothing until someone steps in to take the leader's role. If it is not the librarian, the library may suffer.

School librarians who are democratic leaders will allow others to participate in the decision-making process. Another description of leadership behavior is Jim Collins's graphic pyramid, Hierarchy of Leadership.[1] His first level is the "Highly Capable Individual" who "makes productive contributions through individual talent, knowledge, skills, and work habits." The second level is the "Contributing Team Member," someone who "contributes individual capabilities to the achievement of group objectives." The "Competent Manager," the third level, organizes people and resources to meet predetermined objectives. The fourth level, the "Effective Leader," "catalyzes commitment to and vigorous pursuit of clear and compelling visions, stimulating higher performance standards." The fifth level is the "Executive" who "builds enduring greatness through a paradoxical blend of personal humility and professional skill."

Most school librarians are highly capable individuals who understand contributing to a team to meet objectives. They are also organized or most libraries would be in total chaos. However, helping others reach higher performance levels is essential if students are going to do the best they can do.

Followers of an effective leader or one who builds greatness know that in most situations that leader will use the same style. For a leader to act in any unexpected way unless in critical circumstances confuses all.

In the book *The Many Faces of School Library Leadership*,[2] readers are given a look at leadership from school library leaders with a combination of theory and practice. The various roles and their leadership components are described.

After you have analyzed your leadership style, you are ready to begin the process of managing those around you. Those closest will be the library staff.

Library Staff

In the present economic climate, many schools operate with a single person assigned to the school library. In very large schools, the school library may have two or more professionals and paraprofessionals. Professional staff may include others who are not necessarily certified librarians such as technology professionals. If reading specialists are assigned to the school, a good place for them to have an office and even classroom space is in the library.

One of the most important tasks is to make sure staff members are working with a common goal and a common vision. Once the staff has established and accepted the goals and objectives, the librarian works to build a common vision of information and instructional services with the other teachers in the building, defining the role of the librarian—as a part of the teaching staff. This is especially important as changes in curriculum or other requirements are put into place.

Tasks to be performed in the library have been developed over time by practitioners who manage library programs on a daily basis. However, in recent years these tasks have been changing with every new technology and every new educational trend. The librarian leading the library is also responsible for helping staff, preparing for advances in technology, for learning about additions to the collection such as new databases, implementing new services such as a makerspace, and developing new relationships with agencies outside the school.

When more than one professional is assigned to the library, each will expect the person in charge to direct their actions so they can complete their assigned tasks in a satisfactory manner. Such decisions may be group decisions. Nevertheless, all staff members including students, and volunteers who can work independently, should be allowed to establish how to do a job once the job has been defined. When improvement is needed, the librarian must help staff understand the problem and how to solve it.

If the library is to run smoothly, you must assign job responsibilities to specific personnel, and you will then need to supervise the staff to see that they carry out their duties efficiently and thoroughly. This is not always a pleasant job. Supervising personnel means decisions must be made that may not be readily accepted by staff; at the same time, you have the responsibility of maintaining staff members' job satisfaction.

Finally, if you have been given these responsibilities, you will also be asked to evaluate staff performance. This is pleasant when staff is unusually competent, but a little more difficult if merit raises are given for outstanding performance. However, it is especially difficult if staff is poorly prepared or incompetent. Evaluation is based on standards of performance.

Standards of Performance

Setting standards of performance and monitoring staff as they perform their jobs is a supervision and management task for the librarian. Supervision of personnel is the process of dealing with the persons who have been assigned the job responsibilities and evaluating performance and competencies individuals have for doing their jobs.

Competencies directly define the personnel carrying out functions in the library. The degree to which any school librarian may participate in any of these functions is not only the training of the staff, but it may be a product of the organization of the school district and the contracts binding personnel in that school district. The school librarian as manager may be in a position to evaluate other professionals working in the library and needs to be aware of these contracts because they often have strict regulations for all personnel in the school district. An awareness of the organization of the district and the union contract is essential.

In many school districts, state departments of education mandate personnel evaluation. For professional staff, the school district requirements may include evaluation of performance to determine reappointment or tenure. As suggested in Chapter 3, the applicant should try to find out about evaluation steps to reappointment and tenure before accepting a position in a school district. When you are responsible for the actual evaluation, you must research the process fully. After an initial evaluation, this will go forward to the principal or the district library director if one is in the district, and the personnel office. It is essential to obtain correct information about the latest policies or requirements in the state or district. Evaluation may continue to be required even after tenure is granted.

When the state department of education provides forms to school districts to evaluate the teaching and clerical staff, these forms seldom cover the unique tasks of the school librarian. A generic form will be for the evaluation of all education personnel. If this is the case, the librarian helps the principal by defining the evaluation criteria in library terminology. With little specific evaluation criteria, administrators may not understand how to monitor the librarian's behavior and performance and may not understand the competencies being measured.

Evaluation forms specific to school librarians are usually available from the state school library organization. This group, often in cooperation with the state department of education's school library director, may provide a better form for evaluating the performance of the building-level librarian. When no published form is available, other means of evaluation are used.

The most efficient form of evaluation is direct observation. However, this method is usually uncomfortable for all concerned. Students are uneasy because the library staff person being observed is uneasy. It is difficult for the observer to be at ease because this is an evaluation situation. The performance is strained, and the process seems contrived. However, library professionals must be evaluated as they interact with students and teachers. If this is not to be an arbitrary judgment, it must be based on concrete facts. One way to get these facts is through direct observation.

Unfortunately, when the person in charge of the library is reviewing a less efficient employee, evaluation means keeping a detailed record of inefficiency to build the steps for improvement, or, in the case of consistent lack of improvement, to support dismissal. School librarians hope that they will not need to dismiss personnel, but when the situation occurs, the principal and the district library director will expect the librarian to follow appropriate procedures. Dismissal requires a carefully documented record of tasks done incorrectly or not done at all. It is not a pleasant assignment, yet it is irresponsible to allow inefficient, ineffective, and even harmful employees to remain when the education of students is at stake.

Because clerical and technical staff members are seldom tenured, evaluation determines salary increases and continuation of position. Records must be maintained at all levels. Efficient staff must be rewarded, and merit pay raises often must be documented as carefully as refusals to grant merit pay raises. The dismissal of inefficient clerical and technical staff requires careful and thorough documentation just as with professional staff. In our litigious society, many persons who are dismissed will sue.

Hiring Staff

A school library management book needs to discuss the school librarian in a situation where staff is to be added to the library. In a situation where additional staff is needed for the library, the librarian must clearly analyze those factors that dictate requirements for more staff and prepare appropriate documentation to justify the positions. Administrators must be convinced of the need for a new or expanded position, especially in times when budgets are tight. The foundation established in the job description may become the justification for funding. Calculating actual costs of clerical tasks in relation to professional salary to establish cost accountability is one way to do this. The responsibilities for adding staff are described below.

Larger school districts have a human resources department with staff and a director. In smaller districts, the hiring is assigned to a single person within another department of the district. These persons will be very knowledgeable about hiring teachers, but they may be much less familiar with the competencies of the various persons working in school libraries, and their vision of this person's assignments, if based upon their past experiences, may be in need of an update. Writing job descriptions could become the school librarian's responsibility.

Most jobs have titles and job descriptions. School librarians receive their titles and job descriptions from two professions: librarianship and education. As a part of librarianship, they are described by that profession as librarians. In 1975, the American Association of School Librarians (AASL) changed the title of the person responsible for the school library to "media specialist"; and in 2011, the AASL Board changed it back to "school librarian." However, California has adopted its job title as "teacher librarian," a title that has been used in Canada.

Within the school district, titles may be the choice of the person running the school library who, because this person is in charge of the technology in the building, may choose to be called "educational technologist" or some other title. The title is usually a part of the job description. The job description is used to post in the media for applications from interested school librarians. These must be written very carefully because they are what are applied to the applications that come into the office. The stated criteria are used to "test" for the person's ability to fill the position.

When the school librarian has the responsibility for recruiting and terminating personnel, the process for interviewing and hiring usually is a very established process and one that the school librarian needs to learn if this is one of his or her responsibilities. In any event, human resources personnel will welcome some help with interview questions again because they have very little experience with what is needed in a person who will be working in a school library.

Another person who may be assigned to the library is the preprofessional who is coming to learn about school libraries. Many universities and colleges need exemplary situations to place practicum students.

Practicum Students

Supervision of practicum students from nearby colleges introduces the next generation of school librarians to the real world. Locations for practicum placements are made in schools when the university faculty considers a program location that will provide a student with the best possible experience. This is a great deal of work on the part of the school librarian and the teaching staff as they provide these experiences.

The school librarian as a practicum assignment allows the student to carry out a wide variety of assignments and should work with teachers and students following best practice. If you have been asked to host a practicum student, confirm with teachers that they are willing to let the practicum student help build a unit of instruction or other learning activity with their students.

A faculty member will likely come from the university to see the student in action. Preparing a scenario that will allow the student to truly demonstrate skills learned is essential. The student will also anticipate a letter of recommendation about the activities completed during the practicum. Finally, students seeking positions after graduation need the networking their practicum supervisor can offer.

Support Staff in the Library

All of the information about assigning work for professionals in the library applies equally to assigning tasks to support staff when school librarians are lucky enough to have nonprofessional staff assigned to the library. This may be library technicians who carry out a wide variety of tasks.

Some support staff will have had training at a nearby community college. Others may be hired from the same pool of persons who are applying for secretary positions in the school district. The skills and knowledge of support staff will be very wide, and they need to be asked about these skills before assigning them a task. The amount of training you will need to do will depend upon the responsibilities they have had in the past and the years of experience they have had in your library.

Managing personnel may also be defined as getting along with the clientele. In the next sections suggestions are offered for managing with students, teachers, administrators, parents, and volunteers. The chapter closes with suggestions for managing in the community that includes other libraries and librarians.

Students and the Library

Students who consider the library "theirs" will work to see that it remains a pleasant place to visit and a welcome place to learn. They will see that this warehouse of information runs smoothly. A quote from Chapter 6 on assessment is applicable here because it outlines a major reason why students feel ownership in their library. Frances Henne writes,

> For some students, and in certain schools this may be many
> students, the only library skill that they should have to acquire
> is an awareness, imprinted indelibly and happily upon them,
> that the library is a friendly place where the librarians are eager
> to help.[3]

This friendly interest and demonstrated willingness to assist are often far beyond the attitude that a public librarian or an academic librarian is required to exhibit. Providing that "friendly place" with the freedom that should exist in the library to allow students to explore their environment, learn from one another, and read or view or listen to materials recommended by their fellow students makes the position of school librarian a very pleasant one. Knowing when this interaction moves from exploration and encouragement into mischief is a skill that may take practice to acquire, but it is crucial to allow students the freedom to explore.

The library is the only room in the school where no student need fail. Students with reading or math problems find frustration in the classroom. They perceive that as a lack of ability to accomplish a task that other students can do easily. For students who cannot sing or play an instrument, music class is uncomfortable. If students feel they have little aptitude for art, the art room may be a greater challenge than they wish to attempt. Certainly many students do not enjoy physical activities, especially if they are chosen last for team sports.

In contrast, the library has no specific curriculum area or grade level that might be found in a classroom. Rather, it should have information at all levels and to satisfy all interests. The librarian should be available to give individual assistance to a student without drawing attention to the process. All students ask for help finding materials, and all students find something with which they can work, and in a truly learning environment, students help one another.

The cardinal rule is to place as few restrictions as possible on student use of resources. Limiting anything such as how many books can be taken home or how much time is allowed to search a database may seem to provide "equal" access, but, in reality, it is frustrating to all. Books are no longer the stalemate they once were because fewer students are using hard-bound resources. Some of this can also be alleviated with e-books. The real challenge is with books for beginning readers who will have read their library book before they get back to their room. To limit these students to one or two books that they check out for a week is truly limiting access to information. It helps if any rules or restrictions are understood by all, and the easiest way to do this is to have others involved in the decisions.

Students themselves can help establish rules if they have the opportunity to analyze the resources available to the numbers who will need them at any given time. The Tech Squad will know how long database searches may take. They can speed up searches by helping less experienced students. This gives technically able students the recognition of their expertise and competent help to those less able.

Students know when assignments require use of materials for a longer period of time. They can also help evaluate a plan to allow everyone to check out materials for a longer time, and they will help the school librarian manage getting resources back when someone else needs them because students have been involved in the planning.

It is surprising just how capable students can be in solving problems with project-based learning and in meeting the challenges and opportunities presented in the school library makerspace. They can set the standards for digital citizenship and analyze why books are damaged or lost and make suggestions for solving these problems with physical items.

Librarians, when they assume the role of teacher, must follow the prescriptions for classroom management and effective teaching. Good planning with teachers for exciting instructional activities to carry out as a part of a unit means students are interested and engaged. When students are able to do their assignments using their own plans for learning whether as individuals or as a member of a group, they are interested and engaged. When the school librarian and the teacher are interested in what the students are doing, the students know this. Students are astute. They will be annoyed by busywork. Work with teachers and students to set objectives. It will not be busywork if everyone helps plan what is going to be needed and how it will be presented when it is finished.

Units should be planned with a variety of activities: some lecture, some discussion, some viewing of media, and some active exercises that allow them to move around. No one enjoys sitting for long periods of time, and the library is one room in the school that truly invites browsing and moving from one place to another.

The library is the place where all students come at some point. Not all students will earn your affection, and in some students, it may be difficult to find redeeming qualities. The counterpoint is that not all students will like the librarian, but that does not define student and librarian interaction. Sharing responsibility does. It is the responsibility of librarians to engage students in learning activities that they will enjoy doing, whether finishing an assignment or reading a book. In a shared environment, it is much easier for the school librarian to get to know as many students as possible, to learn to like them, and to let them know it.

Teachers and the Library

Teachers will come under the "management' aspect of the school librarian who must help them learn and use new technologies and use them appropriately. Managing teachers is easily accomplished when the librarian understands what teachers expect and this becomes the assignment to listen to teachers. They have problems that they can share with you and trying to solve them will be welcomed. One way to be successful is to learn teachers' needs and fulfill them. Your success can often be defined as doing what teachers think should be done. Asking which services teachers want and then offering those services will build a positive image.

The librarian must create the perception that the priority for the library is to be available for curriculum assistance, especially with the implementation of standards. The librarian provides teachers with the help they need as they plan their classroom instructional activities.

Accessibility of resources when they are required is essential. Librarians should encourage teachers to plan ahead for library needs, but instant help must be given willingly, not grudgingly.

Managing with teachers is the same as with students: put as few restrictions as possible on library access. Under this method, the librarian allows access to the library to as many students as possible and works with teachers to ensure the best possible experiences for their students while they are in the library. They welcome students sent to the library to work on group projects that might require space to create items as well as to work as teams to discuss their projects.

One way to help teachers understand the role of the library in instruction is to provide in-service for teachers in information sources, research methods, research in the field of education, and additions to the library. The librarian continues to provide in-service that will help teachers gain technological skills they may be lacking with the new communication devices their students use with such great ease.

Helping teachers expand their skills without implying that they do not have the skills is a successful management method. Overcoming teacher resistance is easier when teachers are involved in planning the in-service activity. Then the program will be based on teacher-developed needs.

When helping teachers, it is always a good idea to be empathetic. When colleagues return from absences such as health leaves or sabbaticals, spending extra time to help them catch up on rules and regulations that have changed in their absence or curricular changes being discussed will contribute to a positive atmosphere for all.

Many teachers and librarians complain that teachers who also coach major sports sometimes misuse the library on a game or contest day. Librarians may consider it an imposition if coaches want to bring their classes to the library on those days. Coaches have enormous responsibility for the health and safety of their players, who are vulnerable in a way far exceeding that of other teachers and their students. Working with teachers who have responsibilities such as the yearbook, the prom, or a field trip will ease their teaching burden for that period of time and can make the day more educational for that teacher's classes. This does not mean that the library becomes a dumping ground but that students are receiving the best possible use of their time in school.

Finally, the librarian should be willing to assist with extracurricular events. When the music teacher needs someone to attend the city choral festival with the school choir, the librarian should volunteer rather than be drafted. Volunteering to go to the museum on the fifth-grade field trip provides an opportunity to talk with volunteer parents and observe what students are learning. Such tasks are not in the job description of the librarian, but they require a teacher-sponsor, and librarians are teachers too. Ignoring the opportunity to assist teachers makes managing more difficult later, when teachers use the library.

The above may seem to relate to the classroom teacher, but it is equally important to other specialists on the staff. If the library has become a learning commons, those teachers may be immediately available. Learning the commonalities among these specialties means helping embed what they have to offer with classroom teachers. It helps students understand the reality of a real world that does not separate into units of time for music, art, and math, but for all students today who wear earbuds listening to music while they complete their homework, this is common practice.

Administrators and the Library

This section might be subtitled "How to Get Along with Your Boss." Certainly, "managing" an administrator means getting along with those in authority in the school district. The focus here is on the building principal, but the methods and the suggestions for activities are equally applicable to working with the director of the library program and the district superintendent. It begins with a word of caution. If the only time a school librarian is in contact with an administrator is to complain about something, it will not take a very long time to find out that these persons will try to dodge any encounter. This does not help the perception of the library and the librarian and is very harmful. It could even result in the program's being closed because that is an easy way to get rid of a pesky school librarian. The suggestions that follow are ways to be seen as an extremely competent and helpful person who is in charge of an indispensable program.

School librarians have management responsibility with their administrators. The librarian should make regular reports to principals and other administrators to keep them informed of activities going on in the library and in the classroom, particularly those activities that increase student learning and add to the general instructional climate of the school. Principals have so many outside activities demanding their time that they have little time left over to focus on the well-being of the school staff. Keeping them informed of special events going on in classrooms is also helpful both when the library is directly involved but at other times when teachers may not have thought it important to inform the principal.

Trying to "manage" the principal can sometimes be a thankless task. If one is so unfortunate as to be in a building with a principal who is inadequate or one who has a mindset in opposition to libraries and librarians, it can be miserable. This situation calls out all the creativity possible to let the principal begin to see the positive features of an excellent school library. Students and teachers can help with this simply by having them select things to highlight to the community and include the principal as a member of the community.

When the principal does not support the library, it may well be that this person is not supportive of teachers and students. At that point, the school librarian should work to do everything possible to improve the climate of the school and to show the community how students are learning. This can often be done through the school library website and community blogs to bring the school and all its activities to the attention of the community. Teachers will welcome this when they have little applause from the principal.

The school library program should prosper if the librarian learns to plan with the principal. Planning with the principal does not mean discussing the titles of databases to which to subscribe. That is a professional task for which the librarian has had training. Rather, planning with the principal should include such topics as the continuing costs of new online reference services now replacing the book and periodical collections that are needed to increase student learning potential in the school. This is a broad and somewhat different approach to the relationship between principal and school librarian. Both touch the educational lives of every student through their interactions with students and teachers. However, the school librarian works with all the students, all the teachers, and all the curriculum all the time. While principals want to do this, too, they are taken away to carry out other duties, often outside the building. This means librarians are in a unique position to keep principals informed when they are away from the school at those other functions. The teaching needs of teachers and the learning needs of students as they are carried out in the library then become continuing topics of discussion.

Successes are detailed in regular reports to the principal. This will help present the library program in such a way that the principal can speak highly of it to other principals. Too often in life, the complaints outweigh the compliments, yet, as stated earlier, complaining is not the way to influence the principal. Regular monthly reports on the use of the library and the positive learning experiences of students outnumber any list of needs, great though they may be. Librarians also submit a yearly report, which is a compilation of the monthly statistics. If the librarian has developed a 3-, 5-, 10-, or even 15-year plan with the principal, this yearly report will cite progress toward each of the goals, point out what has not occurred, and present the plan for fulfilling this objective in the next one or two years. The year-end report should be attractive and easily understood.

Another type of report presents trends in education. As professional periodicals are added to the library collection, the librarian may copy pertinent articles, highlighting the key passages, and forward them to the principal. Making copies of articles or information taken from the Internet and sharing them with the principal provides up-to-date information. Sending abstracts from the latest important books can also help the principal maintain a high level of expertise in educational trends as they develop. This makes you and your principal look good, an appealing perception under all circumstances.

The principal who participates in activity planning will better understand the role of the librarian and the amount of responsibility involved in managing a library. In evaluating performance, the principal must clearly recognize the dual role of the librarian as teacher and manager—and adjust the method of evaluation accordingly.

In some school districts, principals are administrators who are responsible for the day-to-day management of their building and also the discipline of students. They seldom have the opportunity to visit classrooms except to evaluate teacher performances. Inviting the principal to read to students, listen to final reports of research projects, and help judge a storytelling contest gives this official the opportunity to share in library activities with children. The principal's participation also gives the school librarian's project more importance and provides a positive experience for students, library staff, and the principal.

Finally, the school librarian has full responsibility for accomplishing as much as possible in the education of each student. Testing, recording, and reporting the role of the library in the educational progress of students will ultimately make the principal look good, the best of all possible results in managing with the administrator.

Parents and the Library

The parent with the librarian is a different relationship than the one of the parent with the classroom teacher. In order to confirm the role of the library in the education of students, the library should be featured as one of the "classrooms" on nights when parents come to the school to visit their students' classrooms.

Librarians may think that they will see few parents because they are not classroom teachers, but this should not be the case. The librarian is ready to listen to a parent who comes into the library to discuss a child. Situations may range from a complaint about a book or a concern that the child is not reading at grade level or even a request that the child be permitted to take home the unabridged dictionary. The parent may also be interested in helping the library program and may be an advocate for the next budget request or the next effort to update materials or equipment. A parent may also be a potential volunteer in the library.

With the reduction of staff in most libraries, parents who are not working full-time can be encouraged to volunteer in the library, carrying out a variety of roles including some of those clerical tasks that staff once did. They can help with book sales if the library holds these once a year. They can also use their skills in helping with makerspaces and in sharing their expertise in the learning commons when classroom content can make use of outside assistance. School librarians must remember that volunteers are not employees. The following describes their relationship with the school:

- Volunteers are "paid" by receiving personal appreciation.

- Volunteer availability is generally erratic or sporadic.

- Volunteers require more training and direction.

- Correcting performance problems requires a great deal of tact.

Much literature is available on the roles of parents and volunteers, especially on the role of parent as volunteer. Volunteers can be helpful, yet two warnings are in order: (1) The librarian does not monitor the volunteer process, and (2) Care must be taken to keep confidential information about students confidential in the presence of volunteers.

A volunteer coordinator is essential to maintain the regular service of volunteers. Because they are volunteers, other important events—a sick child, an unexpected errand—will cause them to miss their scheduled time. The librarian cannot take time to make the telephone calls to get another volunteer for that day. This is more appropriately the task of a volunteer coordinator. It is almost impossible to expect volunteers to remain silent about interesting events in the library. However, for one parent to see the record of another child and report it to a third parent might leave the librarian open to legal action.

Also, the librarian should be very careful not to leave a volunteer in charge of a group of students. The legal responsibility for students in most states lies with a professional with teacher certification. A student injury while the professional is away from the library could cause much difficulty and perhaps legal action.

Volunteers, who are of great help in the library, can become excellent advocates. They must, however, be carefully managed. A form that may be helpful in the management of volunteers is found in Appendix G.

Friends of the Library

School librarians may be aware of and even members of the friends of the public library in their town. The national organization United for Libraries has been interested in encouraging friends of school libraries. A library friend organization may extend beyond the local parent and teacher organization in the school to include other members of the community. In some schools, these friends help with programs such as Junior Great Books, and in other schools, they act in the same fundraising capacity as they do in the public library domain. More information about FOLUSA is available from the American Library Association.

One librarian recruits his friends group from students in the school. These students are his library helpers, for he has a very large school with a 12-month program and no clerical assistance.

The Community and the Library

Keeping the community informed about the school and the school library was discussed earlier, but this is especially critical when school budgets are under scrutiny. The most important community members as far as impact on the school district would be the school board or trustees, those individuals who hire the superintendent and oversee the budget, regulations, and policies applied to the school district. These persons make sure the district is meeting state guidelines, but they could add to those. For instance, the state may require a student have one year of swimming and the school board might think it more important to have two years rather than another form of physical activity.

The process of managing the school board is to keep them informed, and this is easier when all school librarians within a district report the status of school libraries with examples of learning activities and programming at least one time during the school year. If the principal is able to invite school board members to visit the school, they should be given time to visit the library.

School librarians should be willing to make presentations for local organizations including service groups and churches. This allows the community to learn about school libraries and their importance in the education of students.

Included in the school library's community are those other types of libraries, academic and public. While not all communities have an institution offering courses after high school, those who do should foster relationships.

Relationships with Other Types of Libraries

Invitations from the academic library to bring students onto campus allows them to absorb a little of the higher education community. If this also provides access to resources within the library, it would be an added benefit even if it was only during their visit to the library. When both university and school district join forces, students are able to see that possibility in their lives, and this begins with primary school and continues through high school, where students will understand why taking advanced placement classes in high school has a benefit when they do go to college. Introducing high school students to the community college shows them the ability to continue their education while living at home, and many may take classes while still in high school. Creating the experiences throughout the students' schooling makes finishing high school an expectation rather than something to leave as soon as possible.

The other benefit could be help from professors in conducting research studies as described in Chapter 6. Academic faculty in schools of education are required to research and report their findings as a part of their professional careers. They are often refused access to students in local schools because many administrators object to having students tested even more than they are with required state testing. However, they could assist in studies to analyze the value of the school library in the education of students.

The relationship between an academic community and a school district seems a less direct connection than that with a public library. Cities have public libraries and most rural areas have some type of public library service even if by bookmobile.

Relationships between schools and public libraries have a long history of contact, communication, and cooperation. The length of time such cooperation continues and the degree or the depth of the relationship varies from year to year and from location to location. A public library at one time could have close communication with a school district and at another time no contact at all. In an 1876 speech, C. F. Adams, a trustee of the Quincy Public Library, noted, "Yet though the school and library stand on our main street, side by side, there is, so to speak, no bridge leading from one to the other."[4]

Adams ended his presentation with the following statement:

I want very much indeed to see our really admirable Town
Library become a more living element that it now is in our
school system. . . . To enable you to do this, the trustees of the
library have adopted a new rule, under which each of your
schools may be made practically a branch library. The master
can himself select and take from the library a number of
volumes, and keep them on his desk for circulation among the
scholars under his charge. . . . From that time, both schools and
library would begin to do their full work together, and the last
would become what it ought to be, the natural complement of the
first—the People's College.[5]

While school and public libraries complement each other, they differ in
almost every area of facilities, management, clientele, and services. Schools
should have their libraries located in the center of the building, accessible to
all, while public libraries should be in the center of the greatest population
movement, whether downtown or a branch. Public librarians report to a
board of trustees, while school librarians report to their principal. The youth
librarian at a public library reports to the director (another librarian), while
the school librarian reports to the principal (an educator).

School libraries serve the students who are assigned to their attendance
center; the students are a captive audience because they are sometimes sent
or taken there during the teacher's contractual preparation period. Public
librarians must seek out their clientele. A public library may serve a different geographic area than the school and may not be able to serve all the
students attending a single school.

Librarians in schools exist to collaborate with teachers to provide a
learning environment and work with students to help them learn, while the
public library is more of a research library to serve the needs of all the clientele in its community. Managing this relationship requires the cooperation
between the librarians in both settings.

School librarians need to share the topics assigned at the school each
year so materials can be available to everyone who needs them, and especially when the public library may have a homework center in the library for
those students who have both parents or other caregivers working and aren't
at home at the close of school. Sharing in the purchase of databases can
stretch budgets when contracts allow for this type of use. Helping advertise
programming at the public library, especially the summer reading program,
and helping students who do not have one to get a library card prepares
them to become lifelong users of the public library. They may have suggestions for joint funding proposals that could be written. Public libraries often
have a homework center for students who have no one at home immediately
after school. School librarians and teachers advertise this safe location to
students.

School and public library boards often suggest combining these two entities. This is not a new idea, although many often think so. One of the latest
articles by Bundy and Amey[6] describes what joint use libraries should include and provides a list of planning success factors. It then expresses the
need for evaluation and offers many suggestions for just how this evaluation
should be implemented. The one evaluation that has never been confirmed
is that any savings accrues with the combination. A strong resistance for the
shared facility comes with the mixing of ages during the school day, which
can be annoying for adults and, in some cases, has the potential for danger
to students if adults are in the same areas.

School and public libraries are natural friends because they serve the same children. Among other opportunities, joint proposal writing provides a convenient mechanism for joining forces to interest a funding agency to help raise any required matching funds.

No single library collection can or should attempt to meet all the needs of students in schools. Library services to students is the joint responsibility of school and public libraries with school library activities concentrating upon curriculum-oriented programs and the public library offering its wide range of reading and other varied program possibilities. Much has been done to solve the needs for materials and services for students. Much more can be accomplished if both agencies communicate and cooperate.[7]

This chapter discussed analyzing leadership styles so that the school librarian understands how to fulfill that role. Leading as suggested in this chapter improves the environment in the school and the community. The next part of this text covers keeping up in an ever-changing world.

Exercises

1. Discuss with school librarians the greatest problems and the greatest joys they have experienced in each of the following categories. Then see if you can plan practical solutions to the problems.

   Managing staff
   Evaluating personnel
   Managing with administrators
   Managing with teachers
   Managing students

2. Outline the topics you might cover in a meeting with your principal, including:

   Internet costs
   Upgrades to current computers in the library
   Making library seating in the library flexible to accommodate individual students and small groups as well as a class

3. Create a list of tasks in the library and determine which could be carried out by students or volunteers, freeing the school librarian to collaborate with teachers.

4. Visit the local library and talk with the children's librarian about the programs offered to their clientele who attend your school. What joint projects might you organize?

Notes

1. Jim Collins, *Good to Great: Why Some Companies Make the Lead . . . and Others Don't* (New York: Harper Business, 2001).

2. Sharon Coatney and Violet Harada, *The Many Faces of School Library Leadership* (Santa Barbara, CA: Libraries Unlimited, 2017).

3. Frances Henne, "Learning to Learn in School Libraries," *School Libraries* 15 (May 1966): 17.

4. C. F. Adams, "The Public Library and the Public Schools," *American Library Journal* 1 (August 31, 1877): 438.

5. Ibid., 441.

6. Alan Bundy and Larry Amey, "Libraries Like No Others: Evaluating the Performance and Progress of Joint Use Libraries." *Library Trends* 54 (Spring 2006): 501–518.

7. Esther B. Woolls, *Cooperative Library Services to Children in Public Libraries and Public School Systems in Selected Communities in Indiana* (PhD diss., Indiana University, 1973).

Part III
Keeping Up

11
Leading through Technology

In 1915, technology in libraries was described as Mary E. Hall's lantern slides and projectoscope mentioned in Chapter 2. For over half a century, educators have proclaimed the wonders of technology to improve both teaching and learning. Technologies touted by early audiovisual (AV) pioneers included the 16mm film, the phonograph record, early teaching machines, programmed instruction, sound filmstrips, and videodiscs. Early research comparing students who read a textbook with those who watched videos or other media with the exact same content showed no significant difference in the amount learned.

All those technologies have faded into obscurity and have been replaced by a growing number of new and "fancier" tools, but little is gained by delivering content in various media formats. This chapter looks at the contribution of technology in the school library and examines ways that the school librarian might harness the power of technology and demonstrate its impact to teachers, administrators, and parents and begin leading through technology. This starts with an examination of the infrastructure and management aspects that give technology a platform upon which to make a difference.

Infrastructure and Access

A decade ago when schools were first being wired for Internet access, network administrators came from the business community. They were familiar with locked-down systems and tight controls in a very top-down and directive environment. Since they knew little about the needs of educators and cared very deeply about maintaining tight controls, educators immediately found their systems unfriendly and difficult to use with students. Happily, many tech directors now come from an educational background and have created wireless systems and access that is much more robust.

As mentioned in Chapter 3, during interviews for a position, school librarians should find out about the system in place in the library. Whatever the interviewers described, the best information will come from a few students who actually attend the school. They know what devices they can use and where access is available. They know whether download and upload speeds are fast or slow and how many students can be using the system without a major slowdown. They can do a stress test of the system in place to check on the capacity and coverage of Internet access not only in the library but also in classrooms and availability at home. This information is the basis for the first conversations with tech administrators and administration and for continuing discussions. Certainly, questions about equity as well as digital citizenship including the availability of devices for teachers and students are central.

It is helpful to know the trends across the nation during the last decade or so. Many schools started out with a few computers, perhaps in a lab or the library; then they created larger computer labs, often staffed by a computer teacher. Finally, the total wireless school began to emerge. At each stage, the schools began to purchase more and more computers and tablets for student use; first on carts that could be shared, and then finally the idea of one to one computing using either tablets or small compact computers such as Chromebooks that are given to every student. Some districts preferred to transfer the cost of the computer to the parents and so encouraged students to bring their own devices to school and allowed them to link into the school network.

Another important issue across the decade is filtering, which was discussed in Chapter 9. Is the network robust but locked down so tightly that teachers and students cannot function in the way they need to if technology is actually going to make a difference? A healthy interchange between the technology staff and patrons is essential if access and usability is to be maximized in an open environment yet a safe one. Superintendents often side with tight filtering when they need funding for Internet access or internal connections from the E-rate program (see CIPA, Chapter 9) and out of fear of the district being sued if a single incident of misbehavior goes viral.

The best infrastructure with broad access is a system that becomes almost invisible. It is just there, reliable, available 24/7 at school or from home on a device that any patron prefers; and students can access the tools and resources they need for the entire school learning environment. There is no mystery here, but many times schools and school districts struggle to reach this level of service. Sometimes it takes a long time to get the message across to those in charge that a poor infrastructure actually hinders learning in spite of claims that "we embrace and provide technology." Every librarian can be an advocate for both teachers and students since our code of ethics as a profession demands that we seek equity and access to information whether in print or available digitally. It will take more than one voice in the school promoting a great infrastructure, but it is a goal worth pursuing as a leader for those who usually don't have a voice.

The School Librarian and Technology

Decades ago when AV materials and equipment came on the education scene, librarians were slow to adopt these innovations when they did not fit into books and reading. It was often thought that women could not learn how to thread a 16mm film projector; it required a man. Thus, for a number of years, library ladies and AV guys worked side-by-side or often in different competing areas in the schools. However, so many of those library ladies demonstrated their ability to handle any AV equipment that came into the school, that the library became the center of information and equipment needed for any type of format. One position rather than two became the predominant staffing nationwide.

The same kind of division emerged in the last decade of the 20th century when computers emerged. Men were considered the techy ones. However, after a slow start, the female librarians are again rising to the challenge. Is it the tortoise and hare story all over again?

One thing is certain: the world of digital information and computer expertise is an essential role of every librarian, male or female! Trying to remain focused on only print books and reading enjoyment doesn't cut it. As people in very high places have discovered, technical ignorance can do school librarians in overnight. Teachers and librarians can't fool a generation of young people who are rather impatient with those trying to control their online behavior with little expertise or good reasons. For those entering the profession who profess little expertise, the message is very clear: "There is no hardware or software out there that you can't learn!" The most effective element for librarians is that they will teach it to their teachers as soon as they have mastered the technology. Providing teachers with staff development creates the necessity for the librarian in the school.

Technology does provide a never-ending challenge to keep up and to make sure both technology and assistance is available constantly. It dictates the need to be willing to change.

Willingness to Change

Later in the chapter suggestions for how to keep up and where to learn about all those new bells and whistles are given. Change in technologies in the past began to accelerate on a much slower pace than in this first quarter of the 21st century. Librarians had to learn to type when the typewriter entered their libraries, an innovation that took literally centuries to arrive, but the change from the standard typewriter to one run by electricity took a mere half-century. That technology was obsolete in less than a quarter of a century with word processing equipment that was then almost immediately replaced in the blink of an eye with desktop computers, laptops, and now machines that create words from an author's voicing them and then translate words into other languages.

Learning to type must have seemed an insurmountable task to the cataloger who had learned a special way to create letters for handwriting catalog cards. The human being is not necessarily acclimated to making changes, and the very number of changes that come with technology are simply more than many would like to accept. However, change is not something that one can ignore, nor can teachers continue to ignore what is going on around them. School librarians have to decide to learn new technologies, keep up with their rapid changes, choose the best from the vast array of these, and help your teachers adjust.

You have made the decision to learn and keep up, and to be open to change. You do not need to do this alone, even if you are a single librarian in your school. You can help maintain this with the assistance of your own tech squad.

The Tech Squad

Many librarians surround themselves with student expertise and create an atmosphere in which "I'll teach you, you'll teach me, and we will all succeed together!" Having the trust of student novices and student master hackers is a must for every successful library professional. To let students become allies, create a tech squad who are your eyes and ears, your doers, your devoted supporters. It is not just about a few computer geeks. A broad range of talents and abilities from your students will be invaluable. They can test any new tool and help select the best; they can fan out across the school to teach both students and adults a new skill, help teach digital citizenship, and on and on and on. Just ask other library professionals who have a tech track record using technologies. Mimic what they do and learn what they know, and your confidence will increase every day.

Building the Technology Plan

As with collection development, a plan and any policies should be in place. When the district has a technology coordinator or if individual schools have these persons, such a plan may be in place. If not, the technology person at the school becomes the leader to write one with the advisory committee and teacher and student support. If no technology person is assigned to the school, the school librarian may need to become the leader in developing the technology policy. An outline for what should be included is found in Appendix H.

Thinking about Software

So many entrepreneurs out there are hoping to make a fortune in the world of education. Many try, few succeed; and there are so many promises that cost so much and deliver so little. Again, this is where your network will help in recommending or warning against the high-priced systems that promise more than is needed when a less expensive system serves as well. Many big-ticket educational systems are sold by the vendor on the golf course with the school administrator; the oversimplified pitch is supposed to solve all problems with one size fits all solutions. All it takes is to meet the price tag.

Librarians have been the champions of free and inexpensive software tools that can actually make a difference. The Google Suite of free collaborative tools and the Microsoft 360 system are two worth investigating. In addition, the American Association of School Librarians (AASL) has a committee charged every year with naming the best apps and websites for education; a number of bloggers concentrate their efforts in reviewing the best of the free tools. Again, this is where your student tech squad can help. They can check out updates and changes such as discontinued tools; they can test the new output. When a product is added to the collection, these students then teach others, sharing the best across the school. Such a service is an invaluable skill for their learning and for their career prospects.

Many issues are always arising from each newly adopted app or system. Logging in, passwords, privacy, collaborative possibilities, advertising, and possible hate groups, or predator access will need to be discussed not only with the tech directors but with teachers, administrators, and the students themselves. Everyone needs to learn the possibilities and the problems in an online world. Anyone, adult or child, can make mistakes and open privacy beyond what is desired. The emphasis is on learning how to cope, developing a community of wise users, and that only comes through experiences and sharing. This becomes increasingly important with the ever-growing social networking tools.

The Challenges of Social Networking

Social networking, by its very title, is social, and this aspect of social networking presents two challenges that are very harmful and difficult to overcome. The first is helping students understand the problems that come from being too open with personal information, posting pictures, making comments from their first post on whatever service they are using. Some of the tales about universities checking student pages and dropping them down into a lesser pool of applicants are true, while others may not be. Trying to help students think about any consequences beyond one day's posting of a stupid picture or remark to their distant future is never easy for any adult. Students are children and they mistrust adults. Technology's social media opportunities are so much more viral than was ever imagined even 10 years ago.

Next is the challenge of bullying with social media, and that sometimes expands beyond students to teachers and administrators being victims on social media. Keeping aware of any articles, books, blogs, webinars, YouTube videos, anything that would be useful to help students learn about the effects of bullying should be shared with teachers, administrators, and parents. It sometimes takes a tragedy to define reality, but something may help, even if you aren't aware of it.

Then there are those teachers who try to ignore social media. Some learn how to use popular social networking tools to great advantage with helping their students increase their learning. Others seem to lose control instantly if they try something. They then feel helpless as students either misbehave or unwittingly get into problem areas. Everyone works on crossing the street safely; but what to do if a terrorist comes into the building; what to do about bullying, and so on. It is no different online. Everyone needs to help each other because trying to turn social media off is not a viable solution. The Internet is not going away anytime soon. It takes a community to provide a positive digital learning environment; and librarians need to be leaders.

School librarians who have not transformed their libraries into physical learning commons can transform their one-way library website into a virtual learning commons (VLC) as a great example of a superb and collaborative learning environment. What is a VLC? It is a website or series of websites in which teachers, other adults, and students are learners, all interacting, contributing, solving problems, creating, communicating, and learning together through the entire school, community, country, and across the globe.

Immediately, alarm bells might ring about control, inappropriate posts, predators, or other access problems. However, this has been tried successfully. The students at San Jose State University created templates for a participatory environment that can be downloaded, modified, and used in schools. Theirs was an entire course in fourth-grade California history that encourages students and teachers to contribute or just to download and use as a place where collaborative learning can take place. The URL for this is http://sites.google.com/site/templatevlc.

Schools who subscribe to Google for Education or its new name, Google Suites, have the collaborative tools already in place to allow this to happen overnight. Those who adopt such a technology are showing that isolated teaching, one-way library websites, websites ignored by students and teachers, and information resources that can't be accessed at home are a thing of the past. Librarians are competing directly with Google by using Google

Suites to make comments like, "When you have a project, start first at the VLC and then branch out from there if you need to. The VLC is also a place to document the library's direct impact on teaching and learning. It can showcase and create a museum of fabulous learning experiences and put the library back into the spotlight as the center of teaching and learning, that hub of the school dreamed about in former years."

Keeping Up with Technology

When school librarians need to learn something about technology, all they need to do is Google it. Check out YouTube videos. Ask students to teach you. Be wise about what conferences you attend. The exhibit hall in most conventions will tell you where the vendors think the money is. Few represent book vendors only. Major software systems have huge exhibits and fancy booths. Many companies that had large exhibits in the past are either absent or have downsized drastically,

Check out the conference programs before deciding to attend. Who's talking about what? What's missing? When travel money is tight, it is better to alternate attendance at different sites to get a sense of what's trending. This is not saying that school librarians need to be on the bleeding edge of every whim or hot topic, but staying informed helps build a repertoire, connections, and the ability to talk intelligently about what's happening across education.

The day school librarians completed their initial certification for the job is the day when they start to fall behind unless they consciously decide to learn something new every day. They keep up by reading some of the great tech bloggers who are out there. Here is a list of school library bloggers and their sites:

Carolyn Foote: https://futura.edublogs.org/

Doug Johnson: http://doug-johnson.squarespace.com/

Gwyneth Jones: http://www.thedaringlibrarian.com/

Jennifer LaGarde: http://www.librarygirl.net/

Judy O'Connell: https://judyoconnell.com/

Kathy Schrock: http://www.schrockguide.net/edtech-blogs.html

One both school librarians and teachers might be interested in:

Richard Bryne: http://www.freetech4teachers.com/p/about-richard-byrne -and-free-technology.html#.WMC9sEUrKRs

School librarians subscribe to the best and read what they can. They share the best with their colleagues, asking questions over state and national networks. They are careful not to become limited by just listening to the same voices over the years. Just as in teaching students, be selective and evaluate carefully the messages coming across the networks. Join that fabulous global community of fearless educators out there; every school librarian can be one of them as their expertise and wisdom emerges.

Before attending conferences, school librarians should read in the literature, consult with their personal learning network, and choose from the many choices what seems best for the school. When beginning to make these changes, it is time to consider how to show their "impact" on students and teachers. Evaluation and assessment are discussed in Chapter 6. A further confirmation of impact from the investment in technology begins here.

Level of Impact

Each of the issues already discussed in this chapter only creates the potential for impact, not the actual impact. Putting a technology in place and turning on the switch does not automatically guarantee that anything good will result. Suddenly, when all students have their own computers and scores on tests don't rise, questions abound. Why did the school make this investment? Why are students playing video games all day every day on the devices purchased for the school? Is anything getting better?

The challenge of impact depends on how technology is used and how its impact is measured. Reuben R. Puentadura created the most sensible model of technological impact thus far. Known as the Substitution Augmentation Modification Redefinition (SAMR) model, it was designed to help teachers and librarians determine the level of technology use with their students. This model[1] is explained with the "substitution" level defined as the substitution of digital technology for analog (with no change). The "augmentation" level is an exchange of digital for analog such as a teacher switching from the entire class's read aloud with the teacher leading to students using their hand-held device to read and listen to individual digital stories with the devices augmenting the reading assignment. To reach the "modification" level, the task is significantly redesigned. The example for this is replacing a diagram of light traveling to students manipulating an interactive computer simulation. Finally, at the "redefinition" level, technology is used to create novel tasks. At this level, students can be assigned the task of writing a persuasive essay but presenting their arguments through their individually created and edited videos, a totally different response to the assignment.

His argument was a simple one: If school librarians try to do exactly the same thing with technology that they did without it, they can expect about the exact same result. Thus, for example, if a student listens to a lecture in person or sees it on a YouTube video, the amount learned is about the same. That seems logical, but it is so commonplace that teachers should intuitively figure out why the technology has not been that hoped-for silver bullet. The SAMR model points out that each technology employed must do something unique that contributes something that other technologies or practices cannot.[2] Authors of this article regret that, "Despite its increasing popularity among practitioners, the SAMR model is not currently represented in the extant literature."[3] However, there are simpler ways to test the impact of technology.

A simple and ubiquitous example can clarify what a technology can and cannot do. If a Google document is used as a simple word processor where each student writes and then submits a report or term paper, a bit of efficiency might accrue and access to the software might extend into the home, but no direct impact on the quality of the product or the thinking/learning can be expected over and above the old method of writing and submitting papers. The innovation that a Google doc offers is its collaborative nature. Instantly, many students can be writing, constructing, revising, challenging, thinking through, structuring, and formatting in real time. Suddenly, students can not only demonstrate their own personal expertise as they have done in the past, but they also have the opportunity to do cooperative work and build collaborative intelligence. However, to document the difference, a different assessment will need to be used to measure both individual as well as group learning.

For librarians who are interested in inquiry, the Google doc pushes the demonstration of personal skills into a multidimensional world of possibility. What are the differences in a report created by a single individual or a small or large group? What is the difference in deep understanding? What is the difference in the quality of the product? What happens to the percentage of students who succeed when working as individuals vs. the percentage of those meeting or exceeding expectations when working collaboratively on a Google doc? The result could be worse, particularly when students don't know how to use the tool, but most likely, if introduced to the possibilities, the students are likely to achieve at a much higher level than the adults are expecting.

The librarian needs to examine each new app or technology for what it can contribute and if adopted, that app or technology must be pushed to its limits on what it can do for learning. A few more examples might help.

- New video software is so easy to use that almost all students can create a great-looking product with excellent sound and tight editing. However, has deeper learning of the content happened?

- The librarian has just spent time introducing the available databases. However, does access to high-quality information actually make a difference in the quality of the papers over what the students could have Googled?

- The librarian has put some great lists of books on a wide variety of topics and genres on the library website for students to read. However, do the students read them any more than if they found a bunch of new books displayed in the library?

- The librarian has discovered several excellent YouTube videos that show how the human body's circulation system works. But is there any difference in deep understanding between those who read the textbook and see the visuals there and those who also watch the videos?

- In the egg drop science experiment, the technology included raw eggs, tissues, and some kind of foam. The students have a great time experimenting with how high they can drop their egg without breaking it, but did they actually learn any physics? What technology could they have used that would boost their understanding?

Micro Documentation of Impact

Many of the studies of the impact of school libraries on achievement use macro measures of reading scores or other scores to look across many learners for statistical significance. While those measures continue to be important, there is much individual librarians can do to look for patterns across micro documentation. What is that? This technique looks at the impact of learning experience by learning experience, teacher by teacher, technology by technology to gauge what happens once, then twice, then more times. If the librarian teams with Mrs. Smith's language arts class whose students have various topics across the semester or school year, this teacher has a set of expectations for improvement over time. If the librarian has expectations that using the collaborative elements of Google Docs will help students meet Mrs. Smith's expectations, the two will look at the first products created at the beginning of the year. Both librarian and teacher decide that the students have much room for improvement. In a metacognitive discussion with the students after that first project, everyone tries to figure out what they did right and what they might do better the next time. Then before the second project, librarian and teacher review what each did the last time and together they determine what to teach to achieve the needed improvement skills. Did the students do better on the second project? What percentage of them met or exceeded adult expectations? And, after the third such experience, what can librarian and teacher say about both the sophistication level of using Google Docs and the effect on the deep learning over time?

This means that the librarian must be in on the planning of the learning experience, the teaching, and the assessment. Each time technology makes the hoped-for difference, it is one brick to add to a wall of excellence the librarian is constructing with teachers. Everyone will have stories to tell. The students will have their own stories to tell and demonstrate. Bit by bit, patterns emerge and challenges are solved and the technology delivers on its potential. Over time, librarian and teachers should be able to observe students creating higher expectations for themselves and the groups they are working with. When this kind of engagement and its effect are observable, perhaps a second brick can be added to that wall when the magic happens.

If during the planning of a learning experience librarian and teacher select a technology uniquely suited to boost the type of content learning both are trying to instill, good things are much more likely to happen. It is a challenge that is not only shared with other teachers, but the students themselves will respond with other technologies that they know will help them learn. It is a phenomenon that can rescue student after student from boredom and replace it with engagement; even excitement. Document these successes brick by brick by brick. The big picture will build faster than you expect.

It's Not Going Away

Many school librarians are able to expand the interest of their administrators in the library program through the careful presentation of facts that point out effective use of new technologies in the library and classrooms. The skill with technology and its application for the instruction of students continues to be a wonderful opportunity to demonstrate the worth of the position of school librarian. To many administrators, technologies are little understood. Careful explanation of outcomes in relation to costs, with demonstrations of each application, often sells an administrator on the idea. The decision to implement new technologies brings with it the need to justify increased funding immediately and with the knowledge that this will be a continuing cost. The amount needed is determined by the type and level of technology selected.

Often, administrators respond to requests for equipment if such technology is available in a nearby school district or another school in the district, especially if that library is featured in news articles or other media. Gaining approval for adding the technology means being able to answer any questions about what exactly, how much for how many, and which vendor to select. At this time, the school librarian has learned as much as possible about information technology and is prepared to share that knowledge with teachers and administrators.

It all leads to providing students with the technologies they need when they need them, especially when they come from homes with little information technology in the home, which is daunting. When students attend a school with some who have every imaginable new device and the Internet in the home and other students have maybe a cell phone, the gap between the haves and the have-nots grows. The school librarian is in a position to offer solutions to narrow the gap, to provide access to information for all.

Keeping up with technologies is a necessity. How to remain current and keep your teachers up-to-date is the subject of the next chapter.

Exercises

1. What would you suggest to a teacher who wanted students to be more interested in an assignment? Choose the level of class (elementary, middle, or high) and help develop an assignment through all four SAMR levels.
2. Look at the URL http://sites.google.com/site/templatevlc and consider what you would have to do to use this with a unit of instruction of your choice.
3. Choose a new technology or new app. List the pros and cons you would use in explaining the possibilities if this was purchased for the school.

Notes

1. Erica R. Hamilton, Joshua M. Rosenberg, and Mete Akcaoglu, "The Substitution, Augmentation, Modification, and Redefinition (SAMR) Model," *Tech Trends* 60 (2016): 433.

2. Ibid., abstract.

3. Ibid., p. 433.

12
Professional Development

Today's world is constantly changing in almost every aspect and these changes affect what happens in schools to varying degrees; that effect may be immediate or it may be delayed. Keeping current is a matter of professional development. That development may be a person's choice; however in some districts and states, professional development is mandated to continue employment or to sustain a credential. The premise is that this will improve as participants understand and accept change.

Exactly how change is happening may be hidden rather than immediately observable. A new superintendent with very different ideas is immediately observable. Different priorities are set; new persons at the district level begin suggesting different teaching strategies they present at convocations of the teachers, and different approaches may be made to the curriculum. Not so immediately apparent are what happens at the national level when interest rates are raised, hindering persons buying homes, and suddenly neighborhoods stand empty. School funding depends upon tax revenues from real estate, and vacant homes in neighborhoods mean less for schools. This filters down over time into fewer resources to hire teachers and provide resources to use.

When these changes are put into practice in the schools, it becomes difficult to continue to repeat activities from one semester to the next or to predict how long the change will continue, what may be the new information or invention that will challenge the next semester or year. New events occur in the world, new technologies emerge, new curriculum is proposed, the weather wreaks havoc, and the economy shifts, causing change. The effects these have on the school allow the school librarian to take a leadership role in helping the school community understand, accept, and adapt to change. Some might argue this is a very big challenge.

In the 117-year history of professionals in school libraries, it has seemed difficult at times for many school librarians to become leaders in either role, as librarian or as educator. Difficulty has occurred in the role of educator for these reasons:

1. The first school librarians were more often part-time librarians and part-time teachers in academic classrooms. Or, as librarians, they

were often responsible for two or more schools. This may be true today.

2. School librarians were and are considered specialists rather than essential teachers.

3. School librarians help children check out books.

4. School librarians are quiet, retiring persons.

School librarians who are assigned to more than one school are still able to carry out many of the suggestions in this chapter. However, they may need to concentrate on one school; successes in that school will make other schools want the same treatment. This leadership role will be evident to school librarians as they begin to be dynamic and assertive program advocates demonstrating the knowledge and creativity to help teachers teach and students learn. Helping build a professional development environment will be further evidence.

This chapter explains many ways to stay alert to potential changes in the local, national, and work environment affecting schools. The first is keeping current through using a personal learning network (PLN). The chapter suggests ways to help teachers share the information they learn from their PLNs through the creation of a professional learning community (PLC) in the school. Opportunities for face-to-face and online experiences are given to initiate workplace learning. Finally, opportunities are suggested for school librarians to continue learning. The PLN would seem to be the most constant opportunity for awareness.

Personal Learning Networks (PLNs)

The school librarian is responsible not only for being aware of new developments but for making decisions about which are important. It is not a decision to try to make alone, but something to discuss with others as school librarians build their own PLN. In *Personal Learning Networks: Professional Development for the Isolated School Librarian*, Harlan describes a PLN as "the people with whom you surround yourself, the tools you use, and the resources you rely on to introduce yourself to new ideas and best practices. It is a network that encourages learning and personal growth."[1]

Individual teachers may be interested in developing a PLN. In fact, they may already have a group of teachers as their PLN who share ideas. What happens in a teacher's PLN may be shared later within the PLC, which is discussed later.

Principals may also have a PLN or be on a list that shares state and national government regulations. The librarian can help the principal by preparing frequent collections of resources on particular subjects to help administrators participate knowingly in their PLN with their colleagues who need help in making informed decisions. When school librarians learn about trends and issues from their PLN, they can bring them to share these with faculty and administrators during meetings of their PLC.

Professional Learning Communities (PLCs)

Just as a PLN is essential for school librarians and teachers, having the school population sharing information about what's going on in the education world is easily accomplished when the school has a PLC. School staff shares in the identification of the need for change and ways to make this happen. If no PLC exists, the school librarian helps create a PLN within the school. It becomes much easier to keep teachers and administrators informed about trends in education so they are prepared to adopt any changes they may be asked to implement. The PLC is one place to share professional journals coming into the library. Ideas gleaned from a review of each table of contents can target information to match the subject and interest area of teachers. Announcing other opportunities available on the Internet such as blogs, Ted Talks, and webinars serves to help teachers and administrators expand their knowledge to meet many concerns.

School administrators are under exceptional pressure from the requirements of individual state standards and district mandates. Teachers may be challenged by a community that is interested in outcomes, often defined as high scores on statewide tests, from their education dollars invested in students. What is the number whose college applications are accepted by certain universities, or how many will be able to replace a mechanic who is retiring from their favorite car repair shop? The challenges of educating students are complicated by the needs of various at-risk student populations, students with disabilities and learning challenges, the socioeconomically disadvantaged, English language learners, and ethnic groups. Increasingly, educators speak of PLCs as a strategy for school improvement. Proposed solutions may be small or grand, but this is the place to discuss them all.

When in place, PLCs focus staff development activities on change processes to improve student learning. Kirio and Yamamoto[2] offer the key elements in designing, facilitating, and assessing PLCs and their experiences in their school. It is a recipe for success. PLCs have five important attributes:

- Supportive and shared leadership

- Shared values and vision

- Supportive conditions

- Shared personal practice

- Collective creativity[3]

Librarians can be major players in carrying out these attributes, in leading in the creation of supportive and shared leadership. They understand the values and vision of the school; and they know all the teachers and how they teach, all the students and how they learn, and all curriculum at all grade levels in their building. Librarians lead in developing supportive conditions in which to allow change to happen.

PLCs allow participants to share personal practice, both the successes and the failures, so that successful practice can multiply and probable solutions to failures can be discussed. These truly allow for creativity from all with the librarian in a unique role. Librarians remind teachers of their part in collaborative teaching teams, sharing the development of unit plans.

Because school librarians represent no single grade level or subject area, they are able to lead the PLC, allowing them to help consolidate the collective creativity of teachers, providing an active role within subgroups in the school. Librarians can organize teachers into collaborative efforts to create lessons that use as many different teachers as possible in implementing the curriculum. When the principal is busy with other matters, librarians are uniquely qualified to lead this effort as their part in the PLC.

While setting aside time for PLCs to meet is not an easy task, they allow new relationships between teachers and librarians. These might occasionally replace the weekly teachers' meetings where the principal must provide an agenda. Librarians can collaborate with other teacher leaders to design effective meetings to allow discussion of change in a nonthreatening environment. Creative solutions can be proposed and even adopted to make changes.

Because the PLC is based on continuous adult learning, time must be set aside for teachers to collaborate with other teachers and support staff. Democratic participation leads to consensus about the school culture and environment and, most importantly, how individuals will work together to attain the results they want. Educators talk with one another about their practice, share their knowledge, observe each other, and applaud one another's success.

Harlan suggests that for teachers, their PLN may not go beyond their fellow teachers, and the PLC is an opportunity to introduce the school librarian into the teaching process. Moving into any change in what the library has to offer or how it looks or is scheduled, any proposed small or large change can be better understood when such changes are discussed in a professional learning community meeting.

The PLN is an effective tool for leading teachers through new technologies, new curriculum, or new methods. School districts often set aside times for longer experiences. When these are half-day or full-day events, the school librarian can be very helpful in planning these professional development sessions.

Planning Professional Development

School librarians plan for their two primary audiences: teachers and administrators. Their first audience, teachers, are sometimes a difficult audience. Harvey tells of working early in his career with a group writing a grant proposal for professional development. One member said, "Teaching kids is easy compared to teaching teachers."[4] Making sure teachers are involved in determining the needs and planning the activities begins the process. Evaluating what happens in the workshop helps determine what went well and what went wrong.

The second audience is the principal, who needs to know any new educational strategies and theories. Keeping the principal on the cutting edge of innovation in teaching and learning, strategies for managing teachers and students, and ways to engage parents in the education of their students increases the school librarian's value as a member of the school staff.

With both audiences and in a collaborative environment, the school librarian need not feel totally responsible for this assignment and can work with teachers and administrators to determine what is actually needed and can include gathering suggestions for ways to fill these needs. These should grow out of problems perceived as significant to teachers or administrators. A needs assessment, even as brief as an informal query, can help because few teachers and even fewer administrators are eager to admit they lack skills. They may be reluctant to ask for assistance in finding or using resources or equipment, and they may be fearful of technologies they have not used. They can refuse to use technologies because they don't have the skills they know their students have. It is up to the school librarian to decide the most efficient manner in which to provide training.

Involving those who will receive the training in planning is the best way to get willing participants in the program. Input in the planning will ensure the librarian starts where the group is and takes it as far as possible in the time allocated. Choosing who will conduct the training is another factor.

Others within the district who are aware of trends and issues and the persons who could do training for schools in the district can be helpful at this point. Suggestions for persons to invite from outside the district can be reviewed to see if their expertise is appropriate and some analysis can be made of what costs would be incurred if the person were to be hired. Involving staff in this process makes the session more acceptable with those involved so that they take a personal interest in the content and the implementation of a new idea. If such sessions are planned and announced with no advance input from teachers, one will have that audience whose first row remains attentive, the second is looking at cell phones or plan books, while the third row is viewing the closest exit.

As stated above, school staff can be helpful in choosing the trainer and that essential expertise may be available within the school or the district. Sometimes an outside consultant may be the best if not the only way to do this. In some situations, an outside consultant may be preferable even though the school librarian or another person on the school staff is competent to conduct the training. The aura of a "consultant" may be a better choice when trying to sell teachers on a new technology or a new service. An outside presenter can help strengthen the case without appearing to be self-serving. Once a topic is chosen, one needs to begin the actual plan.

The librarian helps set goals and objectives for any training session and then helps keep these in focus. When one or more participants try to turn the group in another direction, the librarian helps the trainer keep the audience on task even though it may seem difficult with a group of peers with whom one works on a daily basis. This is accomplished more easily when objectives are shared and accepted by the participants.

One of the most important services the librarian can offer staff and also students is training sessions that will keep them aware of and capable of participating in educational innovations and, most especially, using the new technologies as they evolve. This is a complicated issue simply because the technologies change so rapidly.

Keeping the school community aware of educational innovation is an ongoing process, not a yearly presentation. This awareness has several levels. The first is the quick presentation at regular teachers' meetings. This type of update will occur frequently because new resources, new trends, and new technologies are evolving constantly. These presentations must always be interesting and short—a preview designed to draw those interested into the session and perhaps into the library for more.

At a higher level, the librarian is asked to help plan specific training days for teaching staff and to recommend presenters and consultants. Potential presenters may be teachers within the school, or suggestions may have been made to invite faculty at schools of education in nearby colleges. Checking with administrators and teachers in your school and in other schools in the district who attend professional association meetings may add to this list. If they have heard someone who has a message staff needs, the name of the person and the topic are recorded. When going beyond the school district, a stipend may be necessary for the speaker. Honorarium, travel, and per diem for housing may be necessary if the speaker comes from a distance in the state or even another location, nationally or internationally. High-profile speakers may require additional funding support from the district or a cooperative venture with other school districts in the immediate area.

Not all experts at a task are necessarily good presenters. If the librarian has not attended a session with a speaker, confirming the quality of the presentation is critical. The person who is suggesting this presenter should have some assessment of the depth of knowledge and the ability to speak to the size of the audience.

When a training session is scheduled during regularly scheduled in-service days or shorter sessions at a teachers' meeting, the trainer who is trying to teach the use of any resource or technology should allow participants time for ample practice. Nothing is as futile as explaining the use of a technology to a large audience, many of whom cannot see the technology even as a projection on a screen. If the purpose is to teach the use of a phone to take a picture and send it to a class of students, each participant must have a phone, their own or one from a store, and the electronic addresses for the transmission. Hands-on experience is essential.

If teachers are going to learn how to access a new database or use a new website, they must have Internet access on a device and they may need some help with a suggested sample topic to search. Only then should they be shown how to access the database and how to download the information they need. It is a good time to discuss copyright if they want to place this on their website for the class to use or for sharing the database with their students.

To recap, training sessions are more likely to be successful when the librarian or the trainer have the necessary resources, whether materials or equipment, on hand. If the information is online, each participant must have access to the Internet. The size of the audience should be limited to provide sufficient resources to conduct the training session. The time when two people could share a computer is in the past. Substitute individual laptops or an iPad. Each person needs to directly experience the technology being introduced.

The successful trainer takes the group as far as possible in the time allotted. To do this, each participant must be made to feel a vital part of the experience. Careful attention should be paid to individuals in the audience to confirm that they are following the process and understanding the instructions, keeping up with the pace of the presentation, and succeeding at the assigned tasks. One person lagging behind should be helped by someone else, allowing the trainer to continue. This would be a good opportunity for your Tech Squad. When the proposed session covers a great deal of information in a short time, their acting as additional staff will help the presentation move forward. It will also establish the Tech Squad as able and willing to help when the teacher needs a brief refreshing of the equipment.

As mentioned earlier in this section, evaluation of the training session helps determine the audience's approval of the information received or acknowledgment of what was missing, the level of success of the experience, and the need for the next level of this training or a new topic if the audience is comfortable with the result. As with any evaluation process, the changes that are needed before presenting another session will be apparent. The skills of any outside consultant are assessed to determine whether this person should be asked to present again or could be recommended when a colleague asks for suggestions for speakers.

Whatever is planned, the program must be considered as it affects the instructional program of the school and the potential effect on the use of the library. Through effective training programs, the school librarian has an opportunity to reach reluctant teachers and expand the services of the library into all classrooms.

A last audience includes the parents and other members of the community. They need to learn about potential changes within the school, innovations, and changes in curriculum. These are very important to reach when it is time for budget changes with tax increases on the ballot or bond issues to be passed if the school is to remodel or build a new building. Parents who went to school before iPads and cell phones became a major resource for information will not understand how these fit into the curriculum. They will not understand the reason a school is working for 1-1 for electronic devices.

Some parents can be reached at the parent–teacher meetings if schools still hold these evening events. If not, another time may be scheduled and the entire community invited. Using students to help demonstrate what's going on in the school is always an excellent way to draw an audience. Always make sure the media is invited.

PLNs, PLCs, and formal professional development experiences with trainers are ways to provide staff development for the staff. The school librarian participates in this process, taking a leadership role to provide, effectively, cutting-edge visions. To be able to do this, the school librarian makes a plan to keep up-to-date using methods beyond the PLN and PLC.

Professional Development for the School Librarian

School librarians as a catalyst in planning and leading training sessions for teachers must remember the admonishment, "Physician, heal thyself!" They must keep current in their own backyard, the school library. School librarians attending webinars, workshops, institutes, and conferences learn the latest trends and responses to challenges presented by other leaders in the library world. These opportunities are described below.

MOOCs

One of the newest forms of professional development is Massive Open Online Courses (MOOC). They are designed for large numbers of participants; they are online; and, best of all, they are free. It does take a great deal of planning to offer one, but librarians are developing these themselves and assisting others who are planning these experiences. Alman and Jumba's *MOOCs Now: Everything You Need to Know to Design, Set Up, and Run a Massive Open Online Course*[5] explain this new way to share information in larger groups. School librarians can reach many colleagues with a well-planned and executed MOOC.

Webinars

Webinars are workshops or seminars conducted over the Internet. Depending upon who is offering the webinar, they may have a charge or they may be free. Announcements for these come to librarians from a variety of vendors such as companies selling library products and publishers of books and other materials. Personnel in state libraries and state departments of education may have contracted for development, and the webinars are announced to librarians within the state. Some of these may carry credit for attendance if the participant is in a position that requires a certificate of attendance to meet a requirement for yearly updating.

Workshops and Institutes

Workshops may be offered by any number of individuals or groups. When a new process is initiated in a state, the department of education may bring school librarians together to learn about this process. When they are mandated, one or more from the district are invited to attend at a central location covering expenses or instructors may be sent throughout the state. When states have purchased statewide databases for use by all librarians in the state, attending a workshop to learn about the content becomes essential for all to know and then share with teachers and students at their schools.

Institutes are funded by agencies such as the state department of education or even a national body. The participants are usually asked to submit an application for the program and then the number who can attend are selected. These meetings usually come with no cost to those chosen.

Another place to gather information is through membership in professional associations. These may be both library and education associations, and they may be local, statewide, national, and even international.

Professional Associations

This discussion begins with educational associations. The first two associations may have mandatory membership when the school district comes under a union contract. These are discussed not only for their role as a professional development opportunity, but as a place for librarians to work to change perceptions of their role in the school.

Education Associations

Among the variety of education associations for school librarians, at the national level, educators choose to join either the National Education Association (NEA; www.nea.org) or the American Federation of Teachers (AFT; www.aft.org). Conferences of these associations provide speakers and sessions with new information, but they also have another purpose. Both of these national associations have state and local affiliates. School librarians may teach under contract to a local affiliate of NEA or AFT that acts as the bargaining unit. Although affiliation may not be mandatory in a local school district, it is usually an uncomfortable situation for a librarian to refuse to join fellow teachers in the negotiating contracts for their units. Resentment directed at the school librarian who does not join may extend to resentment toward the library program.

When the school district has a local bargaining unit, membership in both state and national associations is required and automatic. Also, the teacher and librarian cannot join only the national association but must join their local and state associations as well. These teachers' associations offer librarians the opportunity to attend local and state meetings and possibly become a delegate to the national association.

Librarians who belong to their education association should work within that association to improve perceptions of the library program. Teachers, especially at the elementary level, often feel the library is their free period. The author is aware of one situation in which a grievance was filed against the librarian because this person was not assigned lunchroom duty. Helping teachers understand the importance of having the library open for students throughout the day is part of the role of the librarian.

It is also important that at least one librarian in a district be a member of the contract unit's negotiating team. In this way, school librarians can represent the need for staffing the library as part of the bargaining team. When librarians neglect this important opportunity, they risk being moved into a special category, apart from the teaching staff. When this happens, additional time may be assigned to the school librarian's role. For example, in one state, it was ruled that, because librarians did not have student work to take home to grade, they were expected to report to school 30 minutes earlier and stay 30 minutes later than classroom teachers. School librarians need to be seen as collaborative teachers who are involved in the planning and teaching of units of instruction and grading student work from these jointly planned units of instruction.

School librarians with interests in specific subject areas may join the relevant associations to help keep the library visible to other educators. Special subject associations include the National Council of Teachers of English (www.ncte.org), the International Literacy Association (http://www.literacy worldwide.org), formerly the International Reading Association, and the National Council of the Social Studies (www.ncss.org), among others.

Related organizations include the Association for Supervision and Curriculum Development (ASCD) and the International Society for Technology in Education (ISTE). Choosing to become active in ASCD (www.ascd.org) brings librarians in direct contact with superintendents, principals, and curriculum directors in school districts. The mission statement states that ASCD is a diverse, international community of educators, forging covenants in teaching and learning for the success of all learners. ASCD represents 160,000 educators from more than 135 countries and 66 affiliates. In 2007, ASCD switched its report of membership to percentage of the total. The membership is comprised of 38 percent principals and assistant principals, 18 percent classroom teachers, 16 percent directors or supervisors, 7 percent superintendents and assistant superintendents, 4 percent professors, and 7 percent building-level specialists; 3 percent are not currently employed, and 3 percent designated "other."

ISTE (www.iste.org) provides leadership and service to improve teaching and learning by advancing the effective use of technology in K–12 education and teacher education. It boasts a worldwide membership of leaders and potential leaders in educational technology. Visiting the websites of these associations helps prospective members determine which they might wish to join in addition to their school library and other media associations.

Library and Media Associations

School librarians who wish to meet others working in school libraries may be able to participate in a local association, which is usually an informal group. Membership is inexpensive and participation time minimal, except perhaps for the officers.

The California School Library Association, located in a very large state in size and population, has two spring meetings each year, one in the north and one in the south. These one-day continuing education events allow school librarians to participate as officers and presenters and to get up-to-date information about what is going on in other schools.

Some states have two library-related associations and others only one. Pennsylvania has the Pennsylvania Association for Educational Communications and Technology (www.paect.org) and the Pennsylvania School Librarians Association (www.psla.org). The Florida Association for Media Educators (www.floridamedia.org) is the only association in that state for library and media professionals. Annual conferences provide workshops, speakers, exhibits, and communication with other school librarians. The success of a state association relates directly to the willingness of members to volunteer their services. Few state associations have sufficient income to maintain paid office staff. Participation in the state association provides an excellent opportunity to build leadership skills. At this level, it is often easy to become active in committee work and present at the annual meeting.

Included among national groups are the Association for Educational Communications and Technology (AECT; www.aect.org) and the ALA and its division, American Association of School Librarians (AASL; www.aasl.org). AECT (www.aect.org) provides members with three publications: *Tech Trends: Linking Research and Practice to Improve Learning*, the bimonthly *Educational Technology Research and Development*, and *Journal of Instructional Development*. Members also have the opportunity to attend a yearly conference. AECT is governed by a president, elected annually; a council; and an affiliate council. AECT members may write articles for *Tech Trends* and make presentations at the annual meeting. Exhibits for this association specialize in audiovisual media and equipment. Many state library/media associations are affiliates of AECT.

A second national association is the ALA (www.ala.org), with 60,000 members representing all types of librarians, information professionals, and trustees of public libraries. The AASL is a division of ALA, and members of AASL receive the benefits of ALA membership, including a lobbying effort in Washington, DC. Two meetings are held each year—a midwinter conference and an annual conference. The midwinter conference is for members of the ALA executive board, council, officers, boards of directors of divisions and roundtables, and ALA and division and roundtable committees. Many exhibitors provide new items for participants to consider for purchase.

The annual conference, a much larger event, offers not only meetings of boards and committees but also speakers, preconference workshops, exciting meal functions such as the Newbery/Caldecott dinner, and a vast array of exhibits. A number of library-affiliated groups gather at the same time, including membership in the Black Caucus of the ALA, the American Indian Library Association, the Asian/Pacific American Librarians Association, the Chinese-American Library Association, and the membership meeting for Beta Phi Mu, International Library Science Honor Society.

In addition to the national conference of ALA, AASL holds its own national conference every second year. These are planned by AASL members, and all programming is directly related to school library services. Many members find these an excellent way to become acquainted in a smaller setting, rather than plunging into an ALA conference. This conference also provides an opportunity for practitioners and researchers to present information on their program and research results. Exhibits are directly related to school libraries.

AASL is governed by an executive board made up of the past president, the president, the recording secretary, the president-elect, a member elected by the board of directors from the board, and the executive director and deputy executive director, ex officio. In addition to the executive board, a board of directors is elected by membership and by other sections in the association and the Affiliate Assembly membership.

A wide variety of committees exist for AASL members. These include the AASL Intellectual Freedom Committee, the AASL Legislation Committee, and several awards committees, among others. The AASL Editorial Advisory Committee reviews the publication of the association journal, *Knowledge Quest*. Their research journal is a second publication, *School Library Media Quarterly*, which is available online. Members also receive the monthly *AASL Hotlinks*, which is sent to them online. AASL maintains relations with state associations through its Affiliate Assembly, which is made up of officers or delegates elected from state associations. These state associations may affiliate with AASL only if their president is a member of AASL.

Some school librarians suggest that dues for national associations seem very high, and they question what they get out of their membership. An article by Helen Adams in *School Library Media Quarterly* listed the following AASL membership benefits:

- Toll-free number to the AASL office
- Provision of the *Information Power* national guidelines
- Written policy statements on such issues as the role of library media specialists in site-based management
- Advisory telephone services by trained library media professionals
- Access to strategies for defending library media programs
- Access to statistics and research about library media programs
- Access to intellectual freedom assistance
- Access to a national network of fellow library media professionals
- Access to public relations information and activities about school library media programs through a variety of media
- Subscription to two AASL publications (*Knowledge Quest* and the electronic journal *School Library Media Quarterly*)
- Reduced registration rates at national AASL conferences, preconferences, and regional institutes
- Discounts on AASL publications
- Eligibility for AASL awards and scholarships
- Opportunity to serve on more than AASL committees
- Leadership training[6]

In addition, the American Association of School Librarians (AASL) has a benefit for its members, eCOLLAB/Your Learning Laboratory, which includes webinars, podcasts, and other professional development events.

International Associations

For school librarians who enjoy meeting their counterparts from other nations, two organizations are available. The International Association of School Librarianship (IASL; iasl-online.org) is open to school librarians from all over the world. A graduated dues schedule allows persons from developing nations to join for a reduced fee, and members are encouraged to adopt a member from a less wealthy nation. Two scholarships are available for someone from this category to attend the annual meeting.

Members can present papers at IASL conferences and hear speakers with national and international viewpoints on education and school librarianship. Many of the social events allow visits to school libraries and homes of school librarians in other countries as well as historical sites. Preconference and postconference tours and educational experiences add to the value of membership in this association.

The governance structure of IASL includes an executive board with a president, three vice presidents, and a financial officer. The board of directors includes the executive board and six directors who represent their regions of the world. The executive secretary serves ex officio on both boards. IASL members receive the online research journal, *School Libraries Worldwide,* an online newsletter, an up-to-date website, and an active email list.

The School Library Section of the International Federation of Library Associations and Federations (IFLA; www.ifla.org) also provides a forum for school librarians worldwide. Because IFLA is primarily an association made up of associations (e.g., ALA and Special Libraries Association) and major research libraries (New York Public Library, Harvard University Library), fewer individuals join as personal members but rather participate as voting representatives of their professional associations.

Both of these associations allow school librarians from the United States to meet and discuss library programs with professionals from around the globe. Because library programs in the United States are usually more advanced than in other locations, discussing activities provided in a library program here helps a professional in a country with less well-developed programming plan for the future. Understanding the state of a library program in another country may encourage school librarians to adopt an international library program and collect funding for materials for that school. As others are able to access the Internet, email will expand the exchange of information and widen the boundaries of schools in countries around the world. Because both associations meet in other countries, active membership means the librarian will travel to an international location and be able to visit libraries of all types. This places a different perspective on cultures and clarifies any impression of persons from that country as well as from other countries. It is obviously a more costly investment in time and funding, but the outcomes as we move into a global society are incomparable.

The School Library Section's elected chair is responsible for planning school library–related programs at the annual meeting of IFLA. These programs are available at the conference on CDs and are posted to the IFLA website. Many of the presentations are often translated to other languages.

Certainly more associations exist than most school librarians can hope to join. Nevertheless, choosing as many as possible and participating actively is essential to the effectiveness of the school librarian and the profession. Membership in an association exposes librarians to the most recent trends in education and librarianship and enables them to join forces with peers to lobby for the continuing expansion of school library programs at local, state, and national levels. Membership information is available from the websites of each professional association.

This chapter explained the leadership role of the school librarian in the organization and provision of professional development for teachers and administrators. It suggested ways for the school librarian to keep personally up-to-date. The next chapter outlines advocacy with the many ways to share the role of the school librarian with the school, the school district, the local community, the state, and the nation.

Exercises

1. Pick a technology application that you think would be new to most teachers and then design a session to teach it. Be sure to indicate the materials/equipment you would need and estimate the time needed for each part of the session.

2. Do you have a Professional Learning Network (PLN)? If yes, using their initials, write a sentence or two about the contributions each makes in your life. If you do not have a PLN, make a list of the people (by initials or by job titles) you would like to have on your PLN.

3. Review the charges to AASL committees found in the ALA Handbook of Organization. Compose a letter to the current president-elect of AASL who will make new appointments and volunteer to serve on the committee of your choice. Be sure to state your qualifications for this committee as well as your desire to serve.

Notes

1. Mary Ann Harlan, *Personal Learning Networks: Professional Development for the Isolated School Librarian* (Westport, CT: Libraries Unlimited, 2009), 1.

2. Carl A. Harvey II, *Adult Learners: Professional Development and the School Librarian* (Santa Barbara, CA: Libraries Unlimited, 2012), xiii.

3. Carolyn Kirio and Sandy Yamamoto, "Improving Practice through Professional Learning Communities," pp. 157–180 in Debbie Abilock, Kristin Fontichiaro, and Violet H. Harada, eds., *Growing Schools: Librarians as Professional Developers* (Santa Barbara, CA: Libraries Unlimited, 2012).

4. Richard DuFour, Robert Eaker, and Rebecca DuFour, *On Common Ground: The Power of Professional Learning Communities* (Bloomington, IN: National Education Service, 2005).

5. Susan W. Alman and Jennifer Jumba, eds., *MOOCs Now: Everything You Need to Know to Design, Set Up, and Run a Massive Open Online Course* (Santa Barbara, CA: Libraries Unlimited, 2017).

6. Helen R. Adams, "Money Talks," *School Library Media Quarterly* (Winter 1994): 127.

13
Advocacy

Advocacy is interpreted in many ways in this chapter. Levitov explains that advocacy is "a gray area for school libraries. It is frequently associated with attributes equivalent to public relations and marketing" and that may be interpreted as "self-serving and motivated by job security."[1]

This chapter begins with a discussion of some of the perceptions of the school librarian with some suggestions for changing those perceptions. It moves to a business view of marketing the school library program and then moves to advocacy as activism.

Each school librarian enters the profession with a perception of the role based on observations of school librarians. Some chose the role because it seemed a quiet place to work and it offered an opportunity to share a love of books with their students. This has not been the accepted role for decades, but it has increased the pressure on others, particularly new professionals, to make up for a veteran's lack of understanding that the traditional role has changed radically. They are no longer that quiet person who creates a dynamic program making sure teachers and students have more than access to the resources they need and works side-by-side with teachers developing curriculum and teaching. School librarians must make sure their programs are recognized as vital in the education of students. This chapter begins with ways to change perceptions some may have of the library and its role in education. It covers ways to make the goals and objectives clear to a wide variety of audiences within your school, your district, your community, and a wider audience to support access for all in your state and your nation. It also brings suggestions for helping librarians around the world.

Changing Perceptions

The importance of the school library program seems apparent to librarians. Unfortunately, this is not an automatic reaction for all users or potential users: students, teachers, administrators, parents, or the community at large. They base their perceptions on previous situations where no library existed or it was poorly stocked and seldom opened or the librarian was not friendly. The reality is that the exact opposite may be true, but the school library program often becomes one of the first areas to be targeted for reduction or elimination when budget cuts are mandated.

What happens when perceptions are inaccurate? School administrators, principals, and superintendents who do not know their teachers' and students' information needs think Google is both acceptable to provide resources and a great savings in dollars. No more book budgets, an open position allowing another teacher to be hired, and what was the school library can become two or three classrooms. This perception can spread when superintendents meet as a group; their discussions of potential savings in difficult budget times may allow one or more to say how much they are saving in closing their libraries. If no administrator makes a counterpoint, this spreads like wildfire. The first step is to work to change incorrect perceptions of the library and its purpose and how the librarian makes this happen.

Some students begin school with memories of story times and shelves of books for them to take home; other students have never been to a library. When the school library is a welcome place, positive perceptions prevail. This begins when they open the door. As has been asked before, is that first impression welcoming? Do they think the library belongs to the librarian? If their library doesn't seem to welcome them, ask them what would help change that image. Those students will tell their parents about the friendly library and helpful librarian. Teach them that the library belongs to them. It is their library. Use available spaces to display student work and encourage them to invite their parents to the library to see their work on display. Suggest they invite their parents to stop in the library if they are visiting the school for any reason.

Think carefully about any negatives that might happen. When students are threatened with fines and limited in how many items they can take away from the library, the positive image changes. Assessing students for overdue items is not teaching responsibility. A student who wants to keep a book might consider that a fine is a "rental" fee, thereby holding it from other students. It penalizes students who may not use the library for fear they might forget the item and they couldn't afford to pay the fine. Students who take ownership because the library is their library can help solve the problem of overdue resources.

Ask them at the beginning of the semester if they would like to check books out for a longer time with the understanding that they will return them if someone else requests them; this is teaching responsibility not only for care of the item but to their colleagues. Let students suggest books they would like to read and, if budgets allow, take a small group to the local bookstore to select books. They should be able to use your OPAC on their cell phones to see if the library already has a copy. Be the go-to person when information is needed for a project or when a small group needs to meet. If they tell their fellow students about the success they have had getting advice from the librarian and using resources from the library, either on the shelf or online, the numbers who come to do both will grow.

Teachers may need to have their perceptions changed or improved, too. Many librarians lament no use or inappropriate use of materials and facility, teachers who send students with no advance warning or do not provide adequate instructions; however, this may be librarians who do not collaborate with their teachers to create assignments that encourage the use of relevant resources, whose teachers do not ask the librarian to participate in unit planning. When teachers are aware of the success from collaborating with the librarian to improve student learning, they become advocates. Working with one teacher at a time, the librarian demonstrates the value of this program that offers the best resources and has the best technologies to share. Learning about these resources happens when school librarians plan and help conduct staff development so teachers learn new technologies. Sharing strategies that ease lesson planning and collaborating to increase student interest in completing assignments makes the librarian an indispensable colleague. Teachers will be well aware of the importance of the library because what happens there gives students cutting-edge educational opportunities. This program and its librarian leader will be recognized by teachers as something they should fight to preserve.

Other activities discussed in this chapter will also help you reach the wider community. Efforts of informed members of the community can point out that the school library is the essential part of education for the students who go to that school. These persons may also be available to volunteer in the school or they may bring expertise to a subject or topic that would increase the students' understanding.

Another group within the community includes those librarians in academic and public libraries who can be very supportive for intellectual freedom, in sharing resources, in their willingness to invite students to their libraries for any number of reasons, and their support in explaining the role of libraries in the lives of students before and after basic education. It all works when perceptions are changed and you have safety in numbers to carry out public relations efforts.

While books are available on the topic of public relations in libraries and specifically for school librarians, many have older copyright dates. They obviously will not cover the power of the communication offered by Facebook, Twitter, Tumblr, blogs, and wikis. The more common term for school librarians today is advocacy, and the discussion between advocacy and marketing as a form of public relations continues. This chapter uses the business model term "public relations" in terms of "marketing" because education systems are being encouraged to run on a business model. The advocacy model is discussed later in the chapter.

Marketing

This section begins with the business view and uses the marketing world for models to build a public relations program. According to Philip Kotler, marketing is the "purposeful coalescence of people, materials and facilities seeking to accomplish some purpose."[2] While dated, the definition remains accurate. If this definition is translated into the coalescence of teachers and librarians seeking to prepare students for adult society, marketing the library should involve the selling of services and use of the collection in all its formats, hard copy and online. The librarian and (if there is any) library staff and the advisory committee plan which services and how to sell these services to teachers. Teachers, in turn, join with the librarian and staff to sell available resources and information to students to increase their ability to learn. These efforts market the library's image to gain budget support for increasing services to administrators, parents, and the community; and the circle continues.

The success of this marketing campaign is confirmed when teachers begin co-teaching with the librarian and when joint curriculum planning is in place. Eventually, it becomes the campaign of teachers and students to resist cutting library services or staff. When teachers and students are able, willing, and eager to articulate the importance and value of their library in teaching and learning, the library will, indeed, be the center of the school.

Marketing begins with attention to the ambiance of the library, both physically and virtually, so it is attractive to teachers and students. Teachers and students are asked what is needed to make the library, its website, and its social media presence more interesting and attractive. The obvious things are changing bulletin boards and showcases frequently, displaying student work, eliminating any negative signage, assuring that social media discussions and postings are up-to-date, and having good signage in the library to locate things easily. One of the major features of ambiance includes the persons who work in that library. If those who venture in are met with that "head down, busy, don't bother me" body language, potential users will be discouraged. A friendly smile will do much to make the library a welcoming, wonderful place to be, a strong marketing tool.

From a business management standpoint, marketing is the "managerial process involving analysis, planning, implementation, and control."[3] In the broadest sense, it is the bringing together of producer and consumer. This marketing function means the librarian must attract sufficient resources; convert resources into products (databases), services (professional development), and ideas; and distribute outputs to various consuming publics, teachers, students, and parents. It is a never-ending process. Getting the needed resources to buy the products so the services and ideas from users can be made available is a challenge that must be met constantly.

The marketer, by giving something, acquires something in return. For most school librarians, that "something" in return will be the knowledge that teachers and students are able to use the library to improve both teaching and learning. The successful marketer researches the anticipated needs of the persons to whom this exchange is directed, designs a product they cannot ignore, generates an absolute need for the product in the potential recipient, and communicates at an appropriate time and in an appropriate place. When the anticipated need, providing access to information for all, is met, students will see the value of their library as they find resources to complete assignments and even generate new information. It is definitely a win-win situation.

School librarians are in the unique position of being able to provide large numbers of resources in a variety of formats for clientele at many locations inside and outside the library at no immediate or apparent cost to them. The library is full of products on the shelves and available online that can easily become "gifts" the teacher or student cannot refuse if those gifts are marketed at the appropriate time and place.

Marketing has three facets the librarian must consider: public awareness, dissemination of information (which may be a part of public awareness), and development of services to meet needs based on marketing research. The first, a public awareness program for the library, is centered on the person in charge and how that person and the staff are perceived.

A basic problem for marketing remains with personnel, a problem not unique to education or libraries. This has been presented earlier, but it is so important it needs to be addressed here. Library staff—both personally and through the programs and information services they offer—must project a strong, helpful image to all the students and adults in the building, from kindergarten through high school, including custodians, clerical staff, cafeteria workers, bus drivers, teachers, administrators, and parents. Librarians represent all persons in the library world to the clients they serve, particularly if those clients make little or no use of any other information agency. How they act is the model for the community showing how all librarians will act, and this is a large legacy to hand down to students before they enter adulthood.

One aspect of public awareness is to demonstrate the value of the library and its services; this includes providing information to users and helping them in learning how to find the information independently. In the age of virtual information, school librarians make sure their users understand how to find information. They also need to provide articles and other information on educational trends, new teaching methodologies, and applications of newer technologies that are of potential interest to teachers and administrators and share them. Helping students analyze what they find is an ongoing task. Notifying administrators, teachers, and students of access to new databases and how to share them in classrooms and at home will draw attention to the value of the library. Posting events, new services, and activities on a virtual message board and maintaining a Facebook page and other social media outlets is another sure way to get the word out to the library community.

The process of developing services based on marketing research is another facet of the marketing process. Obviously, the services offered by the librarian should be a combination of services that users deem necessary (determined through market research). Services are reviewed by the advisory committee and in collaboration with teachers so that they are seen as necessary and appropriate for curriculum integration and support.

A wide gulf often exists between offering services and clientele use of those services. Getting users to the library to use the services is another component of the marketing process. If teachers and students receive a warm welcome every time they appear to collect media, produce a sign, search a database, create a report, or look up the price of classroom materials they wish to purchase, they will carry away with them a positive image of library personnel and services. Providing opportunities to create, invent, test in a makerspace becomes a major attraction to the library.

If the librarian goes to the teacher to suggest collaboration to develop units of instruction and agrees to participate in the teaching and the testing for success, teachers will be more eager to participate. When all teachers in the building are involved in this process, and particularly those seen as special teachers are included, this collaboration will expand exponentially.

When students are treated as serious scholars, they will come. Encouraging them to work in small groups in the library in middle school prepares them for small group work in high school and college and as members of teams in their later jobs. Allowing them to take the numbers of resources needed and providing access to designated Web resources will make their research efforts more successful.

If selection and distribution of materials from the library are simple processes efficiently managed, and if information is provided willingly, correctly, and quickly, the recipient will be willing to enter the library or send an email request to the librarian. Placing as few limits as possible on the use of information in the library or for circulation from the library keeps the customer, administrator, teacher, or student a happy customer. The next question is what offerings will keep the client returning.

What to Market

"Marketing in the firm begins and ends with the customers."[4] To the librarian, the customers are the library clientele. To determine what to market, an organization chooses which of its desirable assets it wishes to place for "trade." The Library Advisory Committee would be useful to help determine which assets are most important to users. The primary commodity for most library programs is its services, but which services, and its access to information for all. The secondary commodities are the resources available either in-house or online. Plans should be developed to market the following:

1. Those services determined as priorities by the majority of users. These are the services that must be provided because they are most often requested.

2. Other services offered because the need exists. Some of these may be the same as those listed above. Once services are selected to be offered, it is important that all teachers and students be made aware of their existence.

3. Those services that are provided but are not requested because teachers or students are not aware of them. Advertising these services will provide a pool of potential users.

4. New services provided and used if an area of interest was developed for teachers and students. These might be requested by one teacher or recognized as needed by the advisory committee.

5. New materials and databases added to the collection and their availability within the school and outside the school building.

6. New equipment made available for use in the library, classroom, or to be taken home.

7. Special collections made available for teachers and students.

Once services to market are chosen, librarian and staff must decide what methods will be most effective to carry out the marketing process.

How to Market

The marketing environment comprises consumers and producers and is part of the societal environment. The marketing environment for school libraries varies from state to state and between regions and local districts within states. Included in the marketing environment is competition from other information agencies, such as bookstores and college, public, home, and classroom libraries. Also included in this environment are the suppliers and producers of products and services that are secured by library professionals to place in centers. Producers of materials for school libraries include commercial vendors as well as staff and services of the production center in the library itself. It also includes any information created by students to share with their peers. Appropriate marketing should result in happy school library users who will become consumer advocates.

Librarians become *producers* who must anticipate the consumer marketplace and then offer something of value to the library clientele as *consumers*. A planned market offering of products, services, promotion, distribution, and, in some cases, pricing (e.g., copying costs) is developed. School librarians need to anticipate the market. Just as commercial vendors send sales representatives out to do just that, the librarian must leave the library and meet the clientele in classrooms and corridors to learn about clientele needs.

In the marketing world, the consumers return something of value to the producers. If the product is offered for a cash value, the return is a dollar amount. For librarians as producers, the value received is a much less tangible reward, such as a satisfied customer's smile, a simple "thank you," or, "This was a great book!" "Look at the good things my teacher said about my research paper." The teacher's returning to co-teach the next unit is another reward. If, in the process of planning a particular unit of instruction, an outside expert is willing to join in the planning and presentation of the information to classes, this should bring applause from the teacher. If a learning activity is particularly successful, being covered in the school newspaper or on local media is a very tangible reward. A note of thanks from the principal or superintendent is yet another tangible reward.

The *market offerings* of products or services for the library program are the media (products) and the methods of using them (services). *Promotion* becomes a marketing plan, which will be discussed in depth later in this chapter. *Distribution* is the system that provides the product, service, or information requested by the consumer. Distribution in the library is translated into access to and ease of use of information. In most areas of the library program, *pricing* is not a consideration because services are and should be free. All types of librarians have been debating fee versus free services, usually connected to a need to be reimbursed for some recurring cost that may or may not be used by all students, such as photocopying or making prints of resources found during database searching. However, funding for photocopying or paper and printer ink might be better provided by a project of a school club. The librarian might be able to limit the number of copies made by a single student. When the ceiling is reached, a student might be asked to help support the system. This is becoming less and less a challenge because students are able to share their coursework online.

Market planning is the "act of specifying in detail what will be done, by whom, to whom, with what and when, to achieve the organization's objectives."[5] Market planning resembles the process described in the section on proposal writing in Chapter 7. It begins with setting goals and objectives for the planning process for the district or school library program, developing a proposal for funding, or writing educational objectives for the project. The four steps in this process and some additional suggestions follow.

The first step is to analyze the situation—that is, conduct a *market analysis*. A market analysis may resemble the needs assessment conducted for program planning or proposal writing. Librarians should not spend time trying to convince teachers or students to use services they consider of little value. Librarians have products to sell that are essential if teachers are to have the best teaching materials and students are to be given the best opportunities to learn. At times, these products may be perceived to be less helpful because of the difficulty of securing them, the lack of quality of the products, or simply the audience's lack of awareness of their existence. To use an example, think of a librarian who is trying to change the Google search for students who are doing single research reports, who is able to move them into a joint effort of small teams of students gathering as much information as possible found in all the resources in the library, on the shelf and online.

The second step is to develop a strategy for what to do and how to do it. This also resembles a step in responding to a request for proposal: that of planning activities. What can be done to meet the need within the constraints of the library and its services yet help students find relevant information? Devise a test where two teachers become involved and work collaboratively with the librarian to design the unit. Then one class will continue to do the one person, one topic approach and the second will use the small-team approach. At the end of the project, two tests use two measures: the quality of papers from each group and the numbers of citations found for both sets of papers.

Step three evaluates the effectiveness of this project. Looking at the quality assessment, did students begin to use a wider variety of resources when they were working in teams, and were their papers of higher quality?

The fourth step is the final evaluation. Since the quality of the papers was covered in the analysis of the use of resources, that part has been finished. Looking at the variety of resources used in comparison to the quality of the papers is the second measure. However, a brief survey of students on how well they did in finding resources is needed. The small team group could be asked if they thought their working together made the task better and if they felt their results were stronger for having shared in the planning and execution of the research process.

In the above example, a marketing strategy is planned and the "sale" is not an easy one. One teacher needed to be sold on having students work as a team to find online information. The objective is to achieve acceptance of a new format for materials in the school library. When a strategy such as team research is successful and the product is important, the librarian should use the marketing process to try to get more teachers to collaborate.

A marketing program is ongoing, and statistics should be available for library staff to respond instantly to inquiries from parents, community members, teachers, and administrators. For example, major corporations and university athletic departments publish fact books for the news media. General information on the library program should include statistics about the physical library—its size, amount of seating, numbers of volumes, media and databases, budget, amount of use by class and individuals, and type of use (e.g., storytelling, viewing, research, online searching). Output measures such as usage of databases, numbers of collaborative units, or topics (by name) should be included, as well as interesting input measures such as the number of new resources purchased each year and the average cost of each, from books through databases and hardware. The fact book might also contain a description and photos of the facility. Actual titles of successful research reports and the authors can give credit to students and teachers.

Marketing experts also suggest that an image be selected for the library—an image that can change from time to time. Students might be asked to help choose a theme for the year and to suggest ways to follow through with an ongoing plan to keep the library in the center of attention at the school. One major change in the school library is the move to a learning commons with a totally different focus. Planning for this change will highlight the true leadership of the school librarian and the focus on a different responsibility for teachers collaborating with others in their school, other schools, the community, and even the global society. This type of image change catapults the school librarian into the information specialist for the school, the go-to person for ideas, information, and assistance, and the library as the true center of the school, not just a center of attention.

Who should do this planning? In a single-person library, the planning may begin with the advisory committee. It quickly includes administrators, teachers, students, parents, and finally members of the community who will have suggestions for how they can participate. It ends with the marketing plan.

As stated earlier, a marketing plan follows the format of proposal writing. Objectives are developed, the current situation is described, and the expected progress is outlined. Alternative strategies are written for achieving the objectives, with reasons given for each strategy. Specific actions are then listed and any needed budget proposed. Staff members are assigned to specific implementation tasks. Finally, evaluation of each step is indicated, with a time line showing how often to review.

Promotion

An important point to remember in developing a marketing plan is that promotion itself is a form of communication. Kotler lists several promotion tools, which have been modified for the school library program setting.[6] They require less expenditure of time than the marketing described above. The first tool, *space and time advertising,* could take the form of an article for the school newspaper. If the school publishes a literary newsletter or magazine with articles by students, the library could sponsor a well-written book review or other media review. A library column with critiques of films in local theaters could be patterned after the entertainment column in the local newspaper. These are all written by students who may also work in the library as assistants. The librarian could host a blog with book reviews contributed by teachers and students or a personal blog of favorite new titles.

Loudspeaker advertising of the library could be offered through school intercoms. Sometimes the only public relations message that school librarians provide is a notice about returning books at the close of the semester (penalty noted: grade cards withheld); this is clearly not a positive marketing mechanism. A better plan would be to announce the winner of the latest reference question quiz. The message should publicize happenings in the library that will attract students and teachers to the library to learn about the resources there.

The equivalent of *mailings,* another method of marketing, could be achieved by putting information in teachers' boxes or distributing notices during students' homeroom period or posting on the Web or, in the age of social media, on those sites. All such messages must be carefully planned with thought given to the type of ads used to sell products. Examples that come to mind are the enclosures highlighting new products or sale items that often accompany billing from credit cards, department stores, or oil companies. If the message is clever, brief, and attractive, it will be read and maybe even taken home to share with parents. If not, it will be discarded immediately.

The *sales presentation* could be equated to the presentation of new materials at the teachers' meeting or a book talk in a classroom. The presentation should be relaxed, with some "reward" at the close of the meeting, when teachers are given sample products described during the presentation. Students may check out the books presented. Demonstrations provided at these meetings may promote the use of a new piece of equipment. Certainly, any demonstration should provide new information and offer something the audience will be eager to use. A brief demonstration should leave teachers and students eager to use the product. Scheduling a follow-up session with teachers who want a hands-on opportunity will also indicate success.

Contests are another successful ploy when they pique the interest of the intended audience. Contests should be planned with specific goals and objectives to expand the market, not just bring attention to an existing service. However, providing a prize for the best research paper using library materials should expand students' use of the center. Considering the ease of publishing online, collecting excellent student papers into an online resource as an e-book provides a new resource for students in the school looking for resources.

Free samples are another marketing tool. Actually sharing new acquisitions on a bookmark designed by art students could be one free sample. Others may be a little more challenging to acquire, but businesses in the area may have things to give away. Fast-food restaurants are one source of such free samples if one can overlook the obvious problem of offering students and their families less well-balanced meals.

Displays of posters, signs, and show cards produced in the library can bring teachers and students in to create their own for classrooms and clubs. Posters, signs, and show cards are also excellent tools to advertise the library. If production of attractive posters is not possible in the school, the district or regional production center should be used. Librarians should try to locate sources for developing in-house posters, because the local aspect of this type of advertising adds a positive dimension. The American Library Association (ALA) offers for a small fee the ability to use their Read posters to put student pictures with their favorite book on display, and then the poster can be sent home with the student. It is a clever way to feature teachers and the principal sharing their favorite books.

Another marketing device is the *point-of-sale display,* often used in grocery stores to feature a certain product. A poster and a stack of books near the charge-out desk encourage students to borrow something to read. Displays of new books at the entrance of the library, just as at the entrance of a bookstore, encourage checkout. Displays elsewhere in the library might show books made into movies or a genre grouping to attract readers.

Sales literature could take the form of bibliographies generated to show users what is available on a single topic. Other forms of sales literature are flyers to describe a workshop or a guest speaker and an exhibition book about a special exhibit that a student or teacher might place in the library.

In developing another marketing device, the *brochure,* one should consider the development of the copy. Most advertising personnel choose a particular theme. If several themes are possible, library staff and students might help select the best via an in-house contest. The possibilities of the product to be "sold" to the audience should always be kept in mind as the "sales" literature is being developed such as a brochure inviting parents to students' demonstration of social media devices with costs at a time when the school is trying to raise money to expand the electronic access for students. A brochure might be a list of the resources available to students so that their parents are aware of the need for electronic devices for their students.

Another marketing tool is the *formal presentation* made by the librarian to groups both inside and outside the school. An enthusiastic, carefully orchestrated talk with interesting visuals can draw far more positive attention to the library than many of the methods discussed earlier. Such a presentation, followed by a lively question-and-answer period, can do much to change any negative images of library professionals and library programs and help to build a positive image of the school library for the community. Suggestions for preparing presentations are given in the next section.

The authors have often been asked to present school libraries to service organizations. These groups meet weekly, and the person in charge of programs is always looking for a new speaker. Offering to show a slide set or video of students at work in the library could provide the introduction to a pleasant after-lunch speech. Often, these organizations will make a small donation to purchase something for the library. Also, the school's parent and teacher association and a local school foundation may respond after you present a program to them. All of these increase the positive perception of the school library to the community. Such programs are not that difficult to prepare, as discussed below.

Preparing Presentations

Many books have been written to help the novice prepare and deliver a speech. Persons who have managed to make as few formal presentations as possible in their high school and college years are probably not as comfortable in front of a group as they perceive their colleagues to be. This may not be an accurate analysis because it may take time to feel comfortable before an audience. Yet it is essential that the function of the school library be described to a wide variety of audiences if the program is to be understood and given the high priority that it deserves. A few simple suggestions may help the reluctant speaker accept this responsibility.

First, the length of the presentation should be predetermined and observed. No audience wants to sit longer than they expect to sit, as demonstrated by people who begin to yawn or wriggle in their seats. Nor does a host wish to have the program come to a close too quickly.

The librarian should prepare an outline of the presentation to confirm the sequence of points to be made. The outline should then be followed. A presentation that wanders will confuse the audience, and the point will be lost. Often, the inclination might be to write out the speech and then read it. This is often very boring to an audience, even those attending a research seminar. If you do write out the speech, make margin notes to help you get through the content without actually reading the paper.

The shy speaker should plan visuals to help illustrate points and reduce the speaking time required. An audience watching a screen may seem less intimidating than an audience focused on the podium. It is useful to distribute copies of important visuals so the audience listens rather than trying to make hasty notes.

It may help reduce tension to remember that most audiences are delighted to listen to a speaker talking about something with which they are unfamiliar. Their empathy is high because they are delighted they are not being expected to give the speech. If you are relaxed, they will be relaxed.

When this is absolutely nothing that will ever be attempted, you still need to get the library and its values into the community. Perhaps the students can be asked to make the presentation. They may be an even better choice.

Successful speakers tell their audience what they are going to say, say it, and summarize what they have said. If the speaker is enthusiastic about the topic, that enthusiasm will be transmitted to the audience. Bring along written testimonies, or, as suggested above, have children present their projects in person. This will add substantially to the audience's enjoyment of the presentation.

Marketing the school library is a continuous activity. It begins with a welcoming facility with a pleasant ambiance through the provision of appropriate resources. However, one of the librarian's easiest marketing techniques is to greet everyone who comes in the door with a smile and an eagerness to help.

Using marketing as a business concept provides suggestions for the library within the school. However, the librarian must move outside the walls of the library into the wide world. This is never easy, but in this century, it is critical.

Advocacy to Activism

Readers of Levitov's *Activism and the School Librarian: Tools for Advocacy and Survival*[7] are introduced to the theoretical foundation for activism, how to move from advocacy to activism, and how to create a culture of advocacy in terms of working with parents, community groups, and local businesses. The process involves understanding exemplary practice, which is discussed throughout this text. School librarians who work to gain support for their libraries and their positions "have to be willing to embrace the future and make changes that will transform and reinvent positions and programs, making them learner centered and essential for education in this century."[8]

While some might argue that this is indeed self-serving and saving one's job, in reality it is saving our democracy. Today's students must not only learn to read, write, and do arithmetic, they must have access to information and be able to assess that information to determine true from false, facts from biased opinion, and real from another person's declaration of reality. To do this, the librarian establishes a "Culture of Advocacy" as stated in the following points, which have been chosen from Kaaland's steps.[9]

- Advocacy must be about student learning.
- Advocacy must be altruistically motivated.
- Advocacy must be ongoing.
- Advocacy must be positive.
- Advocates must be vocal and articulate.
- Advocates must do homework.
- Advocates must anticipate change.
- Advocacy is about access for all.

The authors of this textbook are suggesting that all are very important, but the last one, "access for all," is the critical need to sustain a democracy. When demigods can keep information from people or can convince the population that what is being said to them is in fact the truth, it will be up to school librarians who have a captive audience for their libraries to ensure students have access to information and can find the truth. These students are brought into the library or assigned projects by teachers on a regular basis for 12 or more years of their life, placing school librarians in the best position to develop informed citizens. These librarians who are active in the political process make sure their students have access to information and learn.

School Librarians and the Political Process

Many school librarians are well aware of the need to become effective in the political process, but they think this should be an assignment for someone else without recognizing that they may be the only "someone else." This process begins in the local school.

Lobbying at Home

That school librarians are a public asset is a fact that was discussed in the beginning of the chapter. The perceptions are not always as positive as one would wish. This is found throughout the book, but needs to be repeated here.

Lobbying begins at the local school building when the librarian promotes the values and the needs of the library program to students, parents, teachers, and, most of all, the principal in order to affect budgeting and strategic long-range planning. These persons must understand the impact of the school library program to the education of students from the first day of each school year throughout the year. This starts with the teachers who must understand the many ways to collaborate, co-teach, conduct guided inquiry sessions, and allow the school librarian to share the latest technical advances to teach.

One way to look at this was told by Judy Moreillon to an audience at a state conference. Some teachers feel even more isolated than the librarian. New teachers have all those students and all those parents who expect their children to learn; and they may have very little help from another teacher unless the district places mentors with new teachers. Even then, the mentor may not be available as often as the teacher feels the need for help. Working with new teachers makes their classes more rewarding and helps provide better learning for their students. Ultimately, schools with veteran teachers who seem less interested in co-teaching will see the results of co-teaching with the new teacher.

The school librarian who works closely with the principal and other administrative staff to keep them informed about the learning success in the school will remain essential to the school when budgets are reduced or when a different resource allocation process is put into place. This public relations effort is not a once-a-year effort; it is ongoing and requires constant, well-presented activities and their results in a manner that makes the principal want to see and learn what is happening in the school. It is most powerful when the principal shares this activity with other principals in the district or the region. Principals appreciate looking good to their colleagues, and this may be the beginning of many such opportunities.

At the district level, the superintendent and assistant superintendents and subject area specialists, among others, are shown the activities going on in the school that feature teachers teaching and students learning, again in a presentation that will both demonstrate yet be interesting. These can and should be developed by students and teachers under the direction of the librarian so they demonstrate the quality education going on in the school.

Asking for regular time at a school board meeting with students showing the result of their special projects is an engaging event and generates positive results. Reporting on the progress of any proposal that required board approval should happen during the project, not just at the end. This show-and-tell can be at the school. Most principals would like to show off their school to the superintendent and school board when these are well-planned events that will make the teachers and principal look good. This is certainly easier than getting students, teachers, and even parents to a school board meeting.

Going outside the school to report successes in the efforts within the school, parents are the first group to meet. School librarians need to be available for teacher open-house. If this is not a standard procedure in the district, coffee, tea, and cookies in the library as parents move from visiting one teacher to another in the upper grades or who have just come from a conference with their student's teacher may be welcomed. If you have students demonstrating some of their activities in the library, parents will see and, if they talk to the students, hear what is going on in that room. It could be a place to enlist volunteers to work in the library

The evidence of the value of the school library in the lives of students and teachers must be constant and well documented from the first day of school throughout the school year. The program must be supported by others in the school community, not just the school library staff. This support must also go beyond the local community to the legislative decision makers who are elected to state and national offices.

State and National Legislative Lobbying

Kachel proposes that "school library *legislative* advocacy begins with the development of a relationship between school library advocates—librarians and beyond—and legislative decision makers."[10] The novice lobbyist may go to the ALA's Legislative Action Center (http://capwiz.com/ala/home/) to find not only the names of federal and state legislators, but current issues. Some background research on your legislator will be helpful. Know their educational background and their work history. Learning their hometown allows the opportunity to meet them not only in their legislative office but perhaps in a more social situation. Their political party is also important to see if you are a registered member of that party or another. Other suggestions are made by George Miller and John Lawrence in their *Los Angeles Times* article,[11] which is found in Appendix I. This article gives detailed suggestions such as how to better ensure talking to the actual legislator, adding to your information by locating the numbers of bills they will be asked to support, and even how to encourage the media to listen to your message for your legislators. They also outline how to become an effective lobbyist and that includes having your picture taken when you visit the legislator's office.

School librarians actually plan to lobby and that may seem threatening or beneath or above the abilities of a building-level person. Lobbying is the process of making opinions heard and getting ideas to decision makers. It is collecting appropriate information and using it for advocacy. It can result in influencing legislation. Librarians need not begin their lobbying efforts by trying to change federal laws. It is much easier and obviously much more effective to begin at home in the offices of your state representatives. This allows trying methods before planning to visit a political official.

To secure the consideration of state-level funding agencies and legislators requires a more sophisticated organization for your efforts. At this level, more groups are demanding attention from these agencies and individuals, and one's message can easily be ignored. For this reason, novice lobbyists need to remember that legislators at any level are still elected officials. They serve at the pleasure of their constituents, and, as voters, school librarians and other members of the school staff and the parents of students are their constituents.

The second thing to remember is that these officials who work for us were elected by our votes. They are interested in helping make things better for their constituents. They are elected officials in a democratic society that they and all other citizens wish to remain democratic. To do this, citizens must be informed voters, and, as the leaders who developed the U.S. education system believed, this depends on teaching students to read. In our present information society, this also means citizens who are information literate, who have had access to and learned to test the validity of information as part of the education process. That access has come in and through the library. Elected officials need to be kept aware of the central role of the school library as the information center in the education of youth.

Using the information from the Legislative Action Center or the previously mentioned article by Miller and Lawrence in Appendix I, messages can be sent regularly to members, requesting their action. Office staff will tell you that congressional offices are interested in hearing from constituents; they often do not understand the issues involved in particular pieces of legislation. Sometimes legislators receive no comments from any constituents concerning certain legislation. In some cases, opponents of legislation affecting education may send a few persons to state a case against a bill, and the legislator acts in their favor because no one from the education community has offered another viewpoint. Meeting the legislator with other interested constituents greatly supports the message.

Writing an email message takes only a little time and is of great help in communicating with a legislator. Some suggestions for writing and mailing a letter are given in Appendix J. It is no longer a speedy process to send a letter to a legislator in Washington. Since the threat of anthrax, all mail addressed there goes to a site for checking before being forwarded to the legislator's office. It is better to look up the legislator's name in the local telephone directory's government pages and send the letter there if you aren't sending it by email or fax. However you are sending it, follow the ALA's "Five Basic Rules for Effective Communication."

1. Be brief. A legislator's time is limited. So is yours.

2. Be appreciative. Acknowledge past support, and convey thanks for current action.

3. Be specific. Refer to local library and district needs.

4. Be informative. Give reasons why a measure should be supported.

5. Be courteous. Ask; do not demand or threaten. Be positive but polite.

State and national associations keep their members informed of issues that should be addressed and urge support as soon as these messages arrive in your email. These associations often support Legislation Days, when members of the association go to the Capitol to call on legislators; this can be effective. Although school librarians often cannot be away from school on these days, that does not mean they cannot be effective lobbyists. Indeed, Miller and Lawrence suggest it is more effective to meet legislators at their local offices. The local offices of state legislators and members of Congress are listed in the government pages of telephone directories (usually blue pages).

Legislators most often hear from constituents when they want something. It is desirable to establish communication with legislators and their office staff before a need or crisis arises. This can smooth the way for a visit in time of need. Again, remember that legislators need information from their constituents to better understand issues. As a reliable information provider, you can convince your legislator that school librarians are friends of lawmakers, there to help them understand the educational needs of students.

Sometimes the librarian must move to block proposed legislation. Professional associations usually have a legislative network in place to notify members when it is necessary to visit legislators, write letters, or make telephone calls against, as well as for, a bill. When a call comes, it is important to act quickly.

For the librarian who becomes immersed in local, state, and national politics, there are some simple rules:

1. Give legislators carefully researched and correct information. To tell a state legislator that the average per-pupil expenditure for media materials in a state is a very low figure only to have incorrect information contradicted will be embarrassing to everyone, perhaps critically so to the legislator.

2. Follow legislation of interest to school librarians from introduction through signature. Carefully choose legislators to support the issue. Learn to gather support from news media—local newspapers and television—as well as lawmakers.

3. Learn to write letters to lawmakers, and then write them. The image of library programs must be a positive one, and lobbying will help create a positive image of school librarians and their programs.

For librarians who have never considered it necessary to lobby, one is reminded of the Little Red Hen. People are out there planting the wheat, gathering it, and making bread. When it is time to eat that bread, they will not be eager to give away slices to those who have not been active participants in the process. For the continued improvement of information services for students and teachers in schools, school librarians must lobby every day for their meaningful programs, demonstrating to students, teachers, administrators, and parents that they and the services in library programs make a difference in the lives of children. School librarians also must keep reminding their community members how important information resources are in schools for the education of future taxpayers. Finally, state and national government officials must be told that cutting funds for information resources for school libraries reduces the ability of youth to become effective citizens in a global community and persons who will, as adults, be interested in and capable of lifelong learning.

This is a formidable assignment, but one that must be undertaken. It is not the responsibility of one school librarian but of all school librarians. It is always easier to work with someone else who can then enlist other supporters. Start in your own town to build a group. Your local state school library association will have an active legislative group to join. If school librarians wish to make a difference in students' academic achievement, they must ensure that attention is paid to the continuation of strong school library programs because they are essential to student learning. As Lance and others have pointed out in many states:

- The size of a library media center's staff and collection is the best school predictor of academic achievement.

- The instructional role of the library media specialist shapes the collection and, in turn, academic achievement.

- Library media expenditures affect library media center staff and collection size and, in turn, academic achievement.[12]

A final reminder to those who control the purse strings is that the school librarian and the school library provide equal access to information to support the education for all the students in their school. Without this protection of access to information, students will not have the foundation for effective citizenship in a democracy.

School Librarians as Politicians

One way a school librarian might be more effective would be as an elected official. The most direct application of authority is the school board. School boards may be appointed, but they are most often elected. It would be unlikely that school librarians would be able to run for school board in their school district, but they might live in the town next to where they teach. Certainly election to the school board provides a strong voice in the management of a school district.

Being active in a political party can also provide a voice for the platform for many who are running for office. One author is well aware that one state was able to secure funding when two school librarians were active in their political parties; one was county chair of the Democratic Party and another was county chair of the Republican Party.

School Librarians: Advocating in the Global Community

Many school librarians in the United States are aware of the need to participate in the global community and to support school libraries throughout the world. This has a great benefit to the students in schools. The world is shrinking with the expansion of access to communication and movement of resources from one country to another. Language may not remain a problem as computer programs translate texts. Students in schools today need to know how to interact with their peers in other nations. School librarians need to be models of interaction with others throughout the world.

Attending annual conferences of the International Association of School Librarianship (IASL) and the International Federation of Library Associations and Institutions (IFLA) provides an opportunity to meet school librarians from other nations. Those attending from developing nations point out the need for active school libraries in their schools in the face of no funding, no collections, and no perceived value. With the increased capability of electronic transfer, many persons providing service from their small school libraries will become part of the global community as transmission of information becomes available through the Internet. School librarians in the United States should become aware of the problems of schools without libraries in other parts of the world and should begin to help plan solutions to these problems.

Both IASL and IFLA are described in Chapter 12. They both have electronic lists where members post messages seeking other schools to share problems and some suggested and proven solutions.

School librarians provide access to information, opening the world of information to students, teachers, administrators, and the community. They can and do make a difference in the lives of students every day of every school year. They will continue to do so as long as they keep their community aware. Some ways to do this have been described throughout the book. They are placed in a list in Appendix K. They are actually quite simple because most have no real costs attached.

Marketing and advocacy may not seem something that should be in the job description of the school librarian, but they are both essential to school librarians and they will be vital to schools in the future. The next chapter presents thoughts about the future.

Exercises

1. Match a school library activity or service with each of the promotional tools listed below:

   Space and time advertising
   Loudspeaker advertising
   Mailings
   Sales presentations
   Contests
   Free samples
   Displays
   Point-of-sale display
   Sales literature

2. Design a brochure to advertise the addition of new materials or equipment to the library.
3. Outline a presentation for teachers or parents describing a needed addition to the library. Sell this to the group to get their support for administrative approval of additional funds.
4. Describe a presentation you would make for a service organization, including what visuals you would share with them.
5. Compose a one-page document for your school board requesting support for an increase in the per-pupil allocation for materials. Statistics from matching costs of materials from purchase orders for the past three years will demonstrate the rising costs of materials and can be used to support your position.
6. Find out the latest legislation in Congress that would affect school library services, and write a letter supporting the position that would most help improve these services.
7. Gather together evidence of the recent activities in your library and plan how to present them to your state or national legislator. Call your legislator and request an appointment or plan an activity to invite your state or national legislator to your school library.
8. Plan a visit to a state legislator or member of Congress and explain who you would take along with you and why you chose this person and not someone else. What would you want them to share? How would you prepare them for the visit? What would you ask them to be prepared to discuss?
9. Plan an activity that will open your library to the larger world community.

Notes

1. Deborah D. Levitov, ed., *Activism and the School Librarian: Tools for Advocacy and Survival* (Santa Barbara, CA: Libraries Unlimited, 2012).

2. Philip Kotler, *Marketing for Nonprofit Organizations* (Englewood Cliffs, NJ: Prentice Hall, 1975), 5.

3. Ibid., 6.

4. Ibid., 238.

5. Ibid.

6. Ibid.

7. Levitov, op. cit.

8. Ibid., xii.

9. Christie Kaaland and Debra E. Kachel, "School Library Legislative Advocacy Defined," in Deborah D. Levitov, ed., *Activism and the School Librarian: Tools for Advocacy and Survival* (Santa Barbara, CA: Libraries Unlimited, 2012), 39–47.

10. Ibid., 57.

11. George Miller and John Lawrence. "How to Make Your Voice Heard in Washington," *Los Angeles Times,* February 15, 2017, p. A13.

12. Keith Curry Lance and David Loertscher, *Powering Achievement: School Library Media Programs Make a Difference: The Evidence,* 2nd ed. (San Jose, CA: Hi Willow Research and Publishing, 2002).

14
The Future

The person with the half-empty glass might propose that this chapter is a nonentity since all types of libraries have no future. Norman D. Stevens in his *American Libraries* tongue-in-cheek article, "The Last Librarian," credited school libraries as the first crack in the demise of all types of libraries.

> As school libraries began to assume varying degrees of responsibility for computers, beginning in the late 1970s and early 1980s, the use of the term media center, or other variations, became increasingly widespread. As best as Amy could determine, by 2020 almost every unit in elementary and secondary schools throughout the United States that had responsibility for providing access to books, computers, electronic media, and other information formats had abandoned the term school library. Seeking to maintain some element of tradition, a number of schools still maintained the term media center, but most had adopted information center. A recent handwritten note (itself an oddity) had alerted her to the fact that the elementary school in East Machias, Maine, still maintained a school library and had proudly staked a claim—recognized in the Guinness Book of Universe Records—to be the last school library in the United States.[1]

Stevens names the next culprit, "library education," followed by the demise of academic libraries, which remained only as names on buildings, benefactors to the university. According to his prediction, the last public libraries, mid-21st century, received an enormous influx of funding from the Gates Foundation, and all those former Carnegie buildings still standing and all other public libraries became Gates Information Centers.

The name flaw written about in 2001 was repaired when the Board of Directors of the American Association of School Libraries (AASL) changed the name of the professional in the school library media center from "media specialist" back to "librarian" at their Midwinter meeting in 2010. However, a name does not save or destroy a profession. It is the persons in that profession who build the image and create the necessity for the things that a professional offers to clientele. This person becomes the school library to those observing those things, and when the observations are bland or even negative, it may take much more than one new event or a new person to create a different image to change those past perceptions.

Names do sometimes set the stage. In many countries and some states the title is now "teacher librarian" to reflect the role as a teacher as well as someone who administers or manages a library. In the role of "teacher," the school librarian collaborates or co-teaches with other teachers. The school librarian leads teachers in helping students become better students, creating new information from their research projects and building their infrastructure to become informed citizens in a democratic society and lifelong learners. In this role school librarians are an essential, necessary partner in the school. School librarians who accept a leadership role in the education of students very definitely have a future and are the catalysts to revising and improving perceptions. They do this in a world where everything is in a state of constant change.

How Fast Everything Changes

A major challenge to anyone working in today's information environment is that awareness of how rapidly things change, but it is very difficult for people to change. One of the things that changes is the unbelievable amount of information made available through the constantly being invented and updated technologies. Information is created and placed in this flood of resources already available. But it is happening, and the school librarian has become the person to keep current and to help teachers and students find the best and most accurate information available while making sure those teachers and students are able to use the steady stream of new devices that become available.

Keeping up is possible with continuous professional development as described in Chapter 12. Reading the literature and learning trends through participation on blogs and tweets, learning in professional associations, and sharing with colleagues begins the process. The indispensable school librarian not only is personally on top of everything but is responsible for sharing these trends and changes with teachers, administrators, and other colleagues. The person with information who shares it with others demonstrates leadership and the ability to gather, assemble, and analyze. Such analysis of the world outside a single school prepares the school librarian to join with those in the school to plan an appropriate program for the school.

Maintaining a School Library Program
That Is Appropriate

One person cannot hope to decide what makes an appropriate program or be able to maintain this alone. Throughout this text the authors explain the necessity for involving others in designing appropriate school library programs. This planning requires the input and support of teachers, students, and parents who will help to gain the approval of administrators, school board members, and the community. The key to this is the school librarian who accepts a leadership role. But what, exactly, is that role now and in the future?

The School Librarian as Leader

A statement often quoted is if it looks like a duck, walks like a duck, and quacks like a duck, it must be a duck. A school librarian who looks like a leader is managing the resources available, making sure they are accessible for all. This leader is collaborating and co-teaching with teachers. The school librarian as leader approaches challenges with the knowledge that they can be solved, someone who provides suggestions to help with ideas and resources. This leader helps dissolve previous perceptions of those in the school who may have a more traditional concept of the school librarian.

The school librarian at the beginning of the 20th century was delighted to have electricity, the typewriter, the telephone, phonograph, cameras and film, and motion pictures. These seemed to provide all that could ever be desired. Thanks to Mr. Edison, students and teachers could read easily in the library. Librarians could type catalog cards. Mr. Bell provided fast communication between sites, and Mr. Edison also provided canned music. The development of the camera and film created the ability to provide photographs as a resource.

At the beginning of the 21st century, the rapidly expanding information resources and the communication links via computer generate new tasks and new challenges. Even the facility is under scrutiny. The suggestion that a library is not necessary because students and teachers may find all their information on the Internet appears threatening to some, an opportunity to others. Certainly the numbers of school districts faced with budget deficits in the first decade of the 21st century have viewed the school librarian as expendable. Many have been returned to the classroom to teach and a paraprofessional placed in the library. In other districts, school librarians have been assigned to two or more schools. Those situations require a new approach to the role of the school librarian.

Meeting the challenge presented by new technologies and constantly changing educational requirements demands a leadership role for school librarians. They choose from the available technologies which ones will be most helpful and which will help teachers and students access the available information. School librarians help users make the best choices from the vast array before them. School librarians help teachers and students learn how to narrow their queries, thus saving countless wasted hours in searching. School librarians also search the Internet for websites and bookmark them for student use, again saving wasted hours in searching. With the ever-increasing quantities of information available online, it is even more important to help students recognize misinformation they find in online resources. The librarian becomes an information consultant and leader in the use of information.

As librarians become curriculum leaders, helping teachers understand what is being taught in every classroom, they can lead in the development of inquiry learning that will move with students as they go through school. Because librarians have no assigned interest in a subject area or a grade level, they can help teachers move beyond their responsibility for particular content into merging that content with other disciplines and other grade levels. This will help students prepare for a world where disciplines merge or disappear and in which they will change jobs many times during their work lives.

The school librarian as leader is in the appropriate place in every school to ensure that all students have access to accurate, relevant information that they can read, understand, and trust. They teach students to question what they read anywhere, but perhaps most important, what they read on social media.

The present role of helping students understand and plan for their lives as adults will become even more complicated in the future. Recognizing the need to be prepared for more than one occupation, to know how to get training as jobs become obsolete will become more critical as new inventions take over positions formerly held by human workers.

Gathering Support

This text has constantly posed the need to garner support from the broad community, a community that is more than aware of the contributions of the school library in the lives of students and the necessity of the school librarian to ensure access to information for all. These contributions are repeated here.

Student Support

School librarians help their students learn that their library belongs to them and is the go-to place to solve problems, both educational and personal. When students learn the library belongs to them and it is open to them to meet their needs, they will begin taking responsibility for some of their learning. Allowing students to work with other students in groups teaches a skill that students must master and continue to improve throughout their school years and it will lead into more successful adult lives.

Students become library advocates as, from elementary through high school, the library is available to help them prepare for becoming adults through a multitude of educational opportunities they will practice so they are ready when they graduate from high school. Students in today's world need to be ready to change jobs and even vocations as these will be changing throughout their careers. They need to know what skills are needed for any vocation of interest to them, the pros and cons for those jobs, and exactly what training or education is required. They also need to recognize what it takes to keep current in their choice and how to find another opportunity when one is closed. This information they can test and retest whenever they need to find answers.

Students using their library learn what it takes to become an adult, especially in an age when so much has been given to so many of them over such a long time. The opportunities their grandparents had are not the same as those available to their parents and they will be even more different and more difficult for them to achieve. The challenge to prepare our students for adulthood belongs in what happens in their basic education. Students must graduate prepared and not finding themselves stumbling into the world after high school. Beginning in kindergarten, students are given opportunities to learn more than what a police officer or a chef does, but what it takes to be a policeman or a chef and maybe a government official or elected official.

Students must learn how to find answers to questions and how to choose ways to solve problems that will confront them. Many people do not choose to vote in an election for those who will govern them, and if parents do not model this behavior for their children, the school librarian can work with teachers to make clear this responsibility for students as citizens in a democracy. Inviting school board members to visit the school can help students learn that person's responsibilities in their lives. Meeting a city council member or a state legislator is as important as meeting an author or illustrator of a book.

The other responsibility of the school librarian is to help students understand about the global community and how they will be living in a multicultural world. Accepting differences among people, whether it is the food they eat, the furniture in their houses, the way they dress, the religion they follow, or the culture that governs what they do as members of their communities, is a good start to helping students begin to understand their place in the world. The school librarian can help teachers make contact with students and teachers in other countries and learn to celebrate differences.

Teacher Support

Support may be gained with teachers through two major approaches. First, teachers must understand and agree with what is needed to provide an outstanding program within the school library where collaboration and co-teaching with teachers means all the teachers in the building work together to provide the best education possible. They are introduced to this concept from a librarian's first day in a school. Support is built through demonstrations of teachers and librarian working together to build units of instruction, co-teaching, and evaluation of each unit and each student's response to the unit, noting what is most effective and what changes are suggested to make the unit even stronger the next time it is taught.

The second approach is to explain and demonstrate the creative ways that will extend co-teaching and learning throughout the curriculum. Gather all the teachers in the school who believe that sharing in the design and implementation of curriculum is best done with the participation of groups of teachers rather than a single teacher in a single classroom. These groups of teachers include those often considered special: art, music, physical education teachers, the guidance counselor, all teachers in any building. Sharing the effect of these multi-teacher experiences with students will grow, sometimes slowly but often rapidly as students become more active in their learning process. The first person to share these effects is with the school's administrators.

Administrator Support

The support of teachers, students, and parents helps convince all principals, even one who was impossible, to help to revise a previous perception of the role of the school library and the librarian. Presenting examples of successful learning and research assignments, collaboration with teachers, exciting activities going on in the library from a graphic book corner to a wider area for makerspaces, to a presentation from a member of the community to support a unit of instruction, all point out that the school has an outstanding school library program.

Any principal with a model school library program has the ability to convince superintendents, school boards, and administrators in other districts of what a quality information center in a school requires. The school librarian may do this by helping the principal separate the best from all the proposed new developments being proposed by other principals and superintendents.

Parent Support

Parents, as essential in the care and welfare of their children, are interested in what happens to their children in those daily hours in school. They are directly involved in what goes on in classrooms and in the arenas where their children participate in sports activities. They will need to have the importance of the library both explained and demonstrated to them as often as possible. Encourage students to bring their parents to the library to learn about its role in their education; and involving parents in the library program may result in their volunteering to help. Help has many forms from overseeing activities in the library, storytelling to small groups or classrooms, to providing content as a visiting lecturer. They also become advocates for school library improvements when they are presented to a school board for approval.

Community Support

The more members of the community who are directly involved in a school, the more likely issues like bonds for more funding will pass. Members of the community have much to offer when their skills are identified and they are invited to help. This goes beyond the police officer who comes to the school to help with child safety, which is very important. However, high school students need to learn about different occupations in the community; the mechanic who repairs cars, the car salesperson, the plumber, the electrician, the television repair person, the construction worker, all provide information for those students who are not planning to go to a higher education institution. Any member of the community who can help students when they are creating in the makerspace area is golden. Those who have expertise they can share with students related to a topic taught in the school are also to be considered to share this knowledge with students.

Not Jumping onto Every Bandwagon

Bandwagons are always appealing. They are colorful; the people on board are having a great time; they are encouraging you to join them, often with very few concrete reasons why. Speakers at conferences can be very certain that what they are suggesting is absolutely the best thing any school librarian can do. In their 45 minutes, they show you all the bells and whistles, the smiling faces of everyone who is participating, and the speaker and you both go home. The challenge then is to look critically at what is suggested and see exactly what will happen if you are able to get it ready, introduce it, and sustain it, and, most of all, what will happen if it is not sustainable. That is why one always checks a bandwagon very carefully to see if the wheels are sturdy, the wagon itself has sides to keep people from falling off, and there is a good person to drive the horses. A good question is always, is there another similar bandwagon? Does it do the same thing? Where are the bandwagons that lost a wheel? What happens to the bandwagon when the driver moves to another school?

Often administrators need help in seeing all sides of the next proposed change. Is it a good one even though other principals appear to be embracing the concept, which may be an adaptation of an idea rather than an edict? In one area, principals decided that it would be good for high school libraries to model local bookstores by offering a café in the library. Space was cleared and leisure furniture was moved in along with coffee. Little attention was paid to the need for someone to run the café or the effect it might have on students who needed a place to study with a relaxed social area at hand. No one seemed to question why the library was a better space than the school cafeteria, which would have seemed more appropriate to serve as a coffee shop and where chatter would not be a major factor.

Then there are the models that come down from state boards of education or even the U.S. Department of Education. These come back to schools with superintendents and principals when they attend their professional development events, conferences, and professional association meetings. Many times such "good" things are sold as having been carefully researched, but this is most often not the reality of the situation. However, programs can wreak havoc before slowly disappearing when the next concept emerges. Whether it is a political movement or an educational trend, the school librarian assesses the situation and works to help teachers and students survive until the next big happening. They look at what needs to be done and work with teachers to implement it in the best way possible to continue students preparing for their lives as adults. Occasionally something does get a great deal of attention and it may seem to be the best solution when one is making a careful analysis. However, when any cracks begin to form, the school librarian creates ways to move forward. In all of the situations discussed earlier, the school librarian adopts that leadership role.

The Future

Because your authors are in the "half full" category, they believe the school librarian and the school library have a future. This section discusses the future in terms of place, content, and lifelong learning. The first includes the actual location, place, the school's location.

Place

The school librarian is currently a part of a location called "school." It is likely that the bricks and mortar school will continue for the foreseeable future in spite of the proliferation of online opportunities. School librarians will be needed to collaborate and co-teach, making sure concepts, teaching methods, and resources are helping students learn.

Some locations are changing as different concepts appear. When students were isolated from schools in Australia, education was offered over radio transmission. That education was a form of government-provided education. Now commercial entities are offering distance education for parents who want to keep their children at home. In this situation, teachers preparing courses for distant students should have the assistance of a school librarian in the preparation and delivery of the content. The websites needed in the bricks and mortar schools are equally essential here.

Other parents, for a variety of reasons, choose to homeschool their students. For these students, school is wherever they have their lessons. Some parents may ask the school librarian for materials to teach, and they may wish to use online resources available to all students. Making sure parents of homeschooled students know of these resources is a responsibility of the school librarian. School districts have records of students who are being homeschooled, and school librarians send information and instructions concerning online resources to the home. They may also work with public librarians who may be the location for those parents to find information to share resources.

School districts lose students when commercial vendors offer charter schools that compete for tax dollars to finance education. Because these schools must make a profit, extra teaching staff beyond the classroom teacher is not available. Because school districts have difficulty managing on the funding allocated, managing schools to make a profit often fails. When these schools have no librarian, doing small action research studies and reporting the value of a library in student learning may draw students back to the public school.

Some school districts apply for charter school funds and students in these schools remain a part of the "parent" district. However, how students are assigned to charter schools makes a difference in the students who are left behind. When a school district differentiates between teaching staff and students who attend the school, offering a lottery system to allow students to attend, the students who attend schools not designated "charter" become even farther behind their peers. It creates the need for a very dedicated school librarian to help teachers in those schools be affirmative in a difficult role. It is more important that disadvantaged students learn not only how to read, but also what opportunities are available for them through high school and beyond.

In most school districts, the distribution of students goes with the housing around the school. School librarians, as new hires, are probably going to be assigned to that more difficult school. They will meet teachers who are also new hires, and this will provide an opportunity to move forward with exciting opportunities to help students who have learning challenges. They will have started school with fewer skills and so the library becomes even more important to help them achieve. Many of these students are from single-parent homes and many move frequently. It is very difficult for teachers who have a constantly revolving classroom. Helping teachers create an atmosphere where learning is fun and even entertaining will ensure that students will come to school and remain in school until they graduate. For the school librarian to remain in that school is also an incredible challenge because the desire to move will be incredible.

Content

In the not so distant past, children were expected to arrive at kindergarten knowing their letters, numbers, and colors. With more and more children going to preschool, many children are able to read when they begin school. This places a special burden on teachers in schools where children come from homes in neighborhoods described above. These children are labeled "disadvantaged," and it truly describes their situations. Designing school library experiences to reinforce learning in the classroom comes with collaborating with kindergarten and first-grade teachers to do just that. Giving bookmarks cut from colored construction paper can have them line up by color. Have students get in line by their name in alphabetical order or the last name of their book's author or the first word of the title. It takes a little more time to get ready to return to their room, but is a fun learning device.

School librarians collaborate with teachers to offer meaningful assignments regardless of the testing that may be lurking around the corner. Districts basing salary on the students' test scores increase the pressure. This increases the obligation for the school librarian to demonstrate ways to let students learn together, building on their experiences and moving forward, to try to engage high school students and community volunteers to help tutor students. As students find success, they are more likely to come to school rather than skipping and missing even more. School success even with students who move frequently from school to school should keep them interested in moving to the next grade until completing high school. One could surmise that a student who remains in school and doesn't leave to begin the path to prison will save the state the cost of long-term incarceration.

In many elementary schools, teachers may still feel less comfortable teaching science and math. The Science, Technology, Engineering, Math (STEM) movement may offer resources to help. However, librarians can provide ideas for solutions, perhaps encouraging high school students, parents, or other members of the community to help tutor students who are having STEM problems.

In the present, school districts have created magnet schools to give students who are focused on music and theater, science, or foreign language to have more time in school studying those subjects in depth in their curriculum. School librarians in these schools will serve more in the role of the special librarian in a library focused on a subject area. In the case of the foreign language magnet, a school librarian would need the ability to speak in at least one of the foreign languages.

Lifelong Learning

It is often very difficult to identify what is being taught in classrooms with what students will face after they graduate from high school. One example is memorizing and then spelling words that seem to have no relationship to the math problems or history essay assignments they take home, all as homework. What do students need to learn that may not be in the curriculum as such?

Students need to learn what it takes to live: what it takes to be successful as a wage earner, how to manage their finances and their lives. They need to learn what it means to live in a democratic society.

Beginning in kindergarten, as stated earlier, students need to learn more than what a police officer, firefighter, merchant, soldier, mayor, or teacher does, but what it takes to learn how to be one of those. Kindergarten children need to know and perhaps even go visit the first grade to learn how it is different. In many school districts, children move from a single-teacher classroom into different teachers for different subjects as early as grade four. If the change hasn't happened earlier, it does change with middle school.

Middle school students should learn about the different opportunities offered in high school, including what taking accelerated classes offers to those who are going to a college or university because it affects the amount of tuition they will be paying. Many students from low-income homes with parents who may not have graduated from high school will miss an opportunity to attend a higher education institution if they aren't encouraged to begin planning in middle school.

The first year of high school, the librarian, working with the guidance counselor, begins the process of helping students understand the types of education that prepares students for more successful lives. If a student appears to be ready to drop out of high school, that student must be given the directions for completing the GED. All other students are shown the financial possibilities for technical or trade schools as well as colleges and universities. They also need to be shown the long-term costs for borrowing money to pay for that education. Working and saving to go to higher education before starting can mean graduating debt free. Attending a community college may be preferable than trying to attend a four-year college immediately. On the other hand, many universities have excellent financial assistance for low-income students. Helping students find this information is critical.

Students of all ages need to learn how to recognize truth in what they hear and read in all forms of communication from casual conversation including tweets and blogs, to newspapers, radio, and television. We do not always recognize our own biases, and these affect how we react to situations. Broadcasts from stations with opposing political points of view have commentators presenting their news with widely varying commentary. They make it easy to compare what is being said to what might be the actual truth behind every statement. How much that is said is only part of the challenge; what is missing from the story may be an even larger form of bias. If our democracy is to survive, our students must be prepared to enter a world where they can make intelligent decisions about choosing persons to elect for government offices and propositions to support when the result of the count of votes dictates the possible law. Students need to learn that their responsibility as a citizen means voting in all elections, not just for the president of the United States. What are the candidates saying they support? What are they saying about problems local, state, and national? How reasonable is their solution to the problem?

Students must learn at all ages to question what they see, read, and hear. Tracing the ways an event such as a police action against a person is covered in newspaper reports, television news stations, and magazine articles from cities all over the United States is possible in this day of social media. What do the bloggers and tweeters say? What historical facts are used to show how frequently this happens? What is the truth of this?

A study of the promises found in commercials for over-the-counter drugs, even prescription drugs, can be researched and even checked by asking medical personnel about the drugs' ability to cure whatever they are said to cure. How would students research the impact of advertising on the setting of a trend? Why do some students insist on wearing a certain jacket or tennis shoes because of the brand and other students actually refuse to follow such fads?

At the beginning of "lifelong learning," many students leave high school with little knowledge of what it takes to survive, to find affordable housing, to apply and interview for a job, to buy food, to buy and drive a car and pay for the insurance and the expenses to keep an automobile running. They have no idea about credit cards and interest rates for unpaid balances, opening a checking account with the accompanying costs if there is charge for a minimum amount in it, why they need to open a savings account to save part of their salary.

If students are going to have a more successful life, they should continue their education after high school and even beyond. Students need to be aware that whatever and whenever they learn, they will need to continue to add new things to be able to move into new phases of their same jobs, or they need to be ready to look for a different job for which they will need different skills. To prepare students for lifelong learning means to make sure they understand a little of what that means and how they can plan to meet these challenges.

Survival

Pendulums swing and the current downswing in school libraries and librarians may seem to be a slippery slope. However, school librarians survive when they exert leadership in their schools, when they gather teachers to share their skills and creativity to provide a useful curriculum for every student. Teachers will follow the school librarian's leadership to craft better ways to teach and better ways to prepare students for their lives after they have left school.

Librarians have always been the last barricade to save our democracy. We protect the rights of citizens to access information and make sure the information they have is accurate, relevant, unbiased, and complete. School librarians protect access to information for their students who are just learning what it means to become an informed adult accepting their role of full citizenship. School librarians are the persons who will ensure that students will become informed adults, protecting their rights to information from the time they enter school, preparing them to become lifelong learners, and making sure they grow into informed citizens to protect their democratic society.

Ours is truly a noble profession, one that will have many hurdles along the way. However, when each day is over, you will know you have made a little difference in the lives of all the students in your school and a big difference in the lives of many, many others.

Exercises

1. Outline a 15-minute presentation for a teachers' meeting to present how school librarians work with teachers and the community to prepare students for life after high school.
2. Outline a 15-minute presentation for students with suggestions for how students can locate sources of funding for advanced training or enrollment in higher education institutions.
3. Outline a 15-minute presentation about opportunities for students who are interested in apprenticeship opportunities. Check with local unions about how someone becomes a member of that union.

Note

1. Norman D. Stevens, "The Last Librarian," *American Libraries* 32 (October 2001): 61.

Appendix A:
Sample Letter of Application

Your Street Address
City, State, ZIP
Date

Dr. _____, Superintendent
YYY Schools
Street Address
City, State, ZIP

Dear Dr. _____:

    Our University Placement Office has indicated that you are seeking applications for a position as school librarian for your ABC High School, and I am very interested in being a candidate for this position. My résumé is enclosed.

    I have a bachelor's degree in elementary education from the University of Z. When I finish my master's degree in library and information science at the University of X, I will be applying for (K–12) school library certification as an endorsement on my Instructor I certificate in elementary education.

    During the past year, I have prepared a portfolio of work completed in my program, including a proposal for funding (group project), an in-service education workshop to introduce teachers and students on how to use and the uses for a digital camera, a website for a fictional school, a two-page article that has been published in a professional school library publication, and a 45-minute speech written to present at a professional association meeting. During my practicum, I prepared two teaching units, collaborating with high school science teachers for the first where we added experiences for students with the new 3-D copy machine and all first-grade teachers who were revising their unit on community helpers. I also have three examples of senior research projects from three students who were under my supervision.

    My experience with technology includes extensive experience with _____, _____, _____, and _____. In addition, both schools in which I completed my practicum experience gave me the opportunity to share my skills using resources available on the statewide online database and the state's catalog of resources in academic, public, and school libraries available through interlibrary loan.

I am looking forward to hearing from you.

Sincerely,
J— Smith

Appendix B:
Questionnaire

Circle the correct response to each question.	-1	0	1	2	3	4	5
How does the library compare to others in the district?	not very well	don't know	almost as good as	as good as	better than	much better than	best in district
How many print items per student are in the library?	don't know	1	3	5	10	15	more than 15
In general, the collection of print items is:	out of date	of peripheral value	few recent titles, fair condition	some recent titles, some relevant	mostly relevant, most in good condition	mostly recent titles	recent, relevant, good condition
How many databases do you have?	none	1	4	6	6+	share with public library	connected to statewide resources
Do users produce learning materials?	teachers only	groups of students	only when assigned	Teachers produce many materials.	Students produce visuals.	Teachers produce multimedia lessons.	Teachers produce lessons; students produce portfolios.
We have a new technology plan.	don't know	Why?	I think so	took a survey	answered survey	made suggestions	voted on plan
We have new technologies.	don't know	We have a computer lab.	We are a BYOT school.	We have laptops to use in library.	We have WiFi throughout the school.	We have a 3D printer.	We are a 1-1 school.
Our technology and other resources are up-to-date.	don't know	We never discard anything.	We rarely discard anything.	We occasionally discard things.	We discard things yearly.	We discard things semiyearly.	We constantly evaluate and discard.
Library is used for:	discipline	study hall	entertainment	supplementary use	support for curriculum	extension of learning	integral to learning
Library is used by __ % of potential users.	don't know	0–9	10–20	21–40	41–60	61–80	over 80
Library collection print and online is used by at least 50% of students.	don't know	never	once a year	each semester	once a month	every two weeks	once a week

Circle the correct response to each question.	-1	0	1	2	3	4	5
Students enjoy going to the library.	don't know	never	occasionally	some of the time	often	most of the time	always
Library is used by 50% of teachers.	don't know	never	once a year	each semester	once a month	every two weeks	once a week
Teachers choose time for use of the library based on instructional needs.	Never as they follow a rigid schedule.	occasionally	when reminded	some of the time	often	most of the time	always
Library is open before and after school.	never	only for faculty	by special plans	either before school or after school, but not both	often	most of the time	always
Librarian may leave the library.	no, has study hall	don't know	only for lunch	sends classroom collections	seldom visits classrooms	often visits classrooms	regularly visits classrooms
Librarian is a teacher.	don't know	Information literacy only	supports the classroom teacher	co-teaches occasionally	co-teaches with 10% of teachers	co-teaches with 50% of teachers	is an integral part of planning and teaching
Librarian and principal have a five-year plan for the library.	don't know	no plan	The principal speaks to librarian when passing.	The principal meets with librarian yearly to discuss program.	The librarian submits annual report.	The librarian keeps principal informed of needs.	The plan is provided by librarian and the principal approves.
The principal supports the library.	never	occasionally	whenever reminded	some of the time	often	most of the time	always
Teachers support the library.	never	occasionally	whenever reminded	some of the time	often	most of the time	always
Students support the library.	never	occasionally	whenever reminded	some of the time	often	most of the time	always
Library has an effect on teaching and learning.	never considered	don't know	perhaps	occasionally	often	most of the time	always

Appendix C:
List of Research Resources

The books in this list can be helpful in planning ways to find out if your program is successful in meeting your goals and objectives. They describe various ways to conduct research, and it should be noted that research can be a bumpy road. As with any other endeavor in life, one becomes more proficient when one has time to practice. For someone who only occasionally seeks answers, it is helpful to carry out your research with guidance from someone whose main interest is conducting research. This person may be within your school district or may be a professor in a nearby college or university who would enjoy having the opportunity to carry out a research study in a local school district. School districts have become wary of having students "tested" outside of the required testing, and teachers have become less willing to respond to anyone unless they are obligated to do so.

This annotated list shares books that will be helpful as you begin your plans. They will reinforce things you learned in a research class you may have taken. These are listed in alphabetical order by author.

Rachel Applegate. *Practical Techniques for Librarians* (Santa Barbara, CA: Libraries Unlimited, 2013)
"What this does is put in one place, in your hands, an intensely practical evaluator's kit with tools and plans. With this book you and your colleagues can examine individual projects and ongoing services. You can construct effective plans for keeping tabs on how your library is doing. With this book and a general-purpose suite of office software, you can gather, analyze, and report your own evaluation data. You will know what tools are best for what data, and require what staff time and effort. You will be able to knowledgeably solicit assistance and employ consultants, advanced training, or more powerful software." (p. viii)

Susan E. Beck and Kate Manuel. *Practical Research Methods for Librarians and Information Professionals* (New York: Neal-Schuman Publishers, 2008)
This book covers the research process, content analysis, interviews and focus groups, observations, experimental research, bibliometrics, action research, and classroom research.

Mary Snyder Broussard, Rachel Hickoff-Cresko, and Jessica Urick Obelin. *Snapshots of Reality: A Practical Guide to Formative Assessment in Library Instruction* (Chicago: Association of College and Research Libraries, 2014)

This practical book is written for the college librarian who wishes to evaluate classroom instruction with techniques that do not take time apart from actual instruction.

Douglas Cook and Lesley Farmer, eds. *Using Qualitative Methods in Action Research: How Librarians Can Get to the Why of Data* (Chicago: Association of College and Research Libraries, 2011)

Written by academic librarians, this book covers mostly testing the results of teaching information literacy.

Peter Hernon, Robert E. Dugan, and Danuta A. Nitecki. *Engaging in Evaluation and Assessment Research* (Santa Barbara, CA: Libraries Unlimited, 2011)

These authors present the components of the research study, the language of research, designing studies, collecting data, and reporting findings.

Joseph R. Matthews. *The Evaluation and Measurement of Library Services* (Westport, CT: Libraries Unlimited, 2007)

"The intended audience for this book is library directors and managers in all types of libraries who are interested in evaluating one or more services" (p. xix). "The purpose of this book is to provide a set of tools that will assist any librarian in evaluating a particular library service, whether covered in this book or not. The goal is to remove some of the mysteries surrounding the process of evaluation so that many librarians will see the value of performing evaluation in their libraries" (p. xx). Different areas of library service such as reference, electronic resources, and library instruction services are covered in individual chapters.

Lynn Silipigni Connaway and Marie L. Radford. *Research Methods in Library and Information Science*, 6th ed. (Santa Barbara, CA: Libraries Unlimited, 2017)

A basic reference and textbook to teach research methodology in schools of library and information science. Connaway and Radford cover all types of research and statistics to analyze findings. They also describe how to get results published, and for doctoral students, how to write a research proposal.

Ruth V. Small and Marcia A. Mardis, ed. *Research Methods for Librarians and Educators: Practical Applications in Formal and Informal Learning Environments* (Santa Barbara, CA: Libraries Unlimited, 2018)

Judith A. Sykes. *Conducting Action Research to Evaluate Your School Library* (Santa Barbara, CA: Libraries Unlimited, 2013)

This is a workbook with space provided to take notes. A detailed section on tools for each step in the action research project features guiding questions for readers to consider while conducting their own projects. Five action research examples from the data collected are used to explain the process.

Barbara M. Wildemuth, ed. *Applications of Social Research Methods to Questions in Library and Information Science,* 2nd ed. (Santa Barbara, CA: Libraries Unlimited, 2017)
A basic textbook for research courses, it is also an excellent reference. A number of different authors discuss research questions, sampling, methods used to collect and analyze data, and report findings.

Appendix D: Presentation of a Five-Year Long-Range Plan*

For Library Development (2018–2023)

Goal: To bring the Thomas Alva Edison Middle School Library staff, program, and holdings to meet the needs of students and teachers.

Thomas Alva Edison Middle School is one of 25 schools in the Washington Area School District, a district with a varied population, from inner-city to upper-middle-class residential areas. Three of the 20 elementary schools, 1 of the 10 middle schools, and 2 of the 5 high schools are designated magnet schools serving children with exceptional skills in one or more areas. One high school is designated for the performing arts and the other for students interested in science and math. Students interested in vocational training attend a vocational program supported by the county.

All schools, elementary through high school, have librarians, guidance counselors, classroom art, music, and physical education instruction as well as band and chorus for interested students. Students may also participate in intramural sports.

Four high schools, excluding the performing arts magnet, participate in Class A football and baseball programs for boys. Girls' and boys' teams provide opportunities for basketball, indoor and outdoor track, soccer, swimming, and volleyball at all five high schools.

Edison Middle School, the designated magnet middle school, has 1,245 students. Because of its geographical location, 50 percent of the population comes from upper-middle-class homes in the immediate area, and the remaining 50 percent matriculates through an application and testing process. The school features strong science and math programs and offers four foreign languages. Spanish, French, and German are taught by onsite instructors, and Japanese instruction is delivered via an interactive video classroom. Because of the strong foreign language component, other areas of the curriculum stress a more global view than in the other, more traditional middle schools.

---

* Please note that the figures in this model plan are not based on any true costs but are there to serve as an example.

The international emphasis of this school means that students may be given priority for attendance if they are international residents or recent emigrants to the Washington Area Schools. A strong Teaching English to Speakers of Other Languages (TESOL) program resides here.

Because the school is a magnet school and the librarian is a proponent of the Learning Commons concept, this school library is in the process of being remodeled into a more flexible facility. Again, because it does serve as a model for the district, some extra funding for technology has been allocated and the results of providing devices to all students in the school is being tested to see the possibility of doing this in all the schools. While the school is wireless, methods are being discussed to make sure all students have access to resources at home.

A final caution is that this five-year plan is not cast in concrete. Changes in technology mean that what is being projected for even one year may be obsolete, particularly equipment, by the end of the year. Those purchases will be made when it becomes necessary.

Personnel

The Edison Middle School's librarian is a licensed professional who chairs the school's Curriculum Committee. This person is assigned the management of the library and those assigned to work in the program. In addition, the librarian attends departmental meetings as often as possible, and always when changes in curriculum are to be discussed.

Because of the strong technology component, the transmittal of instruction for some classes and the online resources in the library, a full-time technology manager is assigned to the library to handle technology problems, to oversee the school's wireless system, and to train the student Tech Squad as well as helping teachers use technology in their classrooms and any applications needed for units of instruction. Two clerks are assigned, one to the librarian and one to the technology manager to handle routine assignments.

The professional, technical, and clerical tasks can be accomplished with the existing personnel for the first two years. However, by the third year, the expansion of the activities in the Learning Commons and the increased use of the information resources in the school and online and from teachers' and students' homes will require additional materials and hardware and staff development workshops as well as individual help. Training teachers and students on how to make the best use of these resources as well as the circulation and maintenance will require an additional .5 professional librarian and a .5 technology manager. It is hoped that a single individual can be hired for the two half-time assignments. The additional clerical staff member will be able to assume responsibility for communication contacts as the distance program expands to add more variety to the school's curriculum and to assist with the additional teachers, students, and community members working in the learning commons on collaborative projects.

2018	2019	2020	2021	2022	2023
1 FTE Prof 1 FTE Tech	No change	No change	1.5 FTE Prof 1.5 FTE Tech	No change	No change
Total 2 FTE Professionals				3 FTE Clerks	

Facility

The library at Edison Middle School was recently remodeled so that the facility, with 10,000 square feet, easily accommodates 120 seated in the library and 30+ seats in the library classroom. With the installation of a wireless network in the school, students may use their own computers throughout the library and school to access all online resources in the library. The perimeter shelving around the library holds most of the remaining book collection with some on moveable shelves providing easy access for students at all times.

Because most of the newspaper and periodical collections are available online through the statewide database and the additional databases to which we subscribe, the library provides multiple copies of only 20 of the most often requested periodicals. These are available for students to read for pleasure as well as to use for research.

When the area was remodeled, ergonomic, easily moved small desks and tables were purchased to use in the library. These can easily be moved to accommodate individuals and small groups working on projects. The OPAC stations are near the circulation desk.

Because of the recent remodeling, we have made no budget allocation for the facility in our five-year plan.

Equipment

At present, the Edison Middle School Library maintains a collection of 30 laptop computers for student use if they are having problems with their present device. A careful record is being kept of the problems with these to help determine what devices will be placed on our next request for an equipment bid.

In the reading room, five stations support the OPAC and one station is for circulation. Another station is available in the office of each professional and each clerk (four stations until 2018 when staff is added).

Because all forms of media can be transmitted from the library to classrooms, there is little need to provide televisions, VCRs, or DVD players. We do have a television with VCRs and DVD players in case the system should malfunction.

We recognize that equipment purchases must be carefully planned so that equipment remains compatible. New items on the market are carefully tested to see that they provide a needed service and fit the current software collection or have the type of information needed to support the curriculum.

We also recognize that the estimated costs for equipment will seem high. However, the continuous upgrading of both software and hardware dictates a critical need for regular, sustained replacement of equipment. One item, a 3-D copier, will be purchased jointly for the use of three neighboring middle schools. Two other copiers will be shared by the other six middle schools.

Budget

Salaries for personnel must be estimated from the district's salary schedule for years of service and professional education. We've used $50,000 as a base salary for both professionals and $25,000 for the clerks just to help you understand how the increases would look. Calculations were to add 3 percent to each year's salary until 2017. Then salary increases include the additional half-time professional positions and the one additional clerical position.

Professional Salaries

2018	2019	2020	2021	2022	2023
	+3%	+3%	+.5 position	+3%	+3%
$50,000	$51,500	$53,045	$54,636	$56,275	$57,963
50,000	51,500	53,045	54,636	56,275	57,963
			27,318	28,137	28,981
			27,318	28,137	28,981
$100,000	$103,000	$106,090	$163,908	$168,824	$173,888

Clerical Salaries

$25,000	$25,750	$26,522	$54,634	$56,073	$57,755
$125,000	$128,750	$132,612	$218,542	$224,897	$231,643
				Grand Total	$1,061,511

Travel

A budget item also provides support for the librarian and the technology manager to attend workshops, conferences, and training sessions to learn about changes in library management, new technologies and their applications, new resources, and methods of teaching. The librarian also holds an office in the Association of State School Librarians. This funding supports travel to board meetings, conference planning sessions, and conference attendance. A higher increase is made in the year 2021 to accommodate the new persons in the media center.

2018	2019	2020	2021	2022	2023
$9,000	$10,000	$11,000	$15,000	$16,000	$17,000
				Grand Total	$78,000

Equipment

Computers used for the OPAC and other staff use; we would like to continue to purchase a higher level of computer. We have not placed these in this report because we remain unsure of those costs. We will need one replacement OPAC and one replacement for administration. Note in year 2019, a 3-D copier will be purchased for this school's exclusive use, and in 2021, a new server will be added.

Computer Software

Computer software purchase for upgrading systems is now being provided from the school district information technology office. In previous plans we have included purchase of databases here, but they have been moved to expenditures for the collection.

Collection

Analyzing the library collection is carried out to determine the quality of the collection to meet the needs of students and teachers. A schoolwide selection committee assists in the review of new materials that may be considered appropriate for purchase. Teachers and students are queried concerning their expectations for subject areas and interest levels to be met. Weeding procedures ensure that the collection is relevant, up-to-date, accurate, as interesting as possible, and provides the research materials needed to support and enhance the curriculum.

Our collection includes 32,000 books, or 25 books per student. Because we are purchasing e-book readers, we will be adding e-books to our collection as well as new hardbound books and some paperback books. Many of these titles are requested by students for leisure reading. We anticipate spending $10 per pupil for the print collection.

2018	2019	2020	2021	2022	2023
$12,450	$12,450	$12,450	$12,450	$12,450	$12,450
				Total	$74,700

As stated earlier, most of the renewable subscriptions for periodicals and newspapers are available online through the statewide database. The cost of this item includes the duplicate copies of 20 hardcopy periodicals for a yearly cost of $2,400 per year.

Total: $14,000

Budget Analysis

	2018	2019	2020	2021	2022	2023
Salaries	$125,000	$128,750	$133,612	$218,542	$224,898	$230,709
Travel	9,000	10,000	11,000	15,000	16,000	17,000
Collection	12,450	12,450	12,450	12,450	12,450	12,450
Renewables	2,400	2,400	2,400	2,400	2,400	2,400
	$148,850	$153,500	$159,462	$248,392	$255,848	$262,559

Salaries	$1,061,511
Travel	78,000
Collection	74,700
Renewables	14,000
Grand Total	$1,227,311

Appendix E: Publications List

This list has been prepared to assist building-level school librarians who want to share exciting information from their own programs and activities or a paper they have written for a state conference that might have an audience in other states. By reviewing announcements concerning topics of interest to the editor and requirements for submission of papers, school librarians may choose an audience for any article they might produce. This list contains the name of the periodical and, when available, the address, telephone number, URL, editor, information concerning the editorial policy, and requirements for publication. Journals published by professional associations have editors who tend to rotate frequently because the task is often a volunteer position. Commercial publishers, in contrast, hire editors to fill regular positions. Because topics for issues change frequently and submission guidelines may also change, it is wise to use the URL to get the most up-to-date information about publishing in each periodical.

Some basic information shown below includes the following:

1. What is the purpose of the periodical?
2. How long should a manuscript be?
3. Is the journal refereed?
4. Does the journal usually have theme issues?
5. What style manual is required?
6. How do I submit a manuscript?

The information below is very brief and often incomplete. Someone planning a submission must check the website for the most up-to-date and complete information.

Children and Libraries: The Journal of the Association for Library Service to Children

Association for Library Service to Children
A Division of the American Library Association
50 East Huron Street
Chicago, IL 60611-2795
Telephone: (312) 944-6780
URL: www.ala.org
Editor: Sharon Korbeck Verbeten
820 Spooner Court
DePere, WI 54115
Telephone: (920) 339-2740
CALeditor@yahoo.com

1. "Primarily serves as a vehicle for continuing education of librarians working with children which showcases current scholarly research and practice in library service to children and spotlights significant activities and programs of the Association."

2. Scholarly/Research on personal research pieces, assessments, dissertations, surveys and other surveys. 3–10 pages double-spaced.

   "Best Practice" Pieces about a library's successful (and even not-so-successful) children's programs, 1,500 words or less including how funded and promoted, attendance, advance planning, feedback on the program, quotes from staff and attendees, and high-resolution photos from the event.

   Longer features on well-researched topics and themes relevant and of interest to children's librarians and others interested in library service to children; digital books and other technologies; and interviews with children's book authors/illustrators.

   "The Last Word" highlights brief, light essays from children's librarians such as a humorous story about a library experience; a short trivia quiz or puzzle about children's literature; a brief, creatively written insight on library service, children's literature, or programming; a very short question-and-answer interview with a popular author; a funny story about what kids are overheard saying in libraries. Length should not exceed 300 words.

3. Yes

4. Sometimes

5. *The Chicago Manual of Style*

6. Submit to the editor by email as a rich text directly into the body of the email.

Journal of Research on Libraries and Young Adults

Young Adult Library Association
A Division of the American Library Association

50 East Huron Street
Chicago, IL 60611-2795
Telephone.e: (312) 944-6780 ext. 2128
Editor: Denise E. Agosto

1. "To enhance the development of theory, research, and practices to support young adult library services, as emphasized in YAL-SA's National Research Agenda."

2. 4,000 to 7,000 words or 20–25 pages with line spacing set at double space.

3. Yes

4. Yes

5. *The Chicago Manual of Style*

6. Write a 100–200 word abstract with title, author, and author's address and contact on the front page. The second page should have the title and the beginning of the abstract. The manuscript should follow with endnotes at the end of the text. Submit in .doc, .txt. or .rtf files.

Knowledge Quest

American Association of School Librarians
A division of the American Library Association
50 East Huron Street
Chicago, IL 60611
Telephone: (312) 944-6780 ext. 4386
Fax: (312) 664-7459
URL: www.ala.org
Editor: Meg Featheringham
mfeatheringham@ala.org

1. "Substantive information to assist building-level librarians, supervisors, library educators, and other decision makers concerned with the development of school library programs and services."

2. 2,500–3,000 words

3. No

4. Each *KQ* has a mini-theme for the feature articles; the other articles published are unsolicited manuscripts that the *KQ* Editorial Board has accepted.

5. *The Chicago Manual of Style*

6. Submit manuscripts; can be solicited online at http://knowledgequest.aasl.org/write/.

Library Journal

123 William Street, Suite 802
New York, NY 10038

Telephone: (646) 380-0700
URL: ljinfo@mediasourceinc.com
Editor-in-Chief: Michael P. Kelly

1. "Articles reach out to the profession in a broad way, or offer useful information and ideas to others in an accessible and readable style."

2. They "welcome either queries or finished articles, via email if possible. A query can consist of just a paragraph or several. Describe what you plan to cover and your approach. Tell us your connection to it and your expertise. . . . If you have completed a draft of the article, send it attached to your email. If you're attaching a Word document with your pitch or submission, please include your name and contact info in the attachment." 1,800 to 2,700 words.

   Backtalk: "Opinion pieces and rants about topics and concerns in the library profession." 900 words.

3. No

4. No

5.

6. Submit your idea or opinion piece by email to Meredith Schwartz at mschwartz@mediasourceinc.com.

Phi Delta Kappan

Phi Delta Kappa
1525 Wilson Blvd., Suite 705
Arlington, VA 22209
Telephone: (800) 766-1156
URL: www.pdkind.org
Editor: Joan Richardson

1. "Addresses issues related to K–12 edition"

2. Should not exceed 3,000 words.

3. No

4. *Kappan* publishes a call for manuscripts identifying themes of interest to editors in January or February in the magazine. No issue focuses on a single topic.

5. APA

6. Manuscripts must be submitted by email, preferably as Microsoft Word documents. Articles sent by email or as PDF files will not be accepted. Include an abstract (not to exceed 100 words) with your article and a cover letter that identifies the writer and provides complete contact information to manuscripts@pdkintl.org.

School Libraries in Canada: A National Journal Supporting School Library Learning Commons Research & Practice

Following the closure of the Canadian Library Association, CSL became the new home for Canada's school library standards, the journal, and other resources. Please check their website for new information concerning this publication: http://www.canadianschoollibraries.ca.

School Libraries Worldwide

Editors: Marcia Mardis and Nancy Everhart
School of Information
College of Communication & Information
Tallahassee, FL 32306-2100
Fax: (780) 492-7622

1. "Current research on any aspect of school librarianship." "Authors need to be mindful of the international audience."

2. Should not exceed 6,000 words

3. Yes

4. Yes

5. APA

6. Submit manuscripts word-processed or typed, double-spaced to the editors.

School Library Connection

Libraries Unlimited, an imprint of ABC-CLIO, LLC
130 Cremona Drive, Suite C
Santa Barbara, CA 93117
Telephone: (800) 368-6868 x844, 866-270-3856

1. "Articles focus on school libraries—instructional leadership, management and operations, and the library in the context of the educational community."

2. Typically 1,500 words

3. No

4. Yes

5. *Chicago Manual of Style*

6. Submit articles as attachments to an email to their topic center editors:

   - Operations and Management—Carl Harvey: charvey@schoollibraryconnection.com

- Instructional Leadership—Leslie Preddy: lpreddy@school-libraryconnection.com

- Library in Context—Rebecca Morris: rmorris@schoollibrary-connection.com

School Library Journal

123 William Street, Suite 802
New York, NY 10038
Telephone: (646) 380-0700
URL: ljinfo@mediasourceinc.com
Associate Editor: Sarah Bayliss
sbayliss@mediasourceinc.com

1. "Issues of interest to the school library and greater education community"

2. "Our feature articles rarely exceed 2,500 words; opinion pieces are generally 600–700 words."

3. No

4. No

5. Submit a summary of your article in 400 words or less to the associate editor listed above. "Before hitting 'send,' please familiarize yourself with existing *School Library Journal* content to ensure that you are breaking new ground and/or have a fresh, useful opinion on a topic that is relevant to our readers. Please be as specific as possible." Ideas need backup with relevant data that presents new thinking.

School Library Research

American Association of School Librarians
A Division of the American Library Association
50 East Huron Street
Chicago, IL 60611
Telephone: (312) 944-6780 ext. 4386
Fax: (312) 440-9374
URL: www.ala.org
Editors: Mega Subramaniam and Melissa Johnston
mmsubram@umd.edu   mjohnsto@westga.edu

1. "To promote and publish high-quality research concerning the management, implementation, and evaluation of school library programs."

2. 15–30 double-spaced pages in 12-point type with one-inch margins.

3. Yes

4.

5. *Chicago Manual of Style,* 16th ed.

6. Submit your research paper through the form on the AASL website or email directly to co-editor (Microsoft Word files preferred).

Teacher Librarian: The Journal for School Library Professionals

Editor: Deborah Levitov
3401 Stockwell Street
Lincoln, NE 68506
dlevitov@teacherlibrarian.com

1. "Teacher Librarian: the Journal for School Library Professionals is one of the leading journals designed specifically for librarians working with K–12 students as well as with their colleagues teaching in the classroom and with administrators."

2. Features are 1,800–2,200 words, including references.

3. Yes

4. No

5. APA

6. Submit manuscripts via email to the editor: dlevitov@teacherlibrarian.com or associate editor: ckaaland@teacherlibrarian.com.

Tech Trends

Association for Educational Communications and Technology
320 W. 8th St. Ste 101
Bloomington, IN 47404-3745
Telephone: (877) 677-8328 or (812) 335-7675
Editor: Charles B. Hodges

1. "To provide a vehicle for the exchange of information among professional practitioners concerning the management of media and programs, the application of educational technology principles and techniques . . . that can contribute to the advancement of knowledge and practice in the field."

VOYA (Voice of Youth Advocates)

740-294-5878
Editor: RoseMary Ludt
rmludt@voyamagazine.com

1. "Articles from youth advocates who wish to share philosophies, literary analysis, author interviews, research results, experiences, practical project ideas, or controversies that arise from working with youth."

2. Short articles: 800–1,700 words; longer articles: 3,500 words

3. No

4. No

5.

6. "First query the editor to see if your topic is of interest. Describe your article briefly along with your professional background, expertise, and perceived audience for the article and complete contacts for reaching you by mail, phone, and email. A word count of your manuscript."

Attach the double-spaced manuscript in 12-point type with one-inch margins on all sides as a .doc or .txt file.

Young Adult Library Services: The Official Journal of the Young Adult Library Services Association

Young Adult Library Association
A Division of the American Library Association
50 East Huron Street
Chicago, IL 60611-2795
Telephone: (312) 944-6780 ext. 2128
Editor: Linda W. Braun

1. Serves "as a vehicle for continuing education for library staff serving young adults, ages twelve through eighteen."

2. 20 pages, double-spaced

3. No

4. No

5. *The Chicago Manual of Style,* 15th ed.

6. Submit manuscripts up to 5 pages, double-spaced (including references, tables, notes, and bibliographies) via email attachment to the editor.

Appendix F:
Sample Budget

Project Director:
Organization:
Salary and Wages:

Name/Title of Position	Number	How Cost Was Calculated	Funds Requested	Funds Matched	Total
Project Director[a]	1	50% of yearly salary	$15,000	$15,000	$30,000
Project Manager[b]	1	20% of yearly salary	0	7,000	7,000
		Subtotal	$15,000	$22,000	$37,000

[a]The project director is a district employee and will be working on the project half-time or 50 percent of yearly salary. You are asking the funding agency to provide one-fourth of the project director's $60,000 salary, and the district is going to cover one-fourth of the salary as cost-sharing or matching funds.
[b]The project manager is also a member of the clerical staff and will be working on the project one-fifth of the time. You are going to provide 20 percent of the $35,000 salary as cost-sharing or matching funds.

Fringe Benefits					
Rate	Name	Salary Base	Funds Requested	Funds Matched	Total
30%	Director	$60,000	$9,000	$9,000	$18,000
30%	Manager	35,000		10,000	10,000
		Subtotal	$9,000	$19,000	$28,000

Because you have split the director's salary, it is reasonable to split the fringe benefits between the funding agency and the district.
The manager's salary is a cost benefit, and the 30 percent fringe is matching funds.

Consultant's Fees

Name/Type of Consultant	Number of Days	Daily Rate	Funds Requested	Funds Matched	Total
Project Evaluator	5	$1,000	$5,000	$0	$5,000
		Subtotal	$5,000		$5,000

Travel

From/To	Number of Persons	Number of Days	Food/Lodging[a]	Travel	Funds Requested	Funds Matched	Total
x to x	2	2	$800	$1,000	$1,800		$1,800
Various[b]	20	20	20,000	10,000	30,000		30,000
	Subtotal		$20,800	$11,000	$31,800		$31,800

[a]For food and lodging, use the district's per diem established travel amount. Districts sometimes use the government rate for the state. In this example, the flat rate of $200 per diem for lodging and meals is calculated.

[b]One purpose of the project is to bring school librarians to the district for a five-day institute. Therefore, the 20 librarians must have travel and per diem, and you won't know at the application stage from where or how these persons will be traveling. Establishing a flat amount of $500 for travel expenses would mean that most travel was within the state. To make sure you have budgeted enough for all participants, take the highest cost for a ticket within the area where your participants live and $1,000 for per diem.

Supplies and Materials[a]

Item	How Cost Was Calculated	Funds Requested	Funds Matched	Total
Office Supplies			$4,000	$4,000
Flash Drives		500		500
Software		20,500		20,500
	Subtotal	$21,000	$4,000	$25,000

[a]This would be an estimate of what you thought you would be spending based on use of materials in your district's offices for a year. The flash drives are for your participants to take their work home with them. You might need to purchase new software for the institute and send home with the participants if they need it to continue what they learned at the institute.

Services[a]

Item	How Cost Was Calculated	Funds Requested	Funds Matched	Total
Telephone			$1,000	$1,000
Duplication and Printing			4,000	4,000
Books		15,000		15,000
	Subtotal	$15,000	$5,000	$20,000

[a]Here, you estimate what you will spend to make calls to get participants to the institute, travel arrangements, and what it might cost to duplicate materials for the institute, perhaps to buy books for the office to plan the institute, or even to buy books to give to participants.

Other Costs				
Item	How Cost Was Calculated	Funds Requested	Funds Matched	Total
20 laptops	Bid price	$20,000	$20,000	$40,000
Stipends[a]	Per diem	5,000		5,000
	Subtotal	$25,000	$20,000	$45,000

[a]Allocated for the participants' districts to hire substitutes @ $50 per day for 5 days times 20 participants = $5,000.

Total Direct Costs			
Item	Funds Requested	Funds Matched	Total
Salary and Wages	$15,000	$22,000	$37,000
Fringe Benefits	9,000	19,000	28,000
Consultant's Fees	5,000	0	5,000
Travel	38,000	0	38,000
Supplies and Materials	21,000	4,000	25,000
Services	15,000	5,000	20,000
Other Costs	25,000	20,000	45,000
Total Direct Costs	$128,000	$70,000	$198,000

Indirect Costs			
Item	Funds Requested	Funds Matched	Total
Direct Costs	$128,000	$70,000	$198,000
Indirect Costs			19,800
Total Project Costs			$217,800

The indirect cost rate for this project is the state government rate of 10 percent.
If this was a multiyear project, you would need to make those calculations and then submit a figure for the entire grant period.

Appendix G:
Volunteers

Volunteers are asked to assist in the library program in many school districts. Care must be taken to make sure that the use of volunteers does not violate the teachers' contract and that the school administration is aware that volunteers are being recruited. A district-wide policy about the use of volunteers in schools may exist. If the district provides orientation and coordination, the school librarian can be relieved of responsibility for this part of the process.

If no district-wide program is in place, the librarian must do the following:

1. Inform the principal and other appropriate administrators of the scope of the volunteer program and the person or persons designated to take responsibility for it.

2. Develop job descriptions of the tasks expected of volunteers so interested people may anticipate their activities once they volunteer. These job descriptions will help the librarian plan the training for volunteers.

3. Recruit volunteers through the parent-teacher organization in the school, notes sent home with students, pleas to service organizations in the area, and any other means available.

4. Recruit a manager of volunteers. That is, enlist another person to assume responsibility for the attendance of volunteers. The volunteer coordinator frees the librarian from such time-consuming tasks as volunteer scheduling and rescheduling, accepting telephone calls for volunteers who cannot appear on their scheduled day, and so on. Otherwise, the volunteer program could take more time, consequently becoming more trouble than it is worth.

5. Ask volunteers to complete an information form (sample follows).

6. During orientation, explain your expectations to volunteers. If there is no district orientation, volunteers *must* be informed of their expected behavior toward students and information they may learn

about students. All information about the school, teachers, or the program must remain confidential and should remain at school. Volunteers must not discuss the activities in the library with their friends and neighbors, because this may be a violation of students' rights. Any volunteer who is unable to come at the designated time should call the volunteer coordinator well in advance to allow opportunity to call a substitute. Volunteers should also recognize that they will serve as "librarians" while in the library and should dress and behave appropriately.

7. Accurate records should be kept of volunteers' attendance, activities, and comments concerning possible revisions and volunteer program improvement. Careful evaluation can help reinforce good work by volunteers, encourage better performance, and help remove those who are not adding value to the program.

8. Plan a reward system for volunteers. Parties to honor them or other acknowledgements of their efforts will be appreciated and will encourage them to continue. The true test of volunteer devotion is continuing after their children leave the school.

9. Remember at all times that volunteers are directly linked to the school and to those people who can support the library program. Volunteers can be enthusiastic advocates of library activities.

Parent or Other Volunteer Form

Please complete this form and return it to the librarian.

Name_____

Address_____

Telephone Number_____

Cell Phone_____

Days you are available to volunteer:_____

(Please indicate 1, 2, 3 for your preference)

Monday   Tuesday   Wednesday   Thursday   Friday

Times you are available to come to the library:

_____

    a.m. only   p.m. only   a.m. and p.m.

Grades you prefer to work with:

Primary   Elementary   Middle School   High School

I would like to (check as many as apply):

___ read stories to children   ___ prepare orders and book lists

___ prepare a bulletin board   ___ assist with computers

___ duplicate learning materials   ___ help circulate materials

___ other, please specify

Appendix H:
Writing a Technology Plan

Here are some questions to consider before coordinating the writing of a technology plan:

Who will appoint the members of the planning committee? How well does this group represent the school district or individual schools? Are there varying levels of expertise in using these technologies present in your committee—the expert, the average user, the reticent?

How often should the planning committee meet? Consider all the logistics. When will meetings be held? Where can they be held? How long will they last? Who will attend? Who will chair the meeting? Who will design the agenda? Will you use a professional consultant?

Can you collect sample technology plans from similar schools or districts? Is it possible to visit a benchmark school or district? Will committee members be able to attend expositions, conferences, or professional development opportunities to observe best practices?

What technology resources are currently available in your school and district? How are these resources being used?

Will the plan be evaluated and assessed by the same committee after completion?

The Instructional Technology Plan, as a physical document, can run from as few as twenty to several hundred pages long, depending on the size and complexity of the school or district. There is no template to follow when writing the plan, but it will be helpful to look at other school or district documents and use a similar writing style. Match the layout, type, and overall design to what the stakeholders are used to seeing. Share the document in draft status to allow everyone in the group to contribute to and proofread the plan. If possible, send drafts in hard copy as well as posting the draft to a website. Get feedback in any way possible, and use technology to do this (email, discussion boards, wikis, etc.).

The Instructional Technology Plan can be long and overwhelming to nontechnical people, and ultimately, the school board will need to approve it.

Be sure to include an executive summary, which contains concise descriptions of the major initiatives, budget, and time line.

Typically, the Instructional Technology Plan consists of:

Cover sheet
Title page
Table of contents
Acknowledgements
Executive summary
Committee membership
Vision and mission statements (might include philosophy)
Demographics (community, schools, academic ranking)
Data collection, analysis, and reporting
Critical issues
    Infrastructure and facilities
    Equipment
    New and emerging technologies
    Networking and security
    Funding
    Acceptable use policies
Implementation
    Public relations
    Professional development
    Incentives/reward system
    Purchasing
    Community resources
    Legal aspects
    Curriculum, instruction, and evaluation
    Maintenance
Evaluation
Budget
Bibliography or reference list
Glossary
Appendices
Index

Appendix I:
Article for the *Los Angeles Times*

"How to Make Your Voice Heard in Washington"
George Miller and John Lawrence

Since the November elections, we've seen unprecedented numbers of Americans speaking out on public policy. Voters want to influence their lawmakers on high-stakes issues from health care to climate change, education to immigration, foreign affairs to trade policy. The question, for many, is how to communicate effectively, especially when Washington sometimes seems impervious to the average citizen. Between us, we've spent eighty years working in Congress and we know something about effective constituent communications. There are a handful of unwritten rules that can amplify your voice in these tempestuous times.

Every year, concerned groups and individuals flock to Washington to make their cases on Capitol Hill. That's worthwhile, but there is an easier way, and one that may give you an even better chance of meeting face to face not with a staffer but with your senator and Congress member themselves.

Check the "full calendar" listings on Web pages for the House and Senate—or use the portal at the Library of Congress website—www .congress.gov—to see when a district or state "work period" is scheduled. . . . That means your representatives will be in their home districts.

Call your representative's local office to find out when and where he or she will be holding office hours, touring schools and businesses, and holding town hall meetings.

Then call the legislator's D.C. office—the operator at (202) 224-3121 can connect you—and request a meeting in the district office. Be respectful but persistent: if your representatives can't see you during the upcoming district or state work period, when can they?

Make sure to explain that you are a constituent; politicians do not enjoy long careers if they snub their voters. Request a 10 minute meeting. Be clear about the topic and be flexible about when you can meet. If you want to advocate for or against an education matter, include a representative of a teachers group, PTA parents; if health care is your issue, bring along a doctor, a hospital administrator, or a patient advocate.

Know the status of the issue or the bill in question. Is it in committee; is it scheduled for the floor? Again, the Library of Congress website can help. Demonstrating knowledge of the legislative process will make your discussion more effective.

Argue your position clearly and simply, and be very specific about what you expect the legislator to do. Don't issue threats or be confrontational. Keep the small talk brief and the meeting short; former Rep. Morris K. Udall (D-Arizona) used to complain about meetings that go on and on because "everything has been said, but not everyone has said it." Choose your best spokesperson to make the case, take a picture, and say thank you.

If you can't be a part of a face-to-face meeting, emails, texts, tweets, and other communication can be effective. Follow the same rules as above: Be courteous, clear and brief, and always say what action you support. Despite public skepticism, legislators do pay attention when the calls and messages roll in; and don't forget letters to the editor, again cosigned by a diverse group of constituents.

Consider a media strategy: you may be able to arrange to speak with reporters after a meeting to describe what your group requested and the response. And show up at the legislator's town halls and other public appearances: Sometimes, questions and issues need to be raised in public.

A key rule of politics is to assume nothing. You may think you know how your representative will vote, but it never hurts to weigh in to make sure. If your perspective is not heard and the other side's is, the legislator may feel pressured to cast a vote you would never have anticipated. Besides, politicians like to hear from supporters.

Follow-up is crucial as well; if you are granted a meeting, send a thank-you note immediately that reiterates your request. No matter how cordial the encounter, never presume you have persuaded anyone. The other side has cordial meetings too.

Continue to make calls and send emails as the issue is debated and the vote nears. No matter what happens, send another note: a thank you if you got the result you wanted, or a civil note of deep disappointment. Always maintain open communications and good relations; in politics, today's adversary is the crucial ally you may need on another issue.

You can extend your influence by joining or volunteering with advocacy organizations. Our suggestion: Throw your lot in with groups that have proven records of success rather than newly minted, single-issue start-ups.

You don't need to have been in politics for decades to know that you win some and you lose some. We hope this advice will help you win more often than you lose in this critical period for our country.

George Miller (D-Martinez) represented California in Congress from 1975 to 2015 and John Lawrence teaches at the University of California's Washington Center. He was chief of staff for Miller and House Minority Leader Nancy Pelosi (D-San Francisco) from 1975 through 2013.

Originally published in the *Los Angeles Times*, Wednesday, February 15, 2017, p. A13. Reprinted with permission from the authors.

Appendix J:
Sample Letter to Legislator

Although your national legislators' Washington addresses are given here, because of the security checks letters must go through before being delivered, they will arrive much faster if they are sent to the legislators' local addresses in your state. This can be found online.

To Your Senator:
The Honorable (full name)
United States Senate
Washington, DC 20510

To Your Representative:
The Honorable (full name)
U.S. House of Representatives
Washington, DC 20515

You should close your letter with "Sincerely yours," and please sign your full name. If you should wish to add your title (Mr., Mrs., Ms.), please put it in parentheses. This is the same form you would use to address your state representatives or senators when you write them in their state capital offices.

Not all school districts want you to write your letters on your school's letterhead, but if you can, use it. If you must use plain bond paper, you should add your title, School Librarian, your school, and your school district. This tells the recipient that you are competent to write this letter.

Please remember:

1. Your legislators, just like your principal and community, like to have information that keeps them informed of your library activities.

2. If you are supporting a specific bill or opposed to its passage, please state its number and its popular name. Your legislators, both national and state, have many bills before them during the year, and they need to know exactly which bill you are referring to.

3. Please be careful to write a carefully written letter stating your position. Your opinion matters whether or not they agree. However, they must understand your position, and that requires your care not to use poor grammar or punctuation. Also, please do not use acronyms that they, not being experts in our field, wouldn't

understand. Your expertise is very specialized, and you need to share the facts in support of your request.

4. You need to be as brief as possible in writing your letter. Staff members will probably do the first read, and they will be more interested in a brief, well-presented letter than a long, rambling discourse if they are going to share the letter.

5. Please be certain the bill is still alive. If the bill has been passed or voted down, the letter will do no good.

6. Always follow through with a thank-you letter.

7. Write when you are interested in the outcome of any legislation affecting schools and school libraries when you can support or ask to have the bill reconsidered or when you are asked to do so by your colleagues. Many times, legislators hear nothing from your side of the discussion and those who are of another opinion will be the only voice heard. Offer your carefully written arguments about the issue.

It would be better if you didn't:

1. Don't write a letter discussing votes for or against a certain bill without saying what vote you want them to make and why it is important. Legislators need to know why, and if you don't tell them why, they can easily ignore your request.

2. Don't threaten to withdraw your support in an upcoming election or brag about just how influential you are in your community. They can easily find out if you are a registered voter and to which party you belong.

3. Bills that are not out of a committee change when the evidence is heard and the committee's report is made. Wait until you see what the committee is suggesting before you craft your letter.

4. Beware the form letter being sent by an organization. Your carefully chosen wording will show your experience and will be much more influential.

5. Your address identifies you to your legislator. If you write a letter to the legislator in the next district or next state, your letter may be forwarded to the appropriate office, but you are not that legislator's constituent, so your letter will have little or no effect.

6. It's better to write a well-researched letter when necessary rather than flooding a legislator's office on a regular basis. Quantity is very important to legislators, but that quantity should be from multiple constituents, each of whom writes an excellent letter.

Appendix K:
50 Ways

The original "Fifty Ways to Succeed @ Your Library" was created for several conference presentations by one of the book's authors. Most of them have no real cost attached, so implementing these will help you become the professional you should be. They are divided into four categories: managing, teaching, public relations, and "that extra effort."

Managing

1. Make your school library appealing to all who enter. Close your eyes and do a virtual walk into your library. What does the visitor see? How can you make it more attractive? Develop a website and a social media presence. They are a part of your library.

2. Don't put up with broken, scarred, wrong size, mismatched furniture and shelving. This one could cost you some money, so you need to take your principal, a teacher, and a member of your advisory committee to a national or state association meeting where many furniture vendors display their wares and show what the library could look like. Be prepared with the amount that would need to be raised and have some thoughts about how you would raise that money.

3. Improve your signage. If you don't know how to do this, look around at local bookstores and see what they do. You could ask the art teacher to help with this.

4. Take some hints from public librarians. Some children's librarians put their bookshelves on wheels to make rearranging spaces quite easy. They also sometimes hang book racks on the end of shelves and do other things to make spaces more useful.

5. Merchandise your collection. Visit the local bookstore or a local department store and look at how they attract customers to want to buy their products.

6. Weed your collection. Nothing is as negative as shelves and shelves of old, unattractive, out-of-date things that nobody wants. Shelves crowded with "dogs" will keep your teachers and students away because they won't think you have anything that is modern.

7. Change displays, bulletin boards, and exhibitions frequently. What's on that bulletin board or in that display case will draw students into the library.

8. Help students learn about continuing their educations. Guidance counselors cannot reach students as easily as you can because their offices are small and usually require an appointment to enter. You can help every student find something to do when they finish high school. If students knew how to enroll in programs after high school, quitting school might be less of an option. Most of us came from homes where parents let us know what we were supposed to do after high school, so we stayed in high school. You need to do this for students who don't have parents who see any advantage (or possibility) for study after high school.

Teaching

9. Work with teachers and students to make the teaching job easier for teachers and the learning job easier for students. Collaborate with teachers.

10. Meet with teachers informally and formally and plan. Introduce inquiry learning as a possible new and important way to teach. Collaborate with teachers on inquiry units.

11. Teach, with their teachers, things students need to learn. Collaborate with teachers.

12. Teach your teachers all the new bells and whistles technology has to offer. This makes you the hero in the battle to stay current.

13. Welcome all teachers with a smile. Yes, the football coach does like to get rid of classes before the Friday game. You should be thankful that you aren't responsible for the arms, legs, neck, back, and head of 100 young men who may come away from that game with something wrong with any or all of those body parts. Make sure you have a collaborative assignment for the class, and be a good sport.

14. Share with teachers new articles from your professional collection. They will look to you for leadership in educational innovation.

15. Dream up new ways to approach the same old, same old. A teacher may be bored to death with some, if not all, assignments, which means students are going to be equally bored. Help spruce up assignments, and learning will increase.

16. Be especially helpful with new teachers or things new to a teacher. In both cases, the teacher may be quite anxious. It is an easy way to become a hero and leader.

17. Encouraging reading has always been the assignment of school librarians. Students today are bombarded by so many opportunities to do anything except read, while many of these opportunities

require the ability to read. Use all the ideas you can think of and find on the Internet, in professional books, and in other publications to increase students' reading skills.

Public Relations

18. Copy Walmart's greeter policy. Assign students to stand at the door and welcome students into the library. This might be a good assignment for an escapee from study hall if your school still has study halls.

19. Watch rules. My principal always told me that a rule meant a punishment for breaking the rule, and keeping up with those who break ineffective rules and their punishment is more difficult than not having the rule in the first place. Two all-encompassing rules are: Do unto others what you would have others do unto you, and do not do unto others what you would not want others to do unto you.

20. Watch and remove rules that limit students, such as "two-week checkout only," "you can't come to the library if you have an overdue book," or "one book only."

21. Make sure the students understand it is *their* library. This means you ask them what they want and then you try to provide it. If they want to have an area where they can use their cell phones, advocate for that with the administration. After all, it is *their* library, isn't it?

22. Overcome overdues. If you lengthen the checkout time (as you do for teachers) and only require that a student return the book when another student requests it or at the end of the semester, you won't have overdues.

23. Forget fines. Fines cost more in bad public relations and bookkeeping than you could possibly earn.

24. Resist broadcasting negative messages over the public address system. Make these messages about good new books, new things available, and new opportunities.

25. Resist negative reminders in the library. If your library has rules, they should begin with something other than "No" or "Do not."

26. Have great programs. Schedule exciting events in the library. Shopping centers and airports bring automobiles in for people to see. Ever think about a motorcycle in the library?

27. Encourage students to volunteer in the library. This helps them understand what goes on in there. If they understand a database well, they can teach others how to search, effectively easing your teaching load. It also makes the library *their* library.

28. Keep the principal informed of exciting things going on in the library. Give him or her things to brag about to other principals.

29. Maintain a great website with links to great information. Develop a social media presence. If you can't do this alone, draft a reliable student or two.

30. Keep your principal informed about what is new in the professional literature. When principals are cutting-edge aware of all the newest

educational trends, they won't be embarrassed at a district meeting when something new is proposed that they haven't heard of.

31. Have an advisory committee for the library. What they can help you do will surprise you. They become your advocates.

32. Provide at least one event in the library each semester for parents. Make sure the students are involved.

That Extra Effort

33. Watch for opportunities for grant proposal writing. This can be time-consuming at the start, but once you get a list of places and their offerings, you can pick and choose. Also, you need not do this alone. Get your advisory committee members or other teachers to help you or, if you want to get a bigger grant, recruit other librarians in the district to join you.

34. Find out about contests in which your students can participate. You may have to help the teachers collect and submit entries, but a winning student makes the newspaper.

35. Find out about field trips. Sometimes you can tell teachers about special opportunities for students and how to go about getting to the place. Sometimes you can take the training offered by the museum or gallery and become the teacher for all the students, thus relieving all other teachers in your building from participating in the training.

36. Don't miss school events. Students know who attends their special functions, whether it is a football game, the class play or musical, or a field trip. Attending school events is an easy way to become a mentor.

37. Show your worth. You may have to gather some statistics, but when you make a difference, you need a record of that.

38. Keep records of your successful experiences. If something worked well, do it again.

39. Conduct real research. For this, you may need to find a local college or university and an assistant professor in need of research for tenure, but what you discover may have more value than action research you did on your own.

40. Make frequent reports. These should be short and sweet and interesting.

41. Visit your legislators. Take students, teachers, and parents to show off your program. The legislators will know who and what you are when you need to ask for legislation.

42. Invite the school board and legislators to your school. This needs to have your principal's approval, but it may not have occurred to your administrators that having the school board or your legislators visit the school and library just to show off the great programs there would bring applause to your school. It is another way to help them understand education and school library programs.

43. Be a problem solver for little, middle, and big problems. Gain a reputation for getting things corrected, made better, made possible. You may not always be able to do this alone, but you should learn who the best people are to work with to make things happen.

44. Volunteer to present a session at your state conference. You should be able to get funding to attend. If you really want to ensure this, ask your principal and a teacher to present with you.

45. Volunteer to write for a professional periodical. Your teachers, principal, and community will love seeing their school featured.

46. Bring in the media as often as you can. When you do something in the library, perhaps invite legislators to your building, the media will come mostly because the legislator will want this featured in the media.

47. Make sure students understand Frances Henne's description of the ultimate in information literacy: "For some students, and in certain schools, this may be many students, the only library skill that they should have to acquire is an awareness, imprinted indelibly and happily upon them, that the library is a friendly place where the librarians are eager to help." This is what we are all about.

48. Think before you whine; then don't.

49. Most of all, enjoy your job, all day, every day. The contribution you are making to the teachers and students in your school cannot be measured.

50. Smile.

Index

About the Authors

BLANCHE WOOLLS is director and professor emerita from the iSchool at San Jose University.

SHARON COATNEY is a former school librarian in the award-winning Blue Valley Schools in Overland Park, Kansas, and an acquisitions editor for Libraries Unlimited.

Both Woolls and Coatney are past presidents of the American Association of School Librarians and have been awarded AASL's Distinguished Service Award.

CPSIA information can be obtained
at www.ICGtesting.com
Printed in the USA
FSHW020332050821
83681FS